COSMIC MAP

METAPHYSICS DEMYSTIFIED

GRANDMA JANIS

Published by

Meadow Park Press
Post Office Box 14410
San Luis Obispo, CA 93406-4410 U.S.A.

To order more copies:
Use order blanks at the back of this book
FAX: 805-782-9590
Toll Free: 1-800-309-4645

© Copyright First printing 1996 by Meadow Park Press

Library of Congress Catalog Card Number: 95-80439
Janis, Grandma
   Cosmic map, metaphysics demystified / by Grandma Janis — 1st ed.

   Self-help, techniques
   Metaphysics
   New Age movement
   Spiritualistic interpretations
   Shamans
   New Thought
   Religion
   Philosophy

   ISBN 1-888100-60-5
   SAN 298-7937 Meadow Park Press Book Depository
   SAN 298-7945 Nationwide Distributor

   Printed in U.S.A.

   Cover & Book Design: OBI Graphics/Marcie Long, Kelseyville, CA
   Cover Photograph: Roger Hakeman, Kelseyville, CA
   Printed at Barlow Press, Cotati, CA

Unsolicited Comments From Ordinary People

COSMIC MAP – METAPHYSICS DEMYSTIFIED

Psychic reader who had not yet read it (in the ordinary sense): . . . powerful book! Put it on audiotapes so that the blind and elderly can hear the message. [Coming soon from Meadow Park Press.]

Catholic permanent deacon: . . . a very fine book which has a real purpose and fills a real need . . .

UFO buff: I knew it! I knew it! I knew it! . . . tells us where the extraterrestrials are from, why they are here and what they plan to do!

Yogananda devotee: . . . new insights on familiar topics, challenging, exposes me to a number of areas of metaphysics I never knew existed. For this I am grateful . . .

Long–time meditator: [The] image [of Grandma Janis] that comes through the vocabulary, structure and humor is of someone who is ever young, ever spontaneous, ever learning, ever excited, ever on an eternal quest.

Father of five: [Grandma Janis] has had significant metaphysical experiences, has done extensive research and has received a bounty of graces sitting at the feet of her teachers.

New retiree: [Her] "random with purpose" method confused me at first. [Her] thought process is not always linear, even within topic . . . but the style is uniquely "her" with a strong story line and experiences . . . her technique works well . . . this book gets better and better.

Housewife: Finally a God in whom I can really believe! A Godhead, an immense vibrating fountain of light with love vibrations – in charge of the whole thing, a system. . . . and, I, as one of its rays, Souls, am living this life . . . these ideas are exciting and practical.

Real estate salesman: . . . great references to many illuminating works.

Publisher/facilitator: . . . [She is a] master of convergent thinking . . . able to gather and interpret much recent and ancient information to help seekers understand, connect to and enjoy the acceleration/ascension.

There is only one religion, the religion of love.

There is only one language, the language of the heart.

There is only one race, the race of humanity.

There is only one GOD, omnipresent, present everywhere.

— SATHYA SAI BABA

TABLE OF CONTENTS

FOREWORD. vii

INTRODUCTION 1

CHAPTER 1,
    THE IMMENSENESS OF YOUR JOURNEY IS AWESOME 5

CHAPTER 2,
    CLOSE TO HOME 77

CHAPTER 3,
    YOU HAVE TRAVELED IN THE DARK AND THE LIGHT 177

AFTERWORD 277

APPENDIX A – Dedication Pages 283

APPENDIX B – UCM, A Laying-on-of-Hands, Healing Ministry 285

APPENDIX C – Author's Biographical Information 289

APPENDIX D – We Are the Children of the Light 291

APPENDIX E – Memorial Service for a Recreational Drug User 293

APPENDIX F – Harvest, Devaprem Demystified Enlightenment 297

APPENDIX G – Bible Scripture References for Mystical Phenomena 305

APPENDIX H – Bible Scripture References for Troubled Times 307

APPENDIX I – Concept Lists for Chapters 1, 2, and 3 309

APPENDIX J – When Cosmic Cultures Meet 311

RECOMMENDED BOOKS
    for Further Metaphysical Reading, Basic and Advanced 315

INDEX (also see Appendix I). 321

ORDER FORMS 325

Unless otherwise noted, Bible references are from the
King James version *or* the Living Bible.
When the verse is poetic, the older version is used.
When the newer version is used,
clearer understanding is needed.

FOREWORD

Dear old Soul, beloved of the ages,

Years ago, I taught a college sociology course called Humanity and Society. In the course was a long chapter on comparative religions.

One day in class, a young man raised his hand and asked permission to share something his father had told him as a child. I agreed, and this was his metaphor:

> Once upon a time, long, long, long ago, an angel held all the spiritual knowledge in one giant crystal. One day when flying through the sky, the angel accidentally dropped this crystal of truth. It fell to earth and shattered into hundreds of pieces.
>
> As time went by, parts were found. Each crystal–of–truth finder was dazzled by its brightness and enchanting beauty. "Why look further?" Each took for granted that the treasure represented the truth, the whole truth and nothing but the truth.

As the young man had been taught, I, too, have respect for all devout beliefs. It doesn't matter what path you choose, it will lead to the same God.

I do not argue theology. Cosmic Map is *my* "**relative truth**," which simply means "how things looked to me the day I went to press;" in other words, how many pieces of that crystal could I find to share with you?

No finite mind can understand the infinite mind; all I can do is share my insights and experiences.

Dear sister, dear brother, start by reading Cosmic Map lightly as if it is science fiction. You will find ideas which resonate with your Soul, *and* you will find parts that don't fit. Don't let the latter discourage you. Since it takes the human mind so long to accept anything new, as much as you can, read with your heart. Take what seems right for you, and put aside what doesn't. If the idea is neither "right on" or "doesn't fit," I have a useful conception tool called "my **tentative shelf**." If I can't throw out the foreign-sounding idea because it has a "well maybe" ring to it, I mentally place it on that shelf in my mind. Later, more learning may bring the idea to full fruition – or more learning enables me to toss it off my "tentative shelf."

Let me use an example. I love the work of the brilliant psychiatrist and psychic interpreter, David Viscott, M.D. I agree with about ninety percent of what he communicates. If I let the non-resonating ten percent get in my way, I would miss some wonderful education.

Sifting through experiences and printed material, *forging your own philosophy,* is an essential element of the process of connecting with God/your own Soul. And because you are a different Soul than I, different wonders will be revealed to you. Take Cosmic Map for what it is, just one person's survey course in basic metaphysics. Don't make up your mind, ever. Stay open to new insights and revelations and also to new ways of looking at old subjects.

The statement I make to any group of spiritual seekers I lead is: "I believe that truth is relative and you must seek your own truth. Essentially, we come together to create a congenial, supportive and stimulating environment in which each pursues our own path toward spiritual and personal growth."

I am certain, though, that we are here to find a higher form of love, and then, through trial and error, learn to live that higher form of love. And I am certain that the real truth is much greater and more incredible than we can imagine or record.

Today, there is a great urgency! As early as late 1995, but before the year 2012, dimensional windows are going to open.

We are at the dawn of a great spiritual revolution which is rapidly evolving the human race upward. This changing of the guard is sweeping the world and saving our planet, the Planet of the Cross. This is happening because we have the help of the spiritual hierarchy, a dazzling array of celestial intelligences and Beings, including Ascended Master Jesus, Avatar Sai Baba, angels and friendly extraterrestrials. These heroes of expanded consciousness are raising our dimensional windows, enabling us to work more and more with the higher worlds of Light. This on-going revolution started in 1926 with the birth of Avatar, Sai Baba.

Uncountable old Souls have reincarnated at this time of consciousness ascension to help with the practical details; that is, work like cleaning the oceans, lakes and skies. Other old Souls are back saving the trees and teaching us how to take care of our human spirits and human bodies. Others are here to help in the positive transformation of organizations. Still others serve in support roles. You are one of these ancient ones, undoubtedly.

COSMIC MAP offers realizations and practices so you can take your part in this consciousness revolution. As you individually raise your consciousness, the collective consciousness of the planet rises. Indeed, one reason you came to the Planet of the Cross is to help raise this consciousness!

Dear Soul, may your path be filled with blessings and love as you respond to the quickening drumbeat, marching with your brothers and sisters who serve the Light.

In loving service,
Grandma Janis,

November 1995

INTRODUCTION

Dear child of God, let me share with you the joy I have found in traveling the path of metaphysics. To do this, I have chosen a question and answer format which deals with the basic realizations first. I build on these basics as we move along. The book finally evolves into a lifestyle where your daily life becomes your religion.

Please understand, I want to build bridges not walls between the various beliefs. We don't have to be carbon copies of each other. We can learn to enjoy both our common ground *and* our differences. If you are of another faith, please read with a generosity of spirit. Ask "Where are the similarities?" You, too, can help me build bridges.

"Before you start, could you say a bit about yourself, author Janis?" Yes, it is your perfect right to get a sense of the author. I am not anyone special. I write in the first person, so you will learn about my spiritual experiences as you read.

Over a decade ago, I was taking a psychic development class. The awesomely psychic teacher spontaneously turned to me and said, "Janis, through the millennia, the knowledge has flowed through you." In this life, too, I have been a teacher. If you skimmed the Foreword, you already knew that.

I love and appreciate my family and friends, see the Dedication pages, Appendix A. From these pages, you can tell I am not a guru in a monastery, but am a daughter, wife, mother, stepmother, homemaker and grandmother. If you want to know more about my role as a Spiritualist minister, read Appendix B. And if you want biographical information, read Appendix C.

I usually go by just plain Janis, no titles, my given name, because "Janis" means "God is gracious" and that is all that needs to be said. I got the idea for my pen name from my adorable grandchildren who call me "Grandma Janis." I like it because in other cultures "Grandma" automatically means "wise woman."

From past–life regressions I have done with competent past–life ther-
apists (one of them a board certified psychiatrist) I believe myself to
be an old Soul. I have been going around in circles trying to get it
right for a very long time!

My views have been greatly shaped by my teachers. (Anyone who
knows something that I need to know is my teacher.) On my path,
my next teacher has always been there as will be yours, once you *set
your intent*. Your teacher may also come to you through a book, a
dream or a real life experience. It is a metaphysical principle that
once a priority is set to better know God, opportunities come.

I would like to honor my major teachers, but not by name since
they didn't seek a high profile. My first teacher was a Science of
Mind minister, a scientist with a PhD in nuclear physics; then came
a college pottery teacher who had studied metaphysics; then my
shaman teacher; then an "ordinary" housewife (she could bend
spoons with her mind as she did in my kitchen, but when she bent
them back, they had a crook, so I asked her to stop!); then a former
disciple of the Master Muktananda; then a former student of Brugh
Joy, M. D., a registered nurse turned Trager bodyworker; and last, a
newly enlightened German Master. Although they have all moved
out of my life, they are still alive as far as I know. I have been rich-
ly blessed in my passion to know the Divine.

The questions most people want answered in a philosophy book are
"How close to reality is this?" and "Will it enlighten me?" If humanity could have become enlightened by words, we would all be ves-
sels of all–knowing bliss. Unfortunately, words have to be written
and read one after the other, linearly. That is not how reality
operates; in reality many things are happening all at once.

However, words are like a road map. Sometimes a road map helps
you. It might even be essential to get you to your destination, but it
looks nothing like the territory. (Would a road map be helpful if it
came with trees, tall buildings and flowers?) The words in this book
can function like a map, but are not the destination. Becoming intimate with God/your Soul is the journey; then living as *who you
really are* is the destination.

My husband says I left in some of the "big trees." He would have

preferred that more of the details be put in footnotes, which he
could then skip. It has been my experience that students *do* skip
footnotes. Obviously, I wanted you to know. Thanks to him, I can
at least warn you.

"If words are inadequate, how can I come to know more about the
Divine?" **Real knowing** comes from personal experiences, experiential education. Hopefully, this book will set you up to both seek
out and have these wondrous experiences. Knowing and thinking
are totally different. John 4:48: "Except ye see signs and wonders, ye
will not believe."

Usually but not always, the most profound personal experiences
come to those who: (1) meditate daily; (2) get together to worship
with others who seek higher consciousness; (3) set aside some time
every day to do devotional work, pray for others, do yoga, sing or
chant; (4) work on becoming a better person; (5) are productive
interpersonally; (5) are giving back to the world more than they are
taking; (6) become aware of ego's narrow, self-centered pull and
release it at critical times; (7) receive guidance and information from
sources higher than the ego.

"After I finish reading this book, where can I go for more?" To get
you started or to illuminate you at higher levels, a short book list for
basic and advanced metaphysical reading is at the back of Cosmic
Map. I have written an annotated paragraph or two about each
book to help in your selection. Many more resources are mentioned
as we move along. I did my best with the addresses but I can't guarantee they are current. If you get returned mail, a telephone call to
"information" in that area may lead you to that source. Spiritual
organizations change their address as often as an average person. As
you read, do compile your own "resource self-interest list."

Complete books have been written about many of the topics mentioned. Ask at your library, bookstore and metaphysical book store.
My work is intended to be a basic primer – and much, much more.

Eventually, all spiritual terms will be defined. A peek at the subject
index at the back of the book will give you an idea of the topics
covered. However, if you want to see the concepts as presented, see
Appendix I. Now, let's get started . . .

CHAPTER I

The Immenseness of Your Journey Is Awesome

We are *not* human beings
having a spiritual experience.

We are spiritual Beings
having a human experience.

— *Drunvalo Melchizedek,* 1992

He is a Being from a different star
system, an advanced dimension,
living here now. He has come back
to be our teacher.

TERMS AND PHILOSOPHY

"What are **PARANORMAL EXPERIENCES** and have you had any?" Paranormal experiences cannot be explained in terms of ordinary sensing. They are so unusual that they are startling. These usually happen to long–time meditators and are a joy and wonder when they happen in that they almost always erupt spontaneously.

Here is a selection from my personal list of paranormal experiences over a seventeen–year period:

I was started on the spiritual path to find out who I am by a near–death experience (NDE) February 22, 1978. After losing too much blood before and after a hysterectomy, I left my body and hovered above it. I tried to communicate to the operating room personnel that I was fine ("We are losing her, we are losing her!") They didn't hear me – so I went out through the hospital wall, flew over the trees, and out into the universe. It was a marvelous, freeing journey, whereupon I came upon a pulsating white Light Being. I could feel its intense love vibrations and see its emanations and recognized its intelligence and willingness to communicate. Indeed, this Light Being came to meet me. I "talked" to it by forming mental images: "I am not ready to leave yet. I have not finished my tasks on earth. I would like to go back, finish writing my book, finish raising my three sons, and have more time with my husband." The next thing I knew, I was awakening on a recovery room table.

Philosophically, at that time, I felt pretty sure there was a God, but any thoughts I had were random and absent minded; I was devoting no time to exploration or worship.

That NDE forever changed my life and sent me on a passionate quest to know and understand this subdivision of myself that can leave the body, be intelligent, that has the instinct to know what to do and where to go, and that can communicate **telepathically** (thinking of what I wanted to say and having it understood immediately). This experience left me with the definite impression that the Soul has its own sense organs, will and intelligence.

Although at first I believed I had seen God, I now believe that the NDE Light Being who met me was God's helper, not God.

On this quest to know myself, I have been blessed with signs and wonders: I have seen my guardian angel many times (an irregular, many–variations–of–blue crystalline vortex about one–foot high and one–foot wide, not anything like drawings of angels). After a deeply painful personal loss, I saw a spirit band over my bed every night for ten nights. I see auras, but not all the time or in some lights. I have heard angel choirs. I frequently hear a voice giving specific directions. I saw a workshop leader, my shaman teacher, turn into a medicine man and speak from that persona for twenty minutes. I occasionally see people's faces change into a former–life face. And once a man standing in front of me turned briefly into a whole-bodied, ancient–time warrior complete with painted face, long–multiple ear rings, scant clothes and bare feet, with spear in hand.

I have heard "spirit" knocks on the walls when everyone else in the room heard the same thing. I have seen rooms filled with vibrant white Light on at least three occasions. I frequently see clear symbolic pictures just before falling asleep. On two different occasions, I spontaneously astralprojected out of my body into another person's body and felt life as they each did: one was quite sad and the other paranoid. I witnessed a star exploding into a purple pyramid waterfall. I have seen golden Light coming out of my feet. I have seen my favorite teacher, my shaman, break into fractionated shafts of golden Light. I have been keenly in touch with some of my former lives, usually but not always, alerted to it by a devout psychic trained and skilled in hypnotic regression. Always these glimpses have acted as a powerful magnet drawing me on to see and know more.

These kinds of psychic experiences are becoming mainstream. Americans are experiencing more and more unusual and "unexplainable" personal metaphysical events in their lives as reported in a survey by Parade Magazine: In 1973, fifty–eight percent of the population reported having had one or more paranormal experiences. By 1984, sixty–seven percent of the population reported having had at least one **seeing experience** that couldn't be explained in normal–reality terms. I wish I had a current update for you. However, this is a nine percent increase in just eleven years. Something major is happening which is opening us up to experience these intensely personal metaphysical events. If you think back, perhaps you are already experiencing wonders, hearing friend's stories and/or watching TV shows with a paranormal focus.

There is no doubt in my mind that what we know as "space" is teeming with Beings and landscapes which we cannot see with our physical eyes. It is my prayer that Cosmic Map will create a foundation for you to further your own journey.

"What does the term **METAPHYSICS** mean?" The universes are run by natural laws, most of which are not observable with the ordinary senses. Obviously there are sounds you can't hear and energies and objects you can't see. What you are aware of is just the "tip of the iceberg."

It is estimated that what goes on in the universes, or dimensions, or consciousness, is ninety-five percent beyond the awareness of your senses; that is, your seeing, hearing, feeling, touching and tasting. Investigating that ninety-five-percent unknown is a fascinating and unpredictable journey into the inner and outer dimensions of consciousness; perhaps the last frontier.

Metaphysics is the study and practice of using natural laws, the physics of consciousness, the invisible within and beyond the physical. The more you understand these principles and cooperate with them, the more intimate you are with God and your own Soul. Inner happiness and joy come from developing your spirituality. Additionally, a better outer life slowly but surely follows this increasing knowingness.

Outer happiness and joy come from developing your spirituality too.

Metaphysicians have an open system of belief. Knowing there is always more to learn, mystical seekers are learning and experiencing all day long. This is opposed to a few orthodoxies that "know it all," and therefore have a closed system. It is a principle of nature that closed systems die.

The study of metaphysical principles and the disciplined practice of them are therefore extremely practical. But only you can walk your path in this discipline, for your path is totally unique. Sometimes it may seem as though you are wandering around with just a candle in an immense darkness because there is so much to absorb. Just trust. Luke 12:32: "Fear not, little flock; for it is your Father's good pleasure to give you the kingdom."

"Where can I go to find like–minded, open–minded friends?" Studying, discussing and meditating with a group of like–minded friends is so comforting, educational and inspiring. For basic training in metaphysics, Religious Science (Science of Mind), Unity, and Baha'i churches are wonderful. Also, check in your telephone book's yellow pages under "Churches" for these titles: metaphysical; Spiritualist; new age; non–denominational; and scan for other like–sounding titles.

(Please, Yellow–Page editors, could we possibly have just one term, "Metaphysical Churches?" And metaphysical churches, pride in your name doesn't help newcomers find you; consider listing under "Metaphysical" if that option is available.)

Postage costs keep going higher. I don't know how to say it nicely: it is overburdening to spiritual organizations when we expect to get printed handouts or brochures without at least paying the mailing-costs.

Two other organizations you can explore are the Rosicrucians and Eckankar. Write enclosing a self–addressed, stamped envelope to Rosicrucian Park, San Jose, CA 95191 and Eckankar, P. O. Box 27300, Minneapolis, MN 55427.

To find an existing Edgar Cayce study group (founded in 1931) or to learn how to form your own, enclose a stamped, self–addressed envelop when you write to the Association of Research and Enlightenment, Inc., P. O. Box 595, Virginia Beach, VA 23451 (established in 1931).

There may be a Universal Church of the Master church or teacher near you (my church). To find out, write to Universal Church of the Master Headquarters, 501 Washington Street, Santa Clara, CA 95050 enclosing a self–addressed, stamped envelope. (After this one, I will just remind you by saying "Enclose a SASE.")

Always stay tuned to your intuition. Your gut–level reaction to new churches, teachers, groups and friends says everything. There is a place for you that provides just the right amount of both growth and comfort and is *not* taking a chunk out of your wallet. The information is out there for very little cost. Some of the high-priced seminars and classes are padding the pockets of some greedy, partially evolved "gurus."

Also, if after a time your group is not meeting your spiritual needs, you may have absorbed all there is from that source. It is your perfect right to look elsewhere.

"Is the term **NEW AGE** synonymous with metaphysical?" No, not at all. Some astrologers say the New Age and **The Age of Aquarius** are synonymous, approximately from 1930 to 2030. But I like 1926 to 2012 better. (I'll tell you why before the end of Chapter 1.) New Age means, therefore, a period of time.

A new style of music may get labeled "New Age music" because it was composed during these years, while its composer may feel the term is limiting the potential audience.

"New Agers are of satan and are the false prophets warned about in the Holy Bible" according to one fundamentalist church leader. Maybe some are. Later I will talk about negative occult practices. Not all doctors, lawyers or professionals work ethically, either. We can't label *them all* bad.

Laying-on-of-hands healing may get labeled "New Age," but it isn't. On the rare occasion when I use "New Age," my purpose is to hook into other people's frame of reference. It is something like a food ad saying "all natural." What does that mean? Arsenic is "natural." Nevertheless, "all natural" may still get our attention as may "New Age."

Metaphysical principles always operate. An Aquarian Age comes and *goes* every 26,000 or so years.

"Who or what is **GOD**; and is God a man or a woman?" God is a spiritualized energy vortex which may be seen as a *huge* vibrating white Light (but can create visual clothes, a "mask" or persona of a human male or female face if that is what you expect to see). Contained in this infinite *Cosmic Mind* is the knowledge for all the patterns and processes of the universes. God creates by thought.

Thought has sound. Then, the energy (and sometimes matter) follow. John 1:1: "In the beginning was the word. And the word was with God, and the word was God."

The mistranslation of Genesis 2:27 created a major, major gender misunderstanding : "So God created man in his own image, in the image of God created he him; male and female created he them." This is an erroneous translation.

The pronouns "he," and "him," meaning a male God in that mistranslation, are not accurate. A truer translation would have been, "The Elohim created male and female in its own image." The word "Elohim" comes from "Eloha" a masculine word, with "im," a feminine ending. (Elohim is pronounced "Ay-lo-heem." The last syllable, rhymes with "cream.")

God is an immense masculine and feminine energy in union, procreating all that is.

Although God is without gender, God contains therein both masculine and feminine potential, so I resist calling God an "it." I like to call God mother-father. If there were only a pronoun meaning both male *and* female. Since there isn't, I'll use s/he, pronounced shee-hee.

I love to think of God as my "mommy/daddy" Light Being. I am just one of its zillion billion baby Light Beings. Psalms 82:6: "I have said, Ye are gods, and all of you are children of the Most High."

The "masculine" aspect of God is "force," the "feminine" aspect is "form." Masculine force projects in wild abandonment until the feminine draws it in and gives it form.

When actress Shirley MacLaine said, "I am God," she was so right. I do, however, wish she had said, "I am a ray of God;" then she might not have gotten such a negative reaction from the traditional Christian establishment. But her Soul is blessed for the work she has done in the metaphysical sphere, bringing the attention of uncountable numbers of people to metaphysics.

So that immense, awesome, brilliant, unfathomable Light Being is my parent. I am a child of the Light. I am a Light Being. The same is true for you. Even though some people are not yet aware of this, we are *all* children of the Light. There is more on this in Appendix D.

Our Supreme Being waits patiently through thousands of our life-times for us to perfect ourselves. Only as a perfected Being do we have the Soul energy, without fear, to finally cross the final dark void and enter into the seventh heaven (some say nine), the highest consciousness of the Soul, and receive a gracious welcome home.

It is of ultimate importance for us to build our Soul energy. Having a more powerful Soul is like having more gas in our tank. Building Soul energy raises the options of where we can choose to go, whether we happen to be unembodied *or* in a body. The way Soul empowerment works is very beautiful because this greater individu-alized Soul energy contributes to a higher mass consciousness, the **collective consciousness**! Ironically, this collective consciousness has in the past been labeled "**the collective unconscious.**" I sup-pose this is because we have been mostly unaware of it.

God sends nurturing love vibrations ("female side") and the love of stern coaching ("male side"). God is the essential ingredient in everything ever created and is always changing forms. Big fish eat little fish. An owl eats a mouse. I eat my green salad, veggies, rice, seven-grain bread and watermelon. It is all just God changing forms. Light energy changes into matter and matter changes into energy, the physics of consciousness, metaphysics.

Some Western names for God are: Supreme Being, Higher Power, Overself, Being Mind, Central Intelligence, Collective Messiah, Deity, Divine Love, Eternal One, First-Cause Divinity, Divine Mind, God/Goddess-all there is, Heavenly Father, Higher Mind, Lord, Lord of Light, Master of the Universes, Mother/Father God, Radiant Mystery, Radiant One, Super Consciousness, The Force, The Source, Universal Being, Universal Mind, and Universal Soul.

Some Eastern names for God besides the Elohim include Ahura Mazda, Allah, Brahma, Jehovah, Shiva, Vishnu, YHWH, (ancient Hebrew spelling, vowelless) and Yaweh, pronounced two ways, either "yaw-vay " or "yaw-way, " both rhyming with "day".

Actually, in Hindu thought, the Brahma aspect creates, the Vishnu aspect preserves, and the Shiva aspect destroys; all are aspects of a single God process.

In choosing Divine terms to use for yourself, choose those with which you resonate. Everybody has a different spiritual history. As for me, God is just fine. My other favorites in order: Yaweh ("yaw-vay" can be chanted or crooned), Radiant One, and Divine Love.

This higher intelligence is everywhere, and its vibrations are in everything seen and unseen. This invisible Light energy holds together all atoms in vibrational patterns and keeps all stars and planets in their vibrational orbits. Our Milky Way Galaxy's pattern is not random. Notice the computer image on the cover. Our earth is just one dot toward the edge. And our universe has one hundred billion of these galaxies!

Julian of Norwich in the 14th century said, "The fullness of joy is to behold God in everything." For your information, Julian of Norwich was an Englishwoman, known as an "anchoress," a spiritual coun-selor living as a recluse in a small cell, according to a greeting card put out by the conscious Printery House.

At the subtle level, inside, everything is made of this super–intelli-gent Light. Thus God is in everything and sustains everything. In Eastern Hinduism, God is the Absolute, Unmanifested, existing beyond material creation but also existing in it.

Since God sustains the universes, surely God can sustain me.

No words can describe God adequately. Our Radiant One is imper-sonal and eventually, over a framework of multiple–lifetimes, s/he evens out the gifts. The timing depends on the Being's progress, will-ingness to be guided, and willingness to receive.

We do have **free will**, the freedom to make our own decisions. But when we are first born from God's body, we are so jazzed, we do it *our* way, not God's. It takes so many lifetimes before we are willing to listen to the real us, our Soul, so we can do life without pain. We must learn to live in harmony with our Being, our ray, glowing through the dictates of our parents, friends, boss, loved ones, and culture plus our human–animal nature. (The process is infinitely harder to integrate than at the same time rubbing your head with one hand and patting your stomach with the other!)

I personally know only one living person that I trust who has been in the presence of God and returned to teach in a human body. He is Jim J. Hurtak, PhD, who during that visit was given information to share with the human race. In 1991 I attended a class given by Dr. Hurtak, and I saw gold Light streaming out of his eyes.

After his visit with God, Dr. Hurtak wrote a book called THE KEYS OF ENOCH, listed in the back of COSMIC MAP under Advanced Metaphysical Books.

In the following paragraph, from that 1977 masterpiece, is his description of the persona God put on for him in his 1974 visit to the highest heaven. Hurtak had left his human body before he got that far, but later returned to it. Notice that in 1974, Hurtak's image of God, like most folks, was male. (He is quite egalitarian now, speaking of the "higher Brothers and Sisters of Light.")

> And my spirit was so overwhelmed with the presence of the higher Light, I would not have been able to maintain my body of Light were it not for the body of Metatron. [According to Hurtak, Metatron is an incredibly advanced Light Being who is a teacher, guide and creator of the electron.]
>
> Metatron then took me into the presence of the Divine Father. And I went into His presence through the door of omega Orion which serves as a Grand Entrance to regions of pure energy emission. The presence of the Father was so rarefied that only Metatron could take me into the Pyramid of the Living Light, the Throne, where I saw the Ancient of Days face to face, with His flowing white hair and His face of overwhelming love and joy.

I have read only one other description that resonates truth to me, written in 1970 by a man no longer living in that body, Paul Twitchell of Eckankar, the religion of Light and Sound. In his book, DIALOGUES WITH THE MASTER, Twitchell describes being taken by a guide, a man named Rebazar Tarzs, a Tibetan Master, who works as a human, but can easily leave his body for astral travel. Both Twitchell and Tarzs returned to their human bodies after the visit. Notice that Twitchell's image of God was sexless:

> And then a strange cloud hovering over the flowing light seemed to dissolve and a face which filled all space seemed to hang there with eyes gazing upon all . . .

> And then suddenly I was caught up in a sheet of the white flowing light and the singing sound, moving toward that terrifying face.

Twitchell's monumental work lives in his books, only one of which is listed under Advanced Metaphysical Books. Eventually, you may want to read them all. Twitchell's guide, Rebazar Tarzs, has worked in the same human body for over two–hundred years.

Through every faith comes the message as recorded in Deuteronomy 6:5: "And thou shalt love the Lord thy God with all thine heart, and with all thy soul, and with all thy might." As my shaman put it, "Think of the Light *all day long.*"

"What are the meanings of the terms "'**EXISTENCE**' and/or 'THE UNIVERSE?'" Let me start with the term "Existence." This was the word Rajneesh used for "God." "The Universe" was the term my shaman used for God.

The reason these teachers used all–inclusive words is because *"the whole thing" works like a system.* Let me explain this fact in terms of the human body as a system. The human body has a head which contains a brain. The brain is the central place from which the human body is operated. The body has uncountable processes working (many of them automatically) to keep us going.

The God system, or Existence or The Universe simply means that *since God works as a system, we can't escape God because God is in everything seen and unseen.*

The Cosmic Mind or Godhead that put on the face for these two evolved Souls, Jim Hurtak and Paul Twitchell, is only the head of the system.

When I hear anyone say things like, "Why doesn't God do something about that terrible situation?" or "Why does God allow war?" I answer: "We, as the children of the living God, are the material hands, eyes and mouth on the earth plane. It is we that have to right the wrongs." We have more power than we think to do this. Keep reading!

I diligently studied Religious Science from 1980 to 1985 and was tremendously enriched by this experience. Ernest Holmes, the founder of this Religious Science, Science of Mind, is quoted on the church's bookmarks:

> I believe in God, the Living Spirit Almighty; one, indestructible, absolute, and self-existent Cause. This One manifests itself in and through all creation but is not absorbed by its creation. The manifest universe is the body of God; it is the logical and necessary outcome of the infinite self-knowingness of God . . . I believe in the incarnation of this Spirit in man and that all men are incarnations of the One Spirit.

Deepak Chopra, the medical doctor who communicates so eloquently about healing and hope writes in QUANTUM HEALING, EXPLORING THE FRONTIERS OF MIND/BODY MEDICINE ". . . mind and matter join in a dance, moving instinctively together, aware without speaking of where their next step will fall." And he says, "The likelihood that life was created randomly is about the same as a hurricane blowing through a junkyard and creating a Boeing 707."

God is in everything, in the space between the atoms. God is being the quail, the flower, the sink, the ocean, the desk, and you and me. We are all God's forms but we are not the totality, we are just one component of the system.

Pure and imperishable, God is all there is.

When we get together and say "We are One" and sing "We are one in the Lord . . ." we are totally accurate and scientifically correct.

By the way, if you were bothered by being "just one of God's zillion billion baby Light Beings," perhaps your ego-mind got snagged. Conceptually, each of us is just "one cell" in the body of God. And does the awareness that you are living in just one galaxy of this universe's one hundred billion galaxies give you a new sense of proportion?

"In the Foreword, you referred to **ASCENDED MASTERS**?" Could you tell us more about them?" A part of God's system, the Ascended Masters, at their beginning, were first–time rays from God, like us. However, unlike us, after a number of reincarnations, they have mastered the game of life in this dimension–on this planet. These evolved Souls, former partial or full Avatars here, are out of the body, unlimited, omniscient, and infinite, beyond the limitations of ego–mind, time, space and the material world. Because of their great love for humanity, one hundred forty–four thousand strong, they choose to serve our dimension. (This figure is more symbolic than an actual count.) They move with the speed of thought.

There is more to come on both out–of–body Beings, embodied Beings, and extraterrestrial Beings now helping the human race. At the end of Chapter 1, more about the term "Avatar" will be found in addition to information about one embodied Avatar, Sai Baba, and one out–of–the–body Avatar, Jesus, now an Ascended Master. In Chapter 3, you'll find spirit guides, spirit bands, angels, friendly extraterrestrials, walk–in helpers and more!

As you know, our dimension or reality includes the properties of atoms, protons, electrons, solids, liquids, gases, conductors, electro-magnetism, radiation, microwaves, organic and non–organic mole-cules, and fluorescence. To be considered also are the actions of magnetism, spin directions, electrical charges, ions, radiation, electro-magnetic radiation, fission, echoes, radioactivity, chemical bonds, optics, laser radiation, and fusion, to mention a few. That is why big change usually doesn't occur overnight! In our third–dimensional consciousness, we are in a material world that is both mechanical *and* alterable! It is dense and is relatively slow to change by third-dimensional Souls (the vast majority of our planet's population). We need the help of the advanced Souls.

From the book, THE MAGIC PRESENCE (listed in the back under Advanced Metaphysical Books), Ascended Master Saint Germain speaks for all Ascended Masters through author Godfre Ray King: "We have conquered death by complete and Eternal Dominion over the atomic substance of the physical body and the world. All things obey our commands. The laws of Nature and the Universe are Our willing, obedient servants."

During my near–death experience, I wasn't in a material world! Doing my thing, doing what I wanted and communicating what I wanted, was easy. Because of this experience, it is easy for me to imagine how an Ascended Master might operate.

If you know the names of any of these Ascended Masters, just call out their name(s). Any Ascended Master you call will come in spirit to your aid. Both the Ascended Masters and embodied Masters love us and are actively involved in helping to transform the earth. When even one Soul is being dysfunctional or is hurting, this slows down the whole system, the whole race's evolution. Don't just sit there and hurt; call for help! If you can't do it for yourself right now, do it for *us*!

For more comfort, know that about seven thousand Ascended Masters have reincarnated and are now with us on our Planet of the Cross. However, whether they choose to reincarnate or work out of body, they are constantly helping the human race. Even though most of the time we may not even know for sure we were helped, sometimes we get a "hunch" that *something* helped.

"What does the word **DIVINE** mean?" The highest.

"Just what is **THE HOLY SPIRIT**?" God's intelligent love vibration. Even an Ascended Master or an Avatar needs the Holy Spirit to do the work. James 1:17: "All good giving and every perfect gift from above, coming down from the Father of the lights from whom there is no variableness . . . " The Holy Spirit is the vibration of Light of the worlds. It is in every atom and is in between every proton, neutron and electron.

Therefore, the Holy Spirit animates *all* people. In China, an Eastern country, the Holy Spirit in the human body is called "chi."

Metaphorically speaking, the Holy Spirit is like a smoke or gas, quite fluid and flexible. God's Light is the reflection of this "smoke" moving in and among atoms. Or another metaphor is that the Holy

Spirit is like the God system's blood stream.

"How do you divide God from the Holy Spirit?" Since the whole
thing is a system, you don't.

"How does **GRACE** work?" Grace is an intervention. It is the blessings conferred upon you by your karma or by God, or by the God-
System's intervention, which could, therefore, include blessings
bestowed by a Being from the higher realms: an angel, spirit guide,
spirit band, Ascended Master or a master celestial intelligence, such
as Metatron.

The intervention might also be set in motion by an embodied
Ascended Master or Avatar.

You have your part in the workings of grace. Metaphysical teachers
tell you, "Grace is one wing of the bird; your effort is the other
wing."

"There is a scientific discipline developing which has a great deal to
say to spiritual seekers. What is its name?" **QUANTUM PHYSICS**.
Quantum physics informs us that the basic fabric of nature lies at
the quantum level, far beyond or underneath atoms and molecules.
A quantum, defined as the basic unit of matter or energy, is from
10,000,000 to 100,000,000 times *smaller* than the smallest atom. At
this level, matter and energy become interchangeable. All quanta
are made of invisible vibrations – ghosts of energy – waiting to take
physical form.

One of the principles of Light is that an electron is both a particle
and a wave depending upon the energy that drives it. Energy is
vibration. Vibrations go from very fine to the dense black holes we
hear about in space.

Everything that is "firm," including your human body, first takes
form as intense but invisible vibrations, called quantum fluctuations,
before they proceed to coalesce into impulses of energy and particles
of matter.

It is probable that the vibrations of God/Holy Spirit and the vibrations of quanta are one and the same. For this reason alone, God

can now be proven scientifically. Because of this new and unfolding revelation, there is bound to be an acceleration of the merging of physical and spiritual sciences.

By definition, a physicist deals with energy, matter, motion and force. "Quantum vibrations," although most don't know it, are the physicist's words for "Holy Spirit." In my book, the two are inter–changeable, synonymous terms.

"I have heard the term **THOUGHT FORMS**. Why are two words that seem unrelated used together?" First came the word, John 1:1: "In the beginning was the word. And the word was with God, and the word was God." *Thoughts and spoken words are* **pre–matter**, *some might say quanta.* Thoughts, therefore, are vibrations which coalesce into ideas. Ideas vibrate into events and/or physical matter. Words are how God creates – and how you create.

The concept of matter forming from ideas now seems very believ-able. Ideas *are* vibrations.

We have talked about God operating as a system, like the human body is a system. Using a systems approach, we can conceptualize that the "head" of the system is the Cosmic Mind. The Cosmic Mind, the Godhead, thinks and starts creation. Said another way, creation starts by God's thoughts.

Since thoughts are pre-matter, you need to be very careful, use self-discipline in thoughts and speech, to create only what works for good. Every present thought or uttered word solidifies into a future condition. This prin-ciple is basic to metaphysics.

Can you see what the lazy habit of "awfulizing" does? And what about worrying when you are imagining the "worst case" in your dilemma or being a moaner–groaner type, "poor me!"

"**Reverse–thought forms**" do the opposite of "awfulizing" or "poor me-ing." Rather than actively trying to stop *what you don't want* that has already been created, you can put energy instead into *what you do want in its place.* This is a form of non–resistance. For exam-ple, if someone is trying to put you down, demean you by making negative remarks, rather than fighting back, you can visualize them being nice to you. You can change almost anything. There will be more on this in Chapter 3 under "affirmations."

Every atom has thought forms within it. These are intelligent vibrations – even gold knows how to be gold. The kitchen cabinet knows how to be a kitchen cabinet. And skin knows how to reproduce itself and never confuses itself with hair!

To use thought to create, you do not need to understand the details of the process any more than you need to know how electricity or a computer works. You just have to plug into the system.

Thus you can see where the following kinds of thoughts and speech might lead: "I never have any luck." "I can't lose weight and keep it off." "Just the thought of him makes me sick." "My children worry me to death."

Your thoughts and the words you utter are blueprints for the future; they direct the flow and currents of energy vibrations which "harden" into events, the material objects and the Beings that people your life.

"Why is the word **INTENT** a pivotal word in metaphysics?" You will be denied nothing that you want, if your intent is pure, very, very clear and you do not waiver. All you have to do is to *put the intent into clear thoughts, words and prayer; then listen to your intuition for the action you are supposed to take.* In Chapter 2, there is more on building your intuition under "meditation," "intuition" and "psychicness." In Chapter 3, prayer will be addressed.

The noble use of intent includes sharpening your commitment to become acquainted with your Soul and your spirit. After my near-death experience, I went on a passionate spiritual quest to become intimately acquainted with God and my own Soul or Being. After achieving a good degree of closeness, everything about my life slowly but surely fell into place. Now the process of living day by day is no longer a struggle.

"Could you say more about our **SOUL**, or synonymously, **OUR BEING?**" It is your individualized ray or Godself, your fractionated spark or fragment of The Lord of Light. John 15:5: "I am the vine, ye are the branches." It is your perfect gift from God, your universal **Self**, your real Self. Your Soul or Being is always perfect in its present stage of development, as a child is perfect in every stage of development.

Because you do not see enough, you cannot judge someone else's path. Even a murderer's act, if you could see the whole picture, would make sense. This is a difficult statement for most people. So hold that thought as we move along; it should ultimately make sense.

In the human body, two of my teachers said the Being sits close to the heart, center chest area, two to three inches off to the right of center. That is where I intuited it to be before I was told. (I have heard one other respected teacher say it sits in the upper abdomen.)

As individual rays, every Soul or "Being" comes out of the body of Light (God, the Cosmic Mind) and periodically goes home to get a super charge. Thus we are "Light Beings." Exodus 3:14: "I am that I am." This is the creation in the "like" image, our very essence, not our temporary, ever-changing-to-a-new persona or physical body. *We are created exactly in God's image.*

The term "chip off the old block" takes on new meaning.

Songstress Sophia sings, "I am the infinite within my Soul" and "I am opening up in sweet surrender."

This is very important for you to understand: Your Being has a fine vibration. Your human body, with its relatively coarse vibration, *gives the Being protection while on earth.* Your body needs to be healthy, therefore. *Your mind also protects your Being.* It needs to be healthy and drug free.

As already mentioned, your Being's energy will last throughout eternity. Your **persona**, your this-life body/personality/ego-mind, is transitory. Your Being is eternal.

Psalm 46:10: "Be still and know that I am God." If through quiet meditation, you can get in contact with the divinity of your own Being, you come to know it. *If you know your own Being, you know your parent.* Meditation is being intimate with God, going home. Luke 17:21: "Neither shall they say, Lo here! or, lo there! for, behold, the kingdom of God is within you." You experience God through the Being. Individually, to the extent that you concentrate on this process, you increasingly get authority from your own ray, your Being, your Soul, your Self instead of your this–life ego and culture.

Your Being operates in a world of symbol and speaks the language of imagery. It is your Being that speaks in your dreams. The Being expresses itself in work, in creating a home, in friendships, with family and in the arts, such as music, poetry, painting, creative writing and the architecture of wonderful buildings.

Every Being has a purpose and has come to do what no other Being can do. Therefore, copying what someone else has done with his or her life is not going to be comfortable or feel quite right. And at the extreme, not being true to your Soul's purpose can leave you depressed and miserable.

If you only knew what your Being has been through in its many lifetimes, you would love and honor your real Self without measure. You may still have difficulty with some things about the temporary body/personality/ego–minded person you have been and are. But love knowing your Being. Love being your Being. Love doing your Being's work. Love letting your Being play, sing, dance and have fun.

The phrase, "Love thyself" takes on a different meaning when you think of this statement as loving your Being, your Godself. So what if the person others have known as you has not been perfect? Tomorrow you *will* do it better.

Like a golf score, you can always work on yourself and get better. You are not competing against anyone. The army's slogan, "Be all you can be" fits.

Also, the phrase, "To thine own self be true" can mean trying to be true to your Soul's purpose, this time around.

Your Being, operating through your this–life's eyes, is naturally spiritual. You see the vastness of a starry sky, witness the order, sense the magnitude. Reverence is natural.

Your Being, may have been a division from the "big bang." If so, it has been around forever. You may also be a relatively "newer Soul." God continually gives birth to Souls as s/he sees the need. Shaman said, "On this planet, Souls go back to the blades of grass." The Edgar Cayce readings seem to indicate that as Beings we came into semi-animal bodies. It looks like we Souls have evolved the species upward, in physical, mental and spiritual ways.

As a Being, if I started through plant life, insects and fish, I don't remember. It doesn't matter to me *now*. Philosophical arguments over this sort of thing leave me cold. Whatever you think is perfectly fine. In the time it takes to argue, we could have done more of our Being's work and experienced more of its joy.

I do know that Beings are always striving towards higher consciousness. Higher evolution is inevitable over the millennia.

Your Being has two aspects, parts. Your Soul is like a baby. While you are in a human body, you have to teach it, work with it, to make it comfortable in this persona. You have a lot of subtle bodies, sort of like windows that get all fogged up. You have to see through all of them to get to your Being. That is where meditation comes in. You can get so that your Being communicates powerfully with you. Then you can continue at a faster pace, "getting your act together," melding your complex segments to act in beautiful concert.

The second part of your Being is *outside of* you. It is spiritual, but it is beyond spiritual. This "outside of yourself segment of your Being," your **higher self**, is trying to get back into you. Partial seeing (psychicness and knowingness) occurs when it is partially integrated into your physical self. Full power comes when the higher self is fully and permanently in, creating a persona/Being of bliss with complete compassion.

Eastern spiritual teachers talk about the lifting of veil after veil after veil. Behind the ego-mind there is joy.

Drunvalo Melchizedek talks of our higher self like this: It is like you are in a boat on a river. Your higher self is way above you, sort of like flying overhead. Of course, the higher self has a much greater vantage point. If you are approaching a dangerous spot in the river which you can't yet see, your higher self sees. Then it tries to warn you, through your intuition, to change your plans and actions.

Your higher self never sleeps and is potentially there at all times, if you are able to hear or sense it.

I have just recently learned that we have even more **higher selves** above our higher self. After an initial jolt, it makes perfect sense to me that while in the lower dimensions, we will always have a higher guidance that is individually, personally ours. So if we get the higher self into us that has been trying all our life to integrate with us, there is another. Conceptually, we could think of a lateral string of beads above us to use to pull ourselves up.

The Edgar Cayce readings said that the Soul does not project all of its elements into this dimension. Who knows how many aspects or higher selves we really have?

Your Being knows when it is time to stay and when it is time to go. When it is time, your Being will create the terminal illness or accident for your this-life body. Then, the eternal essence of you goes out to do other tasks, processes this life with other intelligent Beings, buzzes off to a planet or two to get re-calibrated, attends some celestial schools, decides what the next learning tasks are, and much, much more that I don't understand enough about to contemplate.

One of the reasons you as Being or Soul came to the Planet of the Cross at this time is that there are particular events you want to experience, special challenges you want to confront and overcome and special people you want to relate to. (Front cover question.)

The Being is very, very fine spiritual energy and this energy exists in the past, present and future. From the Bhagavad-gita, the Hindu "Bible" of Eastern thought written by many religious minds, Chapter 2, verse 20: "For the soul there is never birth nor death. Nor, having once been, does it ever cease to be. It is unborn, eternal, ever-existing, undying, and primeval. It is not slain when the body is slain." (The devotional literature of the Bhagavad-gita took form about the beginning of the Christian era.)

The real you is Soul, Being, Self, essence, a small ray of God, on an eternal journey!

Metaphorically speaking, if I took a piece of 8 1/2 by 11 inch white paper, and cut it into tiny, multiple, unique, different–shaped pieces, I could let each "puzzle piece" represent one Being. Now, please pay close attention to the next four sentences. They are extremely important: *No Soul is superior to another. We all have a place where we fit. We each have a unique purpose every lifetime. We are each beautiful as a single component and as an essential, indivisible part of the whole.*

There is a song with the words in the first line, "We are one in the spirit, we are one in the Lord." Another line says, "And we know that all unity will one day be restored." As said before, since God is a system like the human body is a system, then we each have the importance and function of one cell in the body of God.

Anyone who thinks his or her level of consciousness is superior to someone else's has a **spiritual ego**.

What would Jesus have done without students? Or disciples? Don't you see that Jesus, his disciples, and his followers were all operating within the God system? No Being is more important than another Being because they are all necessary to the integrated whole. Jesus knew he was no more important than the blind man he healed. *Over the long term, everything works together for love.*

Beings are as different as human faces are different. Beings are as alike as human faces are alike. Creativity flows from your Being. Touching your Being in meditation daily keeps you in tune with your Soul's purpose and helps you access your creativity.

By the way, your purpose in this life may be specific, perhaps "to learn medicine" or something more general like "to help a specific person in his or her time of grief." But there is a general purpose for everyone. Writer Lawrence Hinckley said:

> Life has a purpose and only one purpose: it is our Soul-growth. We *must grow* spiritually. This is the only thing that really counts in this world, and we had better be about it. It is something we must do for ourselves. No one else can do it for us.

In some lifetime, we have to come to terms with our Being.

When you set time for devotion every day, your personal wants that take you away from God dim as the Being through your intuition helps you get rid of unwholesome desires by placing before it something of *far greater attraction*, God. This long process occurs slowly, *naturally*. It process doesn't produce feelings of deprivation or guilt.

Few long–time meditators act viciously, practice conspicuous consumption, eat animals, or are greedy. Anyone who has meditated daily for many years can't be anything but generous of heart, kind, respectful of resources, busily doing their Being's work.

There are material objects, people and habits that are cluttering your life and sucking your time and energy. As you gain greater and greater access to your guidance (your Being plus its Higher–Self aspects), you just know what to keep and what to let go, who to move closer to and who to move away from. Shaman said, "Anything you don't need is a burden."

To help my students sort their material possessions, I tell them, "Space in the house gives peace. Only keep what is beautiful, functional or sentimental." Everything else is the outward sign of a neurosis. All great teachers have traveled very light.

Metaphysicians know that the condition of their personal clothes closet represents the state of their consciousness! How does yours look? Are you always cleaning it out, letting go of what you don't want or need, rearranging it, neatening it? And are you thoughtful about what you put in your closet, your life? Or do you have a lot of "stuff" poorly arranged clogging your life? Cleaning out your closet, garage and shelves, leaves consciousness space for the new to come in, space for new vibrations to take form or new happenings to take place in your life.

Eastern Philosophy teaches to first worship the Being within. The West says to worship God. To my way of thinking, both are important. It isn't one *or* the other. I love with a passion my Light Being Mommy/Daddy, God, and I share an equal passion for my individualized ray, the Light Being, who is God's child. They are so interconnected, how could they possibly, in reality, be separate? Probably for the rest of my life, I will be working in some way to encourage a re-marriage of Eastern and Western ideas. The time is ripe. These two great paths to God should never have been in opposition. And they weren't in reality!

God created this world and all worlds in all universes. And hallelu-jah! *Beings are considered by God to be the most wondrous things in all of this creation. Our planet is just one playground for Beings' learning; some say a school. (And others call it a graduate school!)*

The Being as seen by Edgar Cayce in trance was a small dot. My shaman teacher, who had not read Edgar Cayce (or anything meta-physical!), says our Being is the size of a thimble.   P. M. H. Atwater, who wrote COMING BACK TO LIFE: THE AFTER-EFFECTS OF THE NEAR-DEATH EXPERIENCE, gave similar explanations. (In her advanced metaphysical book, a brilliant work, she describes her own NDEs. They differ from mine in that she had already been meta-physically educated, so she watched from a special, educated van-tage point. She could even *see* her own thought forms coming out of her Being as blobs! Even more incredible, she created buildings and trees from her thoughts, got "tired" of them, and disappeared them!)

As I said earlier, our Being, when unembodied, has its own eyes, ears, intelligence and will. And shaman says "nose." Although I didn't smell anything, other NDEers have.

I have altered anonymous' self-esteem-raising paragraph printed in my church's magazine:

I LOVE MY BEING AS PART OF THE WHOLE
I AM THAT I AM
(Hebrew: Ehyeh Asher Ehyeh. Phonetically: "A" as if you were starting to say the English alphabet: A–ya aw–sure A–ya)

I am worth celebrating. I am worth everything. I am unique. In this whole world there is only one me. There is no Being with my talents, experiences, gifts. No one may take my place. God created only one me. I have immense potential to love, care, create, grow, sacrifice. I believe in my Self. It doesn't matter my age, color of skin, my job,   status, or whether my this–life parents loved me or not. Maybe they wanted to but couldn't. It doesn't matter what I have been, things I've done, mistakes I've made, people I have hurt. I am forgiven. I am accepted. I am okay. I am loved in spite of everything or perhaps because of everything. I nourish my Being. I celebrate me. I begin now. I start anew every day. And I know what I say about myself is true also of every other Being.

"Is my human **SPIRIT** the same thing as my Being (Soul)?" No, your spirit is the component of you that gets excited and turned on by projects, people, God, work, leisure and your own Being. Remember when you were "in love?" These "turn–ons" give you energy. Your spirit at its best is vivid, lucid and powerful.

Your spirit comes out of your this–life persona, blended with your Being's vibrations. Your spirit, therefore, is different every life.

It is important that you involve yourself in projects and people that "turn you on." Nothing is better for health and longevity than this practice. Your spirit brings life to living. Poet David Whyte says, "Always this energy smolders inside, when it remains unlit, the body fills with dense smoke."

Your spirit has two divisions, one always resides in your body while you are alive – the other part of your spirit, your subtle body spirit, usually stays in the body, but can move about freely. That part, the subtle body spirit, guided by your mind, has been known to take off for the beach when you get bored, leaving your body sitting or standing. School teachers recognize the vacant stares of students "not really there," especially in the spring.

"With all this out–of–body talk, are we really ever connected to any-thing firm?" Shirley MacLaine talked about a **silver cord** that seemed to tie her to God. Yes, I believe there is a tie, similar to an umbilical cord, a very comforting thought. And we do need com-forting thoughts!

In our home, we have a picture on our fireplace of my beloved shaman's face. It is a three–fourths face shot. Directly behind and "hugging him" is a long–white–Light cord. When I asked him if that was his umbilical cord to The Universe, his term for the God–System, he said, "Yes." Shaman spoke of the photographer who took the shot saying, "He can move into the higher consciousness to shoot his pictures."

"Are the terms **NEW SOULS and OLD SOULS** as self–explanatory as they seem?" Yes, new Souls or Beings are those who have not lived on our planet earth many lifetimes. They fool us at first because their physical body at birth is the same as yours or mine.

Unlike a human three–year–old child from whom we wouldn't dream of expecting grown–up behavior, we innocently expect the impossible of new souls. We don't recognize them! Our unrealistic expectations can lead to very sad consequences. It works in a way very similar to leaving a three–year old child alone in a brand new home with some red, blue and green paint along with the paint brushes.

To solidify your thought process on this concept, we allow new Souls to drive cars, own guns and have babies.

New Souls have not yet come into their potential – as a matter of fact, they have a long way to go! New Souls in bodies cause us stress. By their new–Soul behavior, they "light up" *our* neuroses and negative emotions, "push our buttons," and thus contribute, in the cosmic scheme of things, to the growth of our Being. (As new Souls in former lives, we acted exactly like them!)

New Souls help old Souls grow and vice–versa. It will help you to take things "with a grain of salt" when you *grasp* this principle. How else would you "stretch" if you didn't run into resistance? A hurdler always jumping over a one–foot hurdle will never be able to jump over a four–foot hurdle. New Souls *do* stretch you.

There is a saying that old Souls light up a room when they enter. But new Souls light up the room when they leave! Children like to play with other children. New Souls like to hang out with other new Souls.

My heart goes out to to those in occupations requiring a lot of con-tact with individuals and groups of new Souls, for example, police work. The police are taught that there is a "standard brand" of human Being. But, in their heart of hearts, they know better!

Many old Souls have lived over 5,000 lifetimes and are using some of the later lifetimes wisely.

Most of us can identify with the term **lost Soul**. You see them wandering around with spacey eyes in cities or along the highways. Lost Souls eventually get found and helped by evolved Souls, but maybe not this lifetime. I would be a Pollyanna if I believed that once a human brain has been almost totally destroyed, there is hope for further evolution in this life.

And this leads to a fact that even I, after all these years, have difficulty accepting: Your Soul goes backwards some lifetimes. Not every life is a Soul–energy building life; some lifetimes your Soul gets drained. However, no spiritual *evolution* is ever lost.

Old Souls by their example and by their wisdom and teachings inspire new Souls. Each of us helps some Soul or Souls; that is one of the reasons you chose to come to the Planet of the Cross.

Again, this whole *lifetime's process* works for love. As an example, in one life a new Soul kidnaps and murders a child. The child's community is activated, outraged. They start functioning as a more positive, coordinated town. The members of the child's family become closer, and love blossoms as never before. At the same time, the offender learns from the consequences.

I am not dispassionate toward the child's parents, family and friends. The greatest loss in a life is the loss of a child. We have all experienced the death of our child or children in one lifetime or another.

If you know of someone who has lost a child (or anyone they love), a kind act would be to give them a copy of GRIEF, CLIMB TOWARD UNDERSTANDING, Phyllis Davies, Sunnybank Publishers, P. O. Box 945, San Luis Obispo, CA 93406. Davies lost a little boy in an airplane crash.

As I sit here writing this, in the back of my mind, I am planning how to conduct the memorial services for a couple whose young, grown son was found dead two days ago in his pick–up truck.

Apparently, he got some bad recreational drugs. In the truck was a sack and a that–day store receipt for oil; it is doubtful that he was suicidal. He would not have been thinking of changing his oil. The folks who knew him in our small community are contorted by grief. The loss on this plane is emotionally immense.

I do not believe, however, that he died in vain. Someone may read this, fully realizing for the first time the dangers associated with trusting some greedy new Soul with the quality of their drugs and stop taking that risk.

There is a good chance the passer of the drugs in this case will not be free for long. Because of this death, four other young buyers who have had chest pains just made a sheriff's report.

See Appendix E for a transcript of the above Memorial Service.

Up front, if you knew people were new Souls, you could approach them like you do children. They need an extraordinary amount of love plus discipline, as children and adults, and a terrific amount of understanding. You can be compassionate, but you cannot let them get away with negative behavior. You have to help new Souls grow like you do children. They have to be taught and when necessary, restrained, and when necessary, punished.

I don't believe in capital punishment. I do believe in a life sentence with continued education. Otherwise, newer Souls are going to come back and reincarnate behaviorally right where they left off!

"You have mentioned **HIGHER REALMS** and **OTHER DIMENSIONS**. Could you say more?" It is not my calling to expand in detail on these advanced topics. Read four awesome authors: Dr. Jim J. Hurtak, Paul Twitchell, P. M. H. Atwater and Godfre Ray King. I have already pointed you toward the Advanced Metaphysical Books section in this book, where they are listed.

But, I am not going to leave you completely hanging, either. As a spark of consciousness, you evolve. In most lifetimes, on the Planet of the Cross, you get more "mindpower" or energy, as you embody in different forms. You become a "bigger" Being.

An insect, although physically here, may have its consciousness in the first dimension. A deer may have its consciousness in the second dimension. An ordinary person has his or her consciousness in the third dimension. Jesus and other God–realized Masters, and Avatars, had/have their consciousnesses while here in the fourth dimension, called by metaphysicians the **Christ consciousness**. Many different consciousnesses are experienced by different personas in the same physical location (insect, deer, third–dimensional human.)

The usual human experience has been on a narrow band of consciousness. This is because how you perceive your environment depends primarily on the physical brain in the body you occupy. (I don't think an insect is very jazzed with its life, but I don't remember.) You get greater access to God's intelligence as you expand your consciousness and move up the spiritual and evolutionary ladder. There are so many, many, many incredible things to experience in your Being's future. If you only knew, you would be overwhelmed with excitement. Read the advanced books and you will get more than a clue.

Perhaps because of my near–death experience, traveling without a persona is easy for me to imagine. I was having a wonderful time flying out over the trees and then moving upward toward what I thought at that time was God, the Light Being. From this experience, it seems obvious to me that out–of–the–body, we are not hindered by the limited view that our this–life personality/body/ego–mind projects for us.

As I conceptualize it now, while in a body, it is as if we have a transparency laid over or implanted in our brain. Each new dimension has a different and deeper transparency consistent with the potential of the Being.

Each time, as a Being in a body, we rise to a still–higher consciousness "transparency," life reveals a higher process to us. Advanced metaphysical writer, Elizabeth Clare Prophet, says there are thirty–three astral planes with thirty–three divisions each. There are, correspondingly thirty–three higher heavens with thirty–three divisions each. It is to these higher planes the Soul sooner or later aspires. Now, back to you and me and now.

What I believe is different and dramatic in this current Aquarian

Age is that in order to save this planet, the higher forces have decided they must pull the "third–dimensional transparency" for the *whole human race*. We have gotten ourselves into a terminal mess.

Here comes a shocker – what I believe is the revealing truth: If your physical heart, body and mind are not ready for the consciousness transformation into the fourth and perhaps higher dimensions, your body will not be able to stay here. It will be vibrated to death, indirectly, by the intense love. Your Soul will leave, something like being driven out of a room when someone is playing music too loudly, a type of music or vibration, that you just can't handle.

This is the *evolutionary leap* that will eventually bring peace on earth and conscious living.

To totally integrate this consciousness shift, our bodies' DNA and RNA plus the patterns of our brain waves are actually shifting. Later I will tell you how to take care of your changing body/mind in which *the atoms are actually getting further apart in order to carry more Light, more of God's love vibration.*

We may be the first Beings on this planet to be aware of our own evolutionary leap as it is taking place, our very–own quantum transformation!

This is why things seem to be so crazy all over the world. The love is coming down so strong and is getting stronger. The love is lighting up people's stuck spots, and some are dying already. If you know of some very troubled individual who has been resistant to getting help or counseling, you know they are acting out at their worst. They are not able to properly assimilate the higher energies now entering the human consciousness.

But back to higher realms and other universes. There may be countless universes to visit. According to Dr. Hurtak, there are one hundred million occupied planets. The experiences in sound, color, form, variety, fragrance and thrill are there for us, eventually. The higher experiences are perhaps eons away, but maybe sooner? I am really off my turf on these subjects.

You need not worry about any of this. In the past, your Being has

always been drawn to the right spot for your individual consciousness evolution. In the future, your Being will be drawn to the right
spot for your individual consciousness evolution.

"Who was the **EDGAR CAYCE** you referred to earlier?" Cayce lived
from 1877 to 1945. He was raised on a farm in western Kentucky.
Even though his family was traditional and they were *exceptionally
devout Christians*, he experienced psychic phenomena as natural experiences in his everyday life. Finally, overcoming the disparity in
beliefs, he let himself use his gifts. He gave over 14,246 self-induced,
out of ordinary-consciousness, **trance** readings. His wife was often
present and *most of these readings were recorded by his stenographer.*

As a young woman, from 1958 through 1960, I earned my living as
a stenographer. Later, I taught shorthand at the college level for five
years from 1968 through 1972. So I speak with a little authority: At
high speeds, 120 to 140 words per minute, for a good steno, ninety-
seven percent accuracy is common. In trance work, coming from
another dimension, the voice is greatly slowed. I am guessing, but I
would say Cayce probably brought in ideas at slower than 60 words
a minute. At that slow speed, my estimate is that his stenographer,
devoted to the Cayce cause, and familiar with his style and vocabulary, probably had an accuracy rate of over ninety-nine percent.

Edgar Cayce was not an author and did very little writing. Since
Cayce's death, these accurately recorded trance state transcripts
typed by his stenographer have been read, studied and organized.
Commentaries have been made by many serious and devout metaphysical seekers, including his family.

In spite of his "ordinary awareness" training, *not* believing in reincarnation, these trance readings given to individuals *often* included
past-life information. They also included information about healing
the human body and events that were to happen in the future.
These cures and prophecies have turned out to be quite accurate.
His work has gained the respect of both skeptics and serious psychic
researchers.

After 1972, Cayce's prophesies failed because of events on a cosmic
scale that until recently have not been generally known. A little
later, I'll tell you about the happenings which altered our future and

bought Mother Earth some time to right herself. This protective move for us, conducted by loving extraterrestrial Beings from a higher consciousness, made *all* old prophesies obsolete, including prophet Nostradamus' after-1972 predictions. We'll take a look at that intervention in Chapter 3.

For fifty years, Cayce's family and other responsible individuals, have continued to catalog his work and write books as a component of the work of the Association for Research and Enlightenment. For information, write ARE, P. O. Box 595, Virginia Beach, VA 23451, including a SASE.) The many books about Edgar Cayce's work stand as a cornerstone of metaphysics in America in the Twentieth century. My favorite is EDGAR CAYCE'S STORY OF JESUS edited by Jeffrey Furst. In Furst's Appendix A are twelve pages written by Cayce himself about his life and work, one of Cayce's few written documents.

"Could you say more about the clairvoyant **NOSTRADAMUS**?" He is the first recorded transgenerational psychic, a sixteenth-century prophet and poet, 1503 – 1566. He did his own recording. A respected French physician, he made about one thousand predictions. Deeply devout like Cayce (an absolute necessity with no exceptions if you want an authentic psychic reading), Nostradamus had Jewish ancestors and a Christian background. His predictions until 1972 have been amazingly accurate. He told about the future inventions of planes and rockets and the moon landing. The death-knoll to planet earth was supposed to have come in a terrible nuclear war in 1994.

Nostradamus lamented on man's insatiable need to refine the art of war. He told us that all we have to do is to change our thoughts about what we want and the future will be changed. **Let's do it!**

There is an excellent commercial video on the life and prophesies of Nostradamus narrated by Orson Wells. I once owned it; now I don't remember the name, perhaps "Nostradamus?" It has been shown on TV. If interested, you might ask at your video store.

"Well, nearly everyone these days is talking about **KARMA**. So, how does it work?" Karma is the law of action, "For every action, there is a reaction." You reap what you sow. Or, "what goes around, comes around." Through your many thousands of lives, your thoughts, deeds, acts and attitudes have set in motion future thoughts, deeds, actions and attitudes, all natural consequences of your former behavior.

All you can do is to take your "earned" bad karma gracefully, and try to become, each lifetime, closer to living in harmony with your Being's purposes. Through devotion to God, good thoughts and intelligent acts, your negative karma gets muted somewhat.

Some say this current age heralds in a release from bad karma, but don't count on it! Others say that becoming Self-realized is the way to be released from bad karma. But again, this is not certain. Why was Jesus crucified before he had a chance to make himself clear?

The best way to beat negative karma is to try to live as purely as possible, keeping the needs of your Being/God in the forefront.

You create for yourself the events and conditions in the future of your Soul's journey in this life and future lives by (1) the thoughts you hold; (2) the thoughts you express; (3) the motives behind your acts; and (4) the acts themselves.

The more evolved you are spiritually, the quicker your negative karma comes back to you. This is a hard lesson. You can't get away with much. You probably have seen some new Souls doing greedy or stupid things all their lives, and they never seem to "get theirs."

Parmahansa Yogananda wrote AUTOBIOGRAPHY OF A YOGI before he died. Yogananda said, "An understanding of karma as the law of justice serves to free the human mind from resentment against God and man. A person's karma follows him from incarnation to incarnation until fulfilled or spiritually transcended."

Sai Baba is the great living Avatar, whom I will talk about toward the end of this chapter. Baba speaks of transcending karma in this way:

> You might say that the karma of previous births has to be consumed in this life, and that no amount of grace can save you from that. Evidently someone has taught you to believe

> so. But I assure you, you need not suffer from karma like that. When a severe pain torments you, the doctor gives you a morphine injection, and you do not feel the pain, though it is there in the body. Grace is like the morphine; the pain is not felt though you go through it."

Hopefully, Jesus did not suffer as we might have thought on that cross.

My shaman teacher spoke of this transcendence with an example: "Say in another life you murdered a certain Soul. But since that life, you have really evolved spiritually, learned many, many lessons. In this life, when you cross paths with that Soul, the person comes up to you, gives you a dirty look, and walks off."

Cayce gave this advice on not collecting bad karma, "Think and act as if you are always in the presence of God because you are." Shaman said it this way, "You are always being watched."

As I read the book, EDGAR CAYCE'S STORY OF KARMA by Mary Ann Woodward, I extracted from Cayce's included readings a list of behaviors that create positive karma and a list of behaviors that create negative karma.

Karmic law isn't exactly an "eye for an eye," although it sometimes is. It is more like thoughts and deeds vibrate as either good, indifferent or bad. More specifically, there is a long continuum from extremely good to extremely bad. These register as vibrations of a certain ilk in consciousness. Vibration or wave length is everything. In the journey of your Soul, you get back what you have given out as those vibrations take form in events, relationships and material objects.

Positive thoughts, actions and behaviors build Soul energy. The more Soul energy you have, the more choices you have whether in or out of body. Here is Cayce's list of behaviors leading to positive karma.

Positive karma list. These increase Soul energy:

Being cheerful; being faithful; being forgiving; being generous; being gentle; being hopeful; being humble; being long suffering (means "not thinking of or doing retribution"); being loving; being patient, "For in patience, ye may become aware of your Soul;" being sincere to your spiritual impulses; being the "saving grace" for someone; being tolerant; being truthful; being understanding; demonstrating brotherly love; dividing self and self's surroundings with those less fortunate; doing devotions and worship; doing good deeds; giving thanks; having patience with the wayward; keeping promises; knowing your inner Being; losing self in God; making the best of opportunities presented; praying; seeking higher knowledge; serving fellow man, "Three times a day ask, 'Lord, what would you have me do?'"

More actions producing positive karma: sharing another's burdens; showing concern; showing endurance; showing kindnesses; showing mercy; showing perseverance; smiling often; trying to right wrongs; and working hard.

Be careful now if you do some of these behaviors with the expectancy that tomorrow something good will happen. There is a saying in metaphysics, *"Deeds, not results." That is, you do what your Soul and best impulses say, but you don't look for the return. It will come, sometime, some day when you are least expecting it, but the timing isn't going to seem logical.* Even the good thing itself may not seem logical. Also, if you do something good just to get the return, your attitude and intent are not pure.

Negative karma list:

Being a quitter, giving up: being envious (begrudging another's possession of something, coveting that which belongs to another); being indifferent; being jealous (distrusting, having suspicion, sometimes anger); being resentful; being spiteful; being selfish; condemning self; condemning the traits of others; displaying greed; displaying self-aggrandizement. [Here is the way I look at self-aggrandizement: One woman puts on make-up to look better than other women. Another women puts on make-up to make the most of the individualized beauty God has given her. One man drives a new car as a status symbol to show off his success, making himself superior to others. Another man drives a new car because it rides smoothly enabling him to keep his precious gift, his own body, free from fatigue. *Again, the attitude and intent behind thought and behavior are all important.*]

More behaviors producing negative karma: displaying wrath; disregarding another person's needs; hardening your heart; hating; having doubt; having fear; having rigid attitudes; holding grudges; making "idle" words; overindulgence in appetites; self–indulgence; self–satisfaction (puffed–up ego, conceit); showing malice; "sins" of omission; taking advantage of others; and using self–centered behavior.

In the profound Eckankar materials, some negative karma producers listed are: evil gossip; slander; backbiting; profanity; fault–finding; malice; impatience; resentment; mockery; destructive criticism; lying; perjury; misrepresentation; robbery; bribery; trickery of all sorts; attachment to surroundings, people or credentials; executing the mandates of God in interest of self; having no sense of humor; bigotry; self–assertion over others; scolding; liking publicity; and making a show of religion.

These lists are not totally comprehensive, but you can get the drift!

Some of the most difficult metaphysical questions when life hands you a "dirty deal" are "Where did that come from?" or "Why did I have to go through that?" Or "What did I do to deserve that?"

"Was it bad karma catching up with me from God–only–knows–what life? Am I creating that experience out of my own negative thoughts? Was I given that experience or obstacle to stretch my spiritual and personal growth? Or did overcoming it cause a positive reorganization of my Being after getting rid of some attitudes and blocks that were stunting my spiritual growth? Or was it simply an accident?"

Shaman says accidents are extremely rare, but that accidents do happen. Accidents can be used for growth and even to subtract from the negative karma in your **karma bank**, the place where your records are kept. (I will speak of the record–keeping place in Chapter 2.) I believe that in the cosmic scheme of things, the greatest good for all prevails, always. I have perfect faith that if we could see the big picture, we would totally understand.   And always in my mind is what shaman said, "When your time has come to pay off negative karma, be graceful, bend with it smoothly like a reed in the wind."

Besides, we can inspire people with our patience and lack of resentment.

Although I ask them, I no longer *torture* myself with questions. I just say to myself, "Ouch, sure am glad to get that one out of the way!"

"Doesn't the idea of **FREE WILL** conflict with the idea of karma?" Yes, because of your karma, obviously your "free will" is only partially free. With your own behavior, you have created strong likelihoods or probabilities that specific future experiences will come about. However, life presents you with many true choices and true opportunities. *Not even God knows for sure what will happen for you.*

I explain this with an analogy to metaphysical students: It is as if our life is lived in a dry, giant riverbed. We are in the groove of that riverbed and have freedom, but within its constraints. We can wander all over, but in this life, because of our past karma, we can wander only inside that immense riverbed, never out of it.

These "river walls" are not what they first seem. Let me explain the process to you with a personal example: In my life, there has been nothing set in motion for me to become a concrete worker with such a high-level of skill that I could build a dam; but my husband has that skill. One of his purposes this time around is to gain a complete understanding of how to alter the physical world in positive ways.

In other words, those "river walls" *keep you focused on your own Soul path* during this lifetime. The walls are a help, not a hindrance. This process is not so much different than good human parents setting boundaries for their children, but letting them have freedom within the boundaries.

You can also look at free will this way: In the universe, there are two basic kinds of intelligence. One is "patterned intelligence." This intelligence gets things done *automatically*. A few examples are the natural healing of wounds, the planets' orbits, genetic patterns for trees, bees, or a certain breed of dog produced from mating (two pedigree cocker spaniels are going to produce cocker spaniel pups.) This intelligence is programmed in. Your free will is limited in effecting changes here.

The second intelligence is a creative and problem–solving mind that you plug into with your individual brain. This includes a vast intelligence network, only accessible to you while embodied through the human brain. This second, creative intelligence can affect and change the first intelligence, the patterned intelligence, but usually does not. *This second intelligence, unpatterned and creative is activated by the words you speak and think, your prayers and meditations, higher Beings watching over you* and God. Heaven is definitely interactive; and you can use your free will to do a lot of lifestyle designing. This is the intelligence *you* are in *charge of.*

Please don't be concerned at this point if you cannot grasp the point I am making. There will be more on the brain and mind in Chapter 2 where I try hard to give you a different way of looking at the subject.

"You have spoken about the many lives we live. Could you tell us more about **REINCARNATION?**" It is interesting, but the Holy Bible does not have a statement in it that says, "There is no reincarnation." It is my belief that since reincarnation is an Eastern idea, this concept was so taken for granted that nothing very specific was written into scriptures. It was an established precept because everyone believed in it. If you had been a disciple making statements, you wouldn't write: "The sun comes up every morning." "We go to bed at night." "There are stars in the sky." or "Our Soul lives many lives."

I say from my heart that I believe the scribe got it right in John 3:3, but sadly misinterpreted Jesus' continuing comments, which were not written down until at least fifty years later. This is almost as large a misunderstanding as thinking of God as a big Caucasian male sitting up in the clouds!

John 3:3: "With all the earnestness I possess, I must tell you this. Unless you are born again, you will never get into the Kingdom of God."

See Appendix G, "Bible Scripture References for Mystical Phenomena," under "Reincarnation" for verses where reincarnation *is* mentioned.

One of my devout fundamental Christian sons (fundamental, not
fundamentalist; they are non–denominational), put together this
Bible verse list, the few citations, where reincarnation is mentioned.

If you check out these references, here is what you will find: In
Matthew 11:14, Jesus talks to the disciples saying that John the
Baptist is Elijah who has come again. In Matthew 17:10 again Jesus
talks of Elijah coming again as John the Baptist, saying there had
been another time Elijah had been here unrecognized and was badly
treated. In Luke 1:17 an angel promises Zacharias that his to–be–
born son, John–the–Baptist, will be a replica of Elijah.

In Matthew 27:52-53 we are told that after the crucifixion and Jesus'
death, tombs opened and many godly men and women in the area
who at some time in the past had died came back to life again. This
may mean a resurrection instead of a reincarnation.

And in Malachi 4:5 we are promised a prophet "like Elijah" who will
bring fathers and children together again to be of one mind and one
heart." I will use one more reincarnation quote from the Bible in
Chapter 3.

I was in my forties before I became aware of any of my own past
lives. Until 1988, I had never seriously considered the idea of reincarnation. I thought it was a "cute" idea, something akin to Santa
Claus. Then, one day out of the clear blue, during my favorite
teacher's class, he looked over to me and popped this unusual question: "What did you do with all of those cages?" Startled, I replied, "I
don't know what you mean."

Then he said, "In another life, you were a keeper of animals in cages.
You grew tired of their care and took a vacation, leaving them unat-
tended. When you came back, the animals were all dead. The
shame of this killed you." As he said this, it felt as if he had pulled a
metal splinter out of my heart, and I began to weep.

But, I forgot about this until about a month later when I was in the
presence of another psychic. At that time, she did not know my
teacher. She was doing past–life readings around a circle of people
sitting in my Monterey living room. She told one man he had been
a sailor. He admitted liking pictures of boats and being near the

ocean. She told a woman that she had been a male and a black–
smith. When she got to me, she said, "In another life, you kept ani–
mals in cages, and you sure got tired of cleaning up all that sh. ."

Since then, I have become a believer. I have spontaneously seen
some of my past lives and had psychics pick up the threads of oth–
ers in private readings. I have included drawings of a few of these
past lives as I described them to psychic/artist Jhara, a metaphysical
lady I met at that long–ago workshop (when the leader told me that
through the ages, the knowledge has come through me). Jhara was
able to tune in on these lives and draw the pictures accurately!

In order for you to get a new beginning, usually the Being upon
birth here cannot remember past lives. When you strive toward
higher levels of consciousness, some of your lives are revealed to
help you understand your tendencies, your lessons, and your tri–
umphs over past challenges, as well as how you have stumbled on
the spiritual path.

On the illustration, my current life is in the upper left corner. Since the drawing was made five years ago, perhaps another dozen of my lives have been revealed, a few of these I will speak of later.

The same evening that the second psychic reinforced the animals-in-cages life, she also asked me "How many pairs of boots do you have?" I said, "Oh, I guess at least eight or nine." Then she said, "In another life you lived in a very cold country close to Russia. You thought you would never get your feet warm!" It is true that in this life I tend to have very cold feet and love boots. I find all of this very mysterious. How many other patterns do we bring along with us?

Each Being is comprised of all the lives lived. Each Being has a unique journey in its growth. It is left with free will to help choose its path. It chooses to relate closely with those who do one of two things and usually a combination of the two: give the needed lessons; give emotional support.

We tend to reincarnate in large, extended **Soul families** and take the different roles, like mother, father, sister, brother, boss, servant, etc. Although you chose your human parents this life, the needs of the group were taken into account. Therefore, at the choice point, you might have had to take a second or third choice; the evolution and higher attainment of the species is all important.

Each Being has its own special place in the whole of The Lord of Light's kingdom. (Be good to everyone you contact, he or she was probably a relative in a former life!) Reincarnation is the great equalizer. "If you get to be a peacock in this life, in the next life you may be a featherduster!" Although this is a joke, I might choose to come back to live with a race of people I once scorned.

"Do we ever return to being an animal?" Well, maybe "a blackbird with beady little yellow eyes!" I didn't think shaman was kidding because we were taking notes. He said one day, "I astralprojected my spirit into one of those nuisance birds and much to my surprise, I learned they were reincarnated greedy business people!"

Ninety-five percent of your past lives on the Planet of the Cross have been spent in a survival mode. In comparison, in the United

States, other Western countries, and some of the newly developed Eastern countries, most of us got a relatively good life this time around.

If you are an old Soul, in order to round out your Soul with experiences so that finally your compassion becomes total, you have done just about everything. You have murdered and lived the difficult lives of being handicapped and a homosexual. You have been both sexes, all skin colors, inhabited many nations and climates and have been in most religions.

Your Being's growth or retardation resulting from this life is carried forth into the next life. Almost every life gets a little bit easier as you bring yourself more in line with your Divine potential. However, this doesn't mean that next time you will be wealthier, famous or have more appliances. Shaman said that next life, many of us will be born in the Third World.

It is important to realize that you have looked and acted much like everyone you meet: the people who are pleasing to you, those who annoy or anger you and those you find unattractive.

Shaman urged us to see both uplifting video movies and depressing movies. He said, "Every life you see is one you don't have to do."

In one of his discourses, Rajneesh called your lives akin to "paper sacks." In this life, your Being goes inside to light up and animate for a while, then the external body is easily discarded. However, it may be of interest to you to know that Drunvalo Melchizedek, the Being who has come back from an advanced dimension to help teach us about our past and future, says that not every dimension is so casual about physical bodies. This last fact shows why we have to keep an open mind and remain flexible thinkers.

There is just one Being life, lived inside one persona after another. Approximately every seventh life, you come down just to rest your Being and get centered. You lead an ordinary, relatively easy life. Perhaps you know of someone who is having one of these? I had mine last life when I was a Civil-War-time woman illustrated in the long hoop skirt. (In that life, my this-life husband was my best friend from our little girlhoods on.)

There is a book channeled by Levi and written about one hundred years ago called THE AQUARIAN GOSPEL OF JESUS THE CHRIST. It purports to be what really happened in the life of Jesus and is a required text in the ministry program in which I studied. Below is a beautiful excerpt. Jesus was commenting on a wandering group of singers and musicians who were producing enchanting music:

> All things result from natural law. These people are not young. A thousand years would not suffice to give them such divine expressiveness, and such purity of voice and touch.
>
> Ten thousand years ago these people mastered harmony. In days of old they trod the busy thoroughfares of life, and caught the melody of birds and played on harps of perfect form.
>
> These wandering people form a part of heaven's orchestra, and in the land of perfect things, the very angels will delight to hear them sing and play.
>
> And they have come again to learn still other lessons from the varied notes of manifests.

"You mentioned being a Spiritualist minister. What is **SPIRITUALISM**?" There is a reason the following definition comes verbatim from June G. Blelzer's THE DONNING INTERNATIONAL PSYCHIC ENCYCLOPE-DIC DICTIONARY. While some of my fellow UCM Spiritualist minis-ters say they don't believe in reincarnation, here is an impartial source:

> Spiritualism is "A science, philosophy, and religion using the doctrine of metaphysics; belief in the continuity of life after death and communication with this life for the advancement of civilization and personal growth; scientific study of the etheric world [other dimensions], its properties, functions, and relationship to mankind and God; belief in reincarnation; uses the Bible as a guide to show one how to perfect oneself in his or her many incarnations; uses psychic and mediumship skills for growth and advancement of all."

Along these lines, a few of my colleagues will do some occult practices, but for me, my Being says "No!"

"What do you mean by **OCCULT PRACTICES**?" One example is conducting a **seance** and having what sounds like a dead relative's voice come through the **medium** who is charging for the session. The reason I would never set this sort of thing up is that I have respect for all Beings' paths whether in body or out. And calling a Being back to the earth plane to satisfy some relative's curiosity or longing is just not polite. Unembodied Beings have work to do, and they are busy doing it. Holding them to the earth plan slows down their evolvement.

Another practice I avoid is giving psychic readings to answer mundane questions, "Will my sister visit me in August?" "What color dress should I buy for the dance?"

A program on TV told us recently that **goddess worship** is what the new age is all about. I thought I had seen and heard just about everything but that was news to me. The goddess worship as portrayed in that program showed a group of women (1) choosing a goddess of the evening from their group to honor; (2) bowing down to that "goddess;" and (3) kissing the goddess–of–the–evening's feet. Now, on Mother's Day and Father's Day we might bow down and kiss the feet of a parent in playful fun – and that is what I took the group's rites to be – having fun setting up an ordinary human to worship. Or they may be validating the Holy Spirit in all. However, if someone says, "Goddess worship of individuals is what *metaphysics is* all about," I'll go "toe–to–toe" with them. Thank you, better–educated–now makers of that program, for creating a more broad-viewed sequel.

No ethical Spiritualist minister or psychic would cast **satanic spells**, **hexes**, or **curses**, do negative **voo–doo** (black magic) or **sorcery** (gaining the cooperation of evil spirits). Using the energy and spiritual gifts in this manner to practice witchcraft carries a great deal of negative karma.

But then no ethical evangelical Christian minister would solicit money on TV for unholy purposes. Every profession, unfortunately, has its shady characters.

"Even every day folks are using the term, **CHAKRAS.** "Could you explain them so that I can understand them?" Recently, new scientific cameras with energy–sensing mechanisms have made the subject more complicated to explain, but easier to understand if you are lucky enough to get to see the new photographs. I haven't seen them at this writing; nor do I know where you can get a picture. Nevertheless, I will try to simplify some of the concepts for greater general understanding.

Chakras are an interdimensional transducing system, "plugging" you into your universe, connecting you to the God System, Existence, The Universe, while you are in a human body. The chakras convert God's vibrations or energy into body energy. Chakras can be out of balance when your thoughts, emotions or bodies are sick. When you feel "out of balance," accessing your Being in meditation will help in realignment. Also a good clairvoyant or healer knows how to rebalance chakras. Listening to classical music and other selected calming music can also help to rebalance them.

There is an excellent method in the book, JOY'S WAY, by Brugh Joy, M. D., pages 258 –276. I believe Dr. Joy is a very evolved Soul back in a body to help us now, perhaps a descended, Ascended Master!

For those of you who have already been taught where the chakras are seeded, let's start with the old model. Seven major chakras are associated with the human body, between seven and eight centimeters apart as follows: base of the spine, located behind your body (survival, power); genital area, located in front of your body (sex); navel area, in front of your body (ego, control, will power); heart, in front of your body (love); throat, in front (sound, communication, music); third–eye area, in front, between the eyebrows and up an inch (psychicness; your Light body's geometry patterns for ascension into Christ Consciousness), and top of the head (transpersonal, spiritual connection to higher Self and God). These vibrating "rings" can be sensed and occasionally seen by psychics. There are also chakras above your head for help in your evolvement.

Scientific electronic instruments have recently found more chakras in the body: five at each horizontal level of each chakra; but these chakras are inside the body enabling a spiral movement of energy. A continuing spiral of energy can be drawn between the chakras.

(Also, the one chakra thought to be two inches below the naval instead is straight in *under* the navel.) The subject is getting more complex and now really needs a 3-D picture to do it justice.

I am sure we will continue getting more information as science acquires more instruments. Also, it appears that more chakras may be in the making by the spiritual hierarchy (I like to call them the God Squad) as we make our evolutionary leap: one at the thymus (between the heart and throat, to receive love) and one in the back of the skull where the neck joins, not to mention additional, evolutionary chakras above our head.

For now, it is enough to know that there are places in your body where you are spiritually connected, where you get plugged into God's energy; and you are now being given your new evolutionary hardware! Some say this evolution will give the human body thirteen chakras.

When doing a chakra balancing, I still do it in the same way I always did. It is probably my faith that heals by allowing God's unconditional love to come through my heart and hands with God's patterned intelligence, rather than through my own limited intellectual knowledge.

"You said you sometimes see auras. What are you seeing?" I, and others, see some or all of the **ASTRAL** or **LIGHT BODY**. In 1944, Dr. H. S. Burr and other researchers at Yale University concluded: "Anything living has an aura around it, an electric field."

This Light body radiates from your Soul but is colored by *everything* that is you in this life, such as your culture's impact, your training, your intellect, your body (and its health or disease), your personality, your attitudes, how loving you are, your karma and more. This etheric body is as uniquely yours as is your face and is more than just your Soul shining. It is your Soul shining through every thing you are.

In 1979, I saw a film on Kirlian photography, a process that two Russian scientists developed. On film, a record is made of the electrical discharges from living things. In that particular film, there are two scenes I'll never forget. One was a tree leaf photographed after being pulled from the tree. It was easy to see its aura. The producers tore the leaf in half and photographed the remaining segment of the leaf. You could still see the *entire* outline of the leaf even though you could also see that about half of it was missing! The essential life, the "skeleton of life," had not yet left!

The other scenes involved the hands of two people; first the hands were at rest and the aura was clearly visible. Then they photographed the hands while the two people argued; and you could see sharp and pointed sparks coming out of their finger tips.

Since seeing this process, I have been very aware that if I am speaking angrily, I am actually sending psychic knives into whomever I am addressing. It has made it easier to have a substantial reason to cool down, letting my feelings subside before communicating.

Semyon and Valentina Kirlian invented the high–voltage process that lets you see the invisible behind the physical, the metaphysics of auras. Your Light body continually pulsates and changes in both shape and color. Thanks to these Russian researchers, the explanations of religion and science come closer together. My heart goes out to you two; I hope to meet you soon.

Not the same process, but available in the United States if you attend the right psychic fair, is another process that lets you see the invisible behind the physical. Scientific equipment is available to take a picture of the aura above your head and shoulders as it looked at the time of the shot. To see if there might be one of these psychic fairs in your area soon, write, enclosing a SASE: Aura Camera, 319 Spruce Street, Redwood City, CA 94063.

Your Light body has the five senses like the physical body: sight, sound, taste, touch and smell. Sometimes your dreams are perceived through this body, the astral senses. (In Chapter 2, I write more about "dreams.")

The astral or Light body is invisible to most people. Its ethereal substance interpenetrates the human body and extends outward about five to eight inches. Initiated by the Being, it leaves with the Being at physical death. Recognizable as the person, this Light body is what mourning friends and relatives occasionally witness after the death of a loved one.

It has finer vibrations than the physical body. It "sparkles" and stays with the Being through the beginning of the journey into other dimensions.

The astral body does get shed at some time long before the Being takes on another body to reincarnate. I understand this discarded empty astral shell is sometimes entered and played with by prankster Beings thus becoming one type of **ghost**.

Another type of ghost is a Being who did not have the energy to leave the earth plane after death. So-called "haunted houses" have this type of Being. I had several devout metaphysical friends who specialized in going to these houses and talking to these lost Beings. These ghosts are undoubtedly new Souls without the Soul energy to leave nor the knowledge that they are supposed to. My friends helped them by explaining the way to further their evolution, admonishing, "go back to progression, go toward the Light." These friends laughingly called themselves, "The Ghost Busters." That was a wonderful service they were performing. I have lost track and don't know if they continue now. However, anyone who sees a ghost can help a ghost on its way. Just talk to it as you would a person! If it's the other kind of ghost, so what!

Here is a reminder about some of the ways you build Soul energy. You build Soul energy *by the vibrations* created by your thoughts, behaviors and attitudes listed on the positive karma list. You also build Soul energy by meditating, worshiping God, praying, singing devotional songs and chants, developing and using your unique talents to serve your fellow humans plus reincarnating for more Soul growth and lessons.

For example, if a new Soul was brutally murdered first time around, it would be easy to understand the lack of Soul energy.

"I heard someone say they had a **KUNDALINI** experience. What does that mean?" In our first human incarnation, this spiritual energy rests at the base of the spine. Fed by the chakras, over lifetimes, the energy rises into higher chakras, as we evolve into higher spiritual Beings. This helps explain why a new Soul does not spend time in prayer, and why an old Soul is so very interested in things spiritual.

You can tell the "age" of a Soul by what drives them. Are they interested in power, the lowest chakra, lording it over their fellow humans just for the thrill of it? What would you say about someone compulsively interested in having sex seven times every day (the sexual chakra is the second)?

A new Soul is not at all *balanced*. And to expect them to be, is like expecting a baby to take a college entrance exam and pass it.

An old Soul having a kundalini experience feels the energy "running" all the way through the physical body. Often shaking, quaking and feelings of bliss accompany the kundalini experience. This energy undoubtedly runs *up through the spiral* of chakras. I saw a few people having this experience while meditating in a very large group at a Brugh Joy conference.

My oldest and metaphysical son had an unexpected and spontaneous experience. He and his wife were staying in a motel close to a Yogananda group meeting place which, of course, set up the energy. While sitting on the bed, he suddenly started to quiver. A voice my son heard, but daughter–in–law didn't, gave him directions on what to do step–by–step. He was directed to massage certain areas of his wife's body. After the energy had passed *upward* spiraling through *his* body, the voice told them, "You can make love now." (They told me they kidded each other, then dutifully did.) The kundalini energy experience had lasted perhaps twenty minutes.

I have had another experience of energy, like a bolt of lightening, coming *down* through the top of my head and running down parallel to the spinal column. For just a moment, I saw gold. This experience lasted less than two seconds and happened when I laid my hands on someone's shoulders to say a prayer for them during an Angel Healing Group prayer session. (In Chapter 3, I'll explain how the Angel Healing Group I host functions; perhaps you will want to start one.)

I believe that both directions (going up and spiraling – and coming down straight) and the different timings (twenty minutes vs several seconds) were kundalini energy experiences, but I am not sure. These experiences are just more personal "wonders." Most evolved Souls I know have never had either kind of "kundalini" experience.

I do not advise the seeking out of these experiences. It is possible to create them artificially and get "fried." Shaman got a hole burned in both his leg and tongue. Kundalini experiences should be natural.

"You have talked about 'two Avatars, one alive plus unembodied Jesus.' Could you say more about them?" Yes, but first, I'll describe an **AVATAR**. An Avatar is a special Being, given the right "royal jelly" by God to become a "queen bee." That is not an accurate metaphor, or even a good one, but it is the best I can think of.

(As you probably know, a queen bee is created by the hive bees by feeding an ordinary larvae a special concoction, royal jelly.)

So wondrous are Avatars that many people witnessing miracles directly discount their experiences. They think they are "seeing things," "being fooled as if by a magician," having no intellectual model that enables them to comprehend this supreme incarnation.

An Avatar is fully **God–realized**; that is, has all chakras in balance all the time and has access to the full kundalini spectrum. A fully God–realized Being is by choice selfless in action. He does not marry and have a family. He is not interested in buying a house or having furniture or a bank account.

An Avatar lives for the human race. He emphasizes the unity of religious experience. He moves and works in grace, has an exquisite joyfulness, and works in all dimensions, gross and subtle. A power-ful vibration fills the air around him. These undulations are the purest kind of love being manifested. I am lucky to have experi-enced these powerful emanations from my shaman teacher, evolved, but not a full Avatar.

An Avatar chooses and is permitted to be born to devout parents who let him be and accomplish without interference the things he came to do. These parents are without neuroses. The God–realized Avatar has a *powerful* spiritual presence at an early age. Avatars can produce matter at will, transmute matter and change from one form into another. This includes astralprojecting and rematerializing (going back into Soul form and recreating the body again at a desired destination on earth.) Embodied or unembodied, an Avatar appears in visions, dreams and inner experiences of devotees.

If an Avatar deems it karmically correct, he can heal on the spot or set up the healing to take place over time. Wisdom is constantly flowing from the lips of an Avatar. For every person he meets, he knows the complete Soul/past, Soul/present and Soul/future. An Avatar often predicts events many years in the future. He can bring the dead back to life.

An Avatar, being totally God-realized, is beyond the limitations of time, space, the ego-mind and matter.

Other Avatars: about 10,000 years ago there was Rama. And about 5,000 years ago, there was Krishna. Besides Sai Baba, there was another I will tell you about at the end of this chapter. It will shock you and you probably won't believe it. But put the name on your tentative shelf, please.

These Beings are now arriving on our planet earth with increasing frequency. Now is ripe. We are so blessed.

I use the pronoun "he" because a female Avatar, with the full powers, is unknown to me, but keep an eye on Sai Baba's next incarnation, which he says is due around 2029 or 2030. I believe this future Avatar will take a woman's body because Drunvalo Melchizedek says that women are going to be the leaders of the future.

Over the eons, an ordinary Being takes turns being one sex and then the other – but not rhythmically every other lifetime, because we have a preference – so since we express eventually as both, what difference does it make? Perhaps we can now end "the battle of the sexes" since it is only in-body when we are one or the other.

I'll write about Sai Baba first, and end Chapter 1 of COSMIC MAP with Jesus. Here is my answer to any question about "Which one is 'best?'" All profound spiritual teachers have their place in the cosmic scheme of things, their special tasks, their time in history, the human lives they come to touch directly and indirectly. *There is no such thing as best Avatar, Master or teacher!*

However, I have been privileged to know many devout spiritual seekers with many special spiritual Masters and teachers, some of them partial Avatars. (I have moved thirteen times in the last four years; perhaps just to experience the different devotees and to hear their stories.) Almost all spiritual seekers think their teacher is "best." That, too, is absolutely correct. We attract the one or ones who will be most in harmony with our Being, and we love them with a special devotion because they were the best for our Being at a particular time.

It is time to build bridges, not walls, between the different spiritual groups. And if someone said of me, "She built bridges not walls between the faiths," I would be pleased.

Consider letting go of your spiritual ego. The ego that tells you, "You have had the best spiritual teacher(s) in all the universes." Then listen to the wonderful stories *all* have to tell, and share your stories with them.

"We have been waiting to hear more about **SAI BABA**. Is it finally time?" Yes, I wanted to get your attention so that you would be sure to be mentally present. He is one of the reasons you have chosen to incarnate at this time on the Planet of the Cross. Your Soul knew the Avatar's vibration would Light up the world. And you just had to be here, now!

Alive in India today, his *fifty-six-year ministry* is well-documented on videotapes, audiotapes and by many books by many exceptionally well-educated people. A good book to start with is by a physician specializing in mental health, who was originally a doubter: SAI BABA, THE HOLY MAN . . . AND THE PSYCHIATRIST, by Samuel H. Sandweiss, M.D. Another is A CATHOLIC PRIEST MEETS SAI BABA by Don Mario Mazzoleni. Baba's educational materials are distributed by Sathya Sai Baba Book Center of America, P. O. Box 278, Tustin, CA 92681-0278. Write to them enclosing a SASE, and they will send a brochure.

I have two videotapes which I treasure. The most awesome has two hours of footage of Baba, titled "Sathya Sai Baba, Aura of Divinity." The second video has a group of people, including Christians, who talk about their experiences of Baba (no footage of Baba). This hour-long video is taken from a St. Louis cable TV show, "Loving, A Discussion of Sathya Sai Baba." There are a number of folks on this tape who have received gifts manifested by Baba.

Since 1988, thanks to the Book Center, I have been able to study and worship from afar, five–foot–tall, olive–skinned, kinky–haired Sai Baba. *He is not a partial Avatar; he has the full powers.* Some of our Master teachers who have not had the full power and glory this time around will certainly have it later. These Master teachers vary in their ability to use the energy.

Sai Baba speaks of his last incarnation as a documented holy man, Sai Baba of Shirdi. Shirdi is a small village in northern India.

In this life he was born on November 22, 1926. He says he will leave when he is ninety–five or ninety–six and return again after eight years. One day in 1990 he said, "I am very happy today because my father for my next life was just born."

Simple addition would then have Sai Baba living to the year of 2021 or 2022. Then by adding eight years for his reincarnation, he would return in 2029 or 2030. This means he (she?) will be here for those who make the ascent into Christ consciousness and higher, who choose to be here in body on this planet.

I asked my since–1988 friend, president of the Sacramento, California, Sai Baba group, "How many incarnations has Sai Baba had?" His answer, "I have not seen it written, but devotees give different fig–ures ranging from one hundred to two hundred." That is why com–pared to us ordinary old Souls with perhaps an average of five thousand lives under our belts, I believe Baba got some "royal jelly."

Dedicated to education at every level, Sai Baba has actively initiated and used contributions to financially support India's school system from elementary through college. He says the future for India lies in today's Indian students.

Meditation is an ingredient of this education, and he says *meditation should be taught in every school and college in every land.* Additionally he says, "Education is no education unless it teaches the milk of human kindness."

He is not just for India. A friend who had a private audience in 1988 told a group of us attending a Sai Baba meditation what the great Avatar had said in 1984: "I will not allow a nuclear war. At night, I go into the hearts of the world's leaders."

Baba first thinks of a thing to create, to physically manifest – first comes the word – and then the article appears. Examples that have been seen by millions are bananas and other fruit, necklaces and rings. All jewelry is custom made. For example, a ring might have the stamp of a person's favorite saint. I have seen him on videotape manifest a baseball card for a child. My friend, president of the Sacramento Sai Baba group, goes to India every time he is called, which has been every two or three years. He always manages to get one of those "rare audiences." During his last visit, Baba material-ized a ring for his extra-large hands. The ring looks like gold and has a massive crystal–diamond–like single stone. I was allowed to touch it and I felt great for days.

If karmically correct and a person is spiritually receptive, Baba does daily surgical–like and medical healings. These manifestations and mira-cles are performed at his ashrams. Although Puttaparthi, his main ashram, is in a quiet and remote village in Southern India, millions of people have visited there. He also works at his Whitefield ashram, a township about thirteen miles from Bangalore. Sai Baba says,

> Seek the Light always; be full of confidence and zest.
> Do not yield to despair; it can never produce results.
> It only worsens the problem, for it darkens the intellect
> and plunges you in doubt. You must take up the path
> of Sadhana [spiritual practices], very enthusiastically. Half-
> hearted halting steps will not yield fruit. It is like cleaning
> slushy areas by a stream of water. If the current of the
> stream is slow, the slush cannot be cleared. The stream
> must flow full and fast, driving everything before it, so
> that the slush might be scoured clean.

And . . .

> Let the different faiths exist, let them flourish and let the
> glory of God be sung in all the languages and in a variety
> of tunes. That should be the ideal. Respect the differences
> between the faiths and recognize them as valid as long as
> they do not extinguish the flame of unity.

Sai Baba has come to inspire devotion to the Radiant One and to bring us together.

He has commented many times on Jesus, saying Jesus was very mis-quoted. On the "lost years," he said, "Jesus realized he was Christ in his twenty-fifth year. For eight years following his sixteenth birth-day, he traveled in India, Tibet, Iran and Russia."

Earlier, I said that it is difficult to understand current events and that if we could just see more, we would have peace. Here is a true story of seeing a bigger picture after the reinterpretation of a here-and-now event:

Sai Baba often walks through crowds of tens of thousands of people, sometimes stopping to heal someone along the wayfare. In a crowd one day was an Indian woman holding a badly deformed and retarded baby, begging for Baba's intervention. Baba walked right by, taking no notice. An American woman was standing close and thought, "Why doesn't he help that woman and baby?" Suddenly, in her mind's eye, a blank movie screen was unrolled. Her question had been heard, and she was gifted by Baba with a *seeing experience.* She saw upon the screen the former life of the woman (then a pow-erful male judge) and the former life of the baby (a court clerk to the judge). Then the American woman saw them colluding to hand down unfair and extremely punitive sentences. Baba apparently thought they, in this incarnation, should have to live out the nega-tive karma from their court.

My friend called me just before I began writing about Baba. It is always exciting to hear from him because he is in contact with peo-ple just returned from India. He always has some new Baba stories. I'll share this week's with you because, although the books about him are filled with the stories, *these* stories haven't been in a book yet:

Nine friends from Australia planned a trip to see Baba. They were selected by Baba from the huge crowd for an interview. Baba asked each in turn, "How are you today?" (Baba always addresses people in the language they speak; he just knows.) In turn, the first eight answered in the affirmative. When the last person's turn came, Baba answered for him before he himself could. "I know, your wife is not well, and you want to be home with her." "Yes, you are right, Swami, but I promised my group a long time ago that I would come with them."

"Would you like to go home now?" Startled, the man answered, "Well, if it is okay with you, yes, I would." Baba then turned toward the wall, motioning with his hand and suddenly a map of Australia appeared there. Baba inquired about his hometown's name. Then a map of that city appeared on the wall where the Australian map had been. "On what street do you live?" After the answer, instead of a map, a huge picture of his house appeared. This picture included the door of the house realistically sized. Baba *opened* the door, and invited the devotee to walk through. Startled, the gentleman non-verbally asked permission from his friends. That, having been granted, he walked through the door. The wall returned to its original state – just an ordinary wall in the room.

When the remaining eight left Baba's presence, en masse they rushed to the nearest phone and called their friend's Australian home. The man answered. One of the friends said, "Well, if you really are there, you would have had your passport stamped." Reaching in his pocket for the passport, he checked it. It *had* been stamped!

The second recent story: Baba had invited a car full of devotees to travel with him from Prasanthi Nilayam (the abode of undisturbed inner peace, the name of Sai Baba's main ashram) to Bombay. There was to be a spiritual event at 6 p.m. in the evening. Total travel time by plane and car is six hours.

Noon came, then one, two and three o'clock. Finally, one of the devotees said with some irritation, "Baba! You must have changed your mind about going." "No," said Baba. Then four o'clock and finally at five o'clock Baba said, "Let's go get in the car." Seated, he told them all, "Now I know the wait has been tiring, so I want you to sit back, close your eyes, keep them closed and relax."

Dutifully they did this until Baba finally said, "You can open your eyes now." When they opened their eyes, they were in Bombay, driving up to the building where their greatly anticipated event was to take place. The wristwatch of one of the devotees said five minutes to six!

Here is one of my favorite stories: A group of students was visiting Baba. One of them said, "Baba, your hair is turning grey." Smiling, Baba turned it black right in front of them. And it has been black, as it was in Baba's youth, ever since.

Now for a personal story which just happened as I was writing here about Sai Baba: My Sacramento friend told me of a family's home about an hour and a half by car from where we live where we might go to see some "manifestations." These manifestations include honey flowing out of covered–with–glass pictures; vibuti – a healing ash – randomly appearing on covered–with–glass Baba pictures; and red powder, coming out of a covered–with–glass picture of a Hindu saint. Hindu people dot this red powder on their foreheads. Last, by a mythical picture of Shiva (God with multiple arms), water flows out of a fountain, which is *not connected to anything*. The residing family calls the fountain's water, "Holy Water."

My husband and I stopped off unannounced on a Saturday morning. We were warmly welcomed, even though that afternoon the man, his wife and three children were expecting a party of over fifty people. We ended up staying over an hour. The devotees showed us the promised manifestations. We saw honey being collected in plastic baggies, catching the drips, under six of the pictures. He showed us one huge picture of just Baba's feet. Below the picture was probably a quart of honey collecting in a plastic "pan." The devotee said, "On meditation night, we may have sixty people. And the honey sometimes really flows that night." Then he invited us to put "something to be blessed" in a special closet where there were additional pictures of Baba, other Indian saints and said fountain. I felt *powerful* vibrations in the hall leading to this closet. Awesome vibrations, as powerful as those I had felt so long ago around my shaman teacher. My husband checked the back and undersides of the fountain. He also examined the pictures. We both felt these manifestations were as they were represented to be!

We hadn't brought anything for a special blessing so I suggested we use our rings. My husband handed me his and I laid both very carefully on the shelf, his first, with the jewels *facing out to the front*. Next, I placed mine, jewels also facing out, leaning on his, asking for a blessing for our marriage.

When it was time to go, the home-owner devotee reminded us to go back to the closet for our rings. When we looked in, the rings had moved! On the shelf, the jewel sides were now in tandem, obliquely off to one corner, *facing the back*. They were not touching, but were very close. I said, "Look, our rings have moved!" Stunned, my husband said, "Yes, I remember how you put them down!"

Then I picked up his ring to hand it to him. The jewels were sticky. Then I grabbed mine, and it was sticky, too, but only on the jeweled segment. I lightly touched my jewels with my tongue. Sure enough – honey! (One of the editors of this manuscript asked "Is the honey real honey or just honey-like? And do people taste it?" – It was a very sweet, definite honey, similar to, but not the same as the bees make from orange blossoms. And the owners give it away. They also give away the holy water. At our house, we use the water for saying prayers by giving the prayed-for person a few sips.)

We had expected nothing from the visit except a peek at the manifestations. (I know, your doubting mind may think that someone moved the rings and dipped them in honey. However, the oblique direction of the moved rings was exactly the same angle as a pair of glass love birds sitting on a shelf we have at our home. Also the birds, like the moved rings, are sitting very close, but *not* touching.)

Consider ordering a few books and a videotape of Sai Baba of India. You may become a believer, too. You will love the stories, even if you believe them to be just science fiction! He is so beautiful.

The most helpful information I have learned from Baba is to set priorities: First, he says, take care of yourself. Then take care of your family. Then your friends. Then when you have time, give to your community.

As for the date of the beginning of the Age of Aquarius, I suggested earlier honoring the year of Sai Baba's birth, 1926. God always sends Avatars at very dark times. An Avatar is actually an incarnation of God on the fast track, a child of God extraordinare! As mentioned before, the words "Avatar" and "God-realized" are synonymous.

Baba said in 1992 that The Golden Spiritual Age had begun and that world consciousness would be rising to its own glorious potential. He has told devotees that he is working on the ethereal plane to soften the impact of the earth changes predicted by some psychics.

He has spoken about coming to the United States in this incarnation. But, whether he means "in spirit," as he comes to devotee's homes or in a recognizable–to–the–common–person form, his this–life persona, I don't know. Once I was giving a talk about Sai Baba at a Spiritualist Church. One of the really good psychic seers in the congregation told me later that she clearly saw Baba – in spirit form – walk behind me and the podium, then move over to put a jewel in the ear of a twelve–year–old girl, ironically named Jewel. I did not see him.

We are extremely lucky to be on the planet in the age of a living Avatar. And the flip side is also true. We chose to be here at this time, and we have a duty to do our best to evolve spiritually.

Sai Baba invites all people *not* to accept him on faith but "through inquiry and reason."

"Besides Sai Baba's comments, press articles are saying that some of what **Jesus** is reported to have said didn't come from Jesus. Can you help me come to terms with this 'Jesus Debate?'"

As far as the historical Jesus is concerned, reading the next three paragraphs. Perhaps they will help.

A religion editor writing in <u>Newsweek,</u> April 4, 1994 did an excellent, succinct summary; with about 4,800 Holy Bible scholars inputting, she or he said:

> [Jesus] preached, was a miracle worker and healer, was arrested, tried by Jewish authorities, was convicted and executed by Roman officials sometime between A. D. 30 and 33.

Not in that article, but in other sources such as Holger Kersten's book, JESUS LIVED IN INDIA (his unknown life before and after the crucifixion), there is much academic research which says that before Jesus started teaching, he lived and studied in India. As already mentioned, Sai Baba says this is true.

I deeply respect the work of Bible scholars like Steven Mitchell's, THE GOSPEL ACCORDING TO JESUS, A New Translation and Guide to his Essential Teachings for Believers and Unbelievers and Father Raymond E. Brown's, THE DEATH OF THE MESSIAH. Then there is the group of approximately one-hundred Gospel scholars who have their findings reported in the press (for example, "The Gospels have three different versions of the last words of Jesus.") All of these serious researchers want to know the truth. Once they think they have it, they honestly state their beliefs.

Here is an excerpt from a 1991 Los Angeles Times article:

> A provocative Jesus Seminar has concluded six years of voting on what the Jesus of history most likely said, ruling out about eighty percent of the words attributed to him in the Gospels . . . Virtually all of Jesus' words in the Gospel of John were voted down by scholars meeting in Sonoma . . . in the parallel Gospels of Mark, Matthew and Luke, Jesus speaks regularly in adages or aphorisms, or in parables, or in witticisms created as rebuff or retort in the context of dialogue or debate. *It is clear he did not speak in long monologues of the type found in the Gospel of John.* [Italics mine.]

Staying as valid were the good Samaritan and mustard seed parables, the advice to love your enemies and some Sermon on the Mount pronouncements such as the meek [gentle] are blessed because they will inherit the earth.

I have already stated my fondness for EDGAR CAYCE'S STORY OF JESUS edited by Jeffrey Furst. I feel that in this book are truths, not just the melding together of memories from oral tradition. I can't answer the "Jesus debate" questions for you. A metaphysician really has to come to terms with the man named Jesus in his or her own way. You can study these books, other books, use your intuition and make your own contact. Then be ready to change your view when presented with compelling information.

Now, I'll share with you my personal and difficult, this-life evolution of beliefs about Jesus. It is sad that for most of my life I would not call on him for help.

As a preschooler, my scientific, agnostic Pop refused to let me go to church. But as a college ROTC officer, he was drafted in 1940 and served in World War II until 1945.

During two of those years, my maternal grandmother made it possible for me to go to a Methodist Sunday School. That wonderful, wise woman has reincarnated and is Soul expressing as one of my granddaughters. This was revealed to me when I was looking in adoration at her baby girl face. For a moment, it disappeared and there was a blank oval. Then, as in a black and white movie, I saw my beloved grandmother's face as she had been in her seventies. The picture quickly faded away. Delightfully, my granddaughter is so like my incredible Grandma!

My mom tells about my first Jesus learnings: "You came home and started singing at the top of your five-year-old voice, "Jesus' Britches Shine." My grandmother kindly explained the real words: "Jesus Bids Us Shine." My only memory is of looking at the angelic pictures of Jesus in the classroom and knowing something was wrong, having no emotion whatsoever to the person pictured.

By the time I was a teen, I begged to be allowed to go to church. The answer was still "No," but Pop allowed me to go to Methodist Youth Fellowship because I thought it was a social club and had told him so.

One night at MYF, the leader said, "Jesus died for our sins. Tonight is the night you can stand up for Jesus. You can take Jesus into your heart. Then you won't be lost anymore. Let your faith lead you."

With little background, I was very confused: How could a grown, *dead* man fit into my heart? And how could I be "found" when I was not even lost? And I had to take it on "faith." What was faith?

Nevertheless, I surrendered to group pressure. My three best girl-friends walked up to the altar and I walked with them, parroting, "I accept Jesus as my personal savior," with a knot in my stomach and a sickness in my heart.

I hated that feeling so much I did not go back. And it would be nearly four decades before I again faced coming to terms with Jesus. I was able to push him out of my mind unless I saw one of those pretty pictures purportedly of his face.　My metaphysical teachers rarely referred to him.　All shaman had said was, "Jesus had to leave too soon."

At age fifty–four, after some years of being betrayed by friends, associates, and extended family, I undertook some psychotherapy to deal with all the betrayals.　A Board Certified Psychiatrist was my psychotherapist, a very psychic man.　"Janis," he said seriously, "I believe you are getting karma back from a life at the time of Jesus. Shall we do a past–life regression and find out what you did, so that you can forgive yourself and thus put a stop to these current betrayals?"

No one was more stunned than I.　I had not been drawn to Jesus. But I had been hypnotized many times before, and I had to know.　I wanted to be able to study the session, so I set up my video camera and, with the therapist's permission, video taped it.　I have shown my videotape to a few people I trust who have helped me process the information received.

What came out was that in that past life, I had been Jesus' disciple, Peter.　The therapist prolonged the session until I died as Peter. As Peter, in my sand–colored robe, I was attacked but didn't see the intruders.　Unmercifully, I was speared through the abdomen and then thrown in a grave and buried alive.　In hypnotic trance, the therapist skillfully took me/my consciousness from that grave and the *horrible* choking and sheer *weight* of the dirt into a higher place with a protective out–of–body Being there for me with the healing love.)

This is why you need a very trained, very compassionate, very skilled psychotherapist for regressions.　In Soul regression, you really don't know what you are returning to.　Many of your deaths have been difficult for the body you were in.

After the hypnotic regression, I scurried to a comforting and knowledgeable friend.　After telling her the details of the regression, I asked, "Why, *if I didn't somehow make all of that up*, am I struggling so much in this life.　Why aren't I evolved?"　She gave me peace by saying, "Oh Jesus picked just *ordinary men* to help."

Later I went to the library and read an account of Peter in an encyclopedia. I learned that his death is unrecorded and has been an historical mystery. Another source says Peter was hung on a cross, upside down.

I had to face up to the three times I betrayed Jesus, denying even knowing him. What a terrible shock. But, I told myself, it could have been worse, I could have been Judas! The therapist helped me deal with all of this. And I couldn't ignore Jesus anymore. And the betrayals in my life stopped.

What follows is what I now believe about Jesus some seven years later.

In body, he was a persona of the Divinity who reached perfection as a human Being, according to the Edgar Cayce readings, in just thirty lifetimes. He went through his "babyhood, childhood, and adolescence" on the way to becoming an Avatar by lifetimes in bodies/ personalities known as Adam; Enoch; Amilius; Jeshua; Joseph, son of Jacob; Joshua; and Melchizedek. As Jesus, he was the fully evolved Avatar and prototype or model for fourth–dimensional consciousness, Christ consciousness.

Christ consciousness will happen to us when we fully access our Being and live from it. Statistically, few people can hold the Christ consciousness one hundred percent of the time, as our Planet of the Cross, fully–evolved Avatars have done. (The Avatars can access any higher dimension.)

I don't believe that Jesus died for our sins; he died because some new Souls *thought* they needed the experience of committing murder. I believe he *lived* to set the pattern for love to flow on this planet. His supreme contribution to the human race was creating this pattern to forge the energy of the human race, the collective conscious or unconscious, up from the power chakra (at the base of the spine) to the heart chakra. Other celibate meditators, usually in the East, held it there for centuries to solidify the heart pattern for the race.

Forging a higher consciousness pattern for a race of Beings is a much more awesome and difficult task than giving up and letting oneself be hung on a cross. Jesus was so much, much more than we can imagine.

Seven years ago, I met a young man, about age thirty, who had witnessed a powerful visitation from Jesus. Here is his story: My very devout and beloved Mom had just died. You know, she was so special because she had lived through the Holocaust. Of course, our whole family was in a state of grief. I have never been religious in a 'church' way. Her body was behind a closed bedroom door. I was walking down the hall. All of a sudden, I could see golden Light coming from under that door. I had never seen anything like it. I opened the door. There, in golden outline, was a "Light" figure I knew to be Jesus, although he didn't look like his pictures. I got such a close look before he faded that I could see acne marks on his face. He left me with *incredibly intense feelings* of love in my chest.

I told this young man, "I see you as having had something to do with Buddha." He said, "That is funny, when I was little, I had a collection of little Buddha statues, and I used to play with them all day long." This young man was an old Soul who could handle the vibrations of Jesus. No new Soul would be allowed to have this paranormal experience. Probably, for a new Soul, Jesus would come in thought. He always does it right for the Being involved.

According to Sai Baba, Jesus was born to restore love, charity and compassion in the heart of humankind. By the way, in both the book and videotape I recommended on Sai Baba, you will also get a Baba-produced picture of how Jesus really looked. Or you can visually make the nose much bigger and more bulbous on the Newsweek, April 4, 1994 cover, and you will have a more accurate mental picture. Also the eyes, according to the Edgar Cayce readings, were blue-grey.

Paradoxically, most faiths that do not believe in reincarnation think that Jesus will come again. Until that time though, as my upcoming personal story will attest, sincere and devout prayers called out to him get through to his Being, no matter where he happens to be. I believe he is the Ascended Master in charge of the Milky Way Galaxy; and in the way our minds operate, is relatively close.

There are debates about whether Jesus has reincarnated. I discovered in my travels and moves that some groups with a powerful teacher believed their teacher was Jesus, reincarnated. As you shall soon see, I finally, with much difficulty, accepted one of these seeker's stories: Jesus has come again but is not here now. If he isn't here, will he come again in a body? Let me elaborate.

A series of coincidences lead to the conclusion in the following paragraphs. This is a last–minute addition, no rough–draft readers saw it. I cannot speak in detail here of these events. However, after typing it into the computer, I intuitively knew the decision was right. To solidify it, a long–time friend, out of the clear blue, brought some black and white video film of **Meher Baba**. Keep reading:

Jesus has already come and gone in a body/personality known as holy man Meher Baba from India [1894 – 1969], an incredible, beautiful human Being, an Avatar, who maintained silence, but wrote messages on a board and used non–verbal communication. Determined not to be misunderstood and misquoted, Meher's written communications are extremely clear. He also did not speak in order to hold the planet's energy at the throat chakra. Then Sai Baba, in this incarnation, took the Kundalini for the human race and brought it up to the third eye. He'll do the transpersonal chakra in his next incarnation.

"Meher Baba . . . traveled to the Western world six times, first in 1931, when he contacted his early Western disciples. His last visit to America was in 1958 when he and disciples stayed at the Center established for his work." For further information enclose a SASE and write to Meher Spiritual Center, Inc., 10200 High Way 17, Myrtle Beach, South Carolina, 29572.

Meher Baba communicated: You are loving God when, if instead of worrying over your own misfortunes, you think of yourself as more fortunate than many, many others. And, "Because man has been deaf to the principles and precepts laid down by God in the past, in this present Avataric Form, I observe silence. You have asked for and been given enough words – it is now time to live them. . . . I veil myself from man by his own curtain of ignorance, and manifest my Glory to a few."

So from 1926 to 1969, for forty–three years, the Planet of the Cross had two powerful Avatars publically doing their work, Jesus/Meher and Shirdi/Sai Baba! If you were born during these years, their energy helped draw you here!

My intuition says Jesus is not currently reincarnated. I personally don't think he will take an ordinary human body at our ascension time, but in his Light body, he will continue allowing himself to be seen from time to time. He also channels his messages. Two channelers I have faith in are Virginia Essene (we will talk about her masterful work in Chapter 3) and Jon Marc Hammer of the Shanti Christo Foundation, P. O. Fox 22877, Santa Fe, New Mexico 87502, SASE. Jesus' job as Head of the Spiritual Hierarchy in the Milky Way Galaxy requires flexibility. Will he reveal himself in the clouds as it says in the Bible, Revelations 14:14 and Mark 13:26. Yes, I think so.

While I am being controversial, I might as well mention that Jesus had twelve women disciples in addition to the twelve men we already know about.

Now back to *my* this–life relationship with the man from Galilee. At long last, I had to test to make sure that Jesus had forgiven Peter. I was desperate. My fears that he would not respond had to be challenged when one night in early 1995, my body temperature had dropped to ninety–four degrees and my blood pressure was seventy–eight over thirty–eight; both measurements were still dropping. Not to mention that my sex drive had disappeared. With all of this, my caring husband was in a state of alarm. So I swallowed my pride-fear mixture and called to Jesus in earnest prayer, told him my predicament, explained that four doctors didn't know what was wrong, said I would be glad to cross over if I was needed on the other side and asked for quick help if I was intended to stay. I asked that his intervention not be "faint" but so powerful I could recognize the grace.

The next morning, I awoke with an enormous pain in the back of my neck – a pain like you might sustain if someone had whopped you with a baseball bat. Immediately I called my chiropractor. As he worked, he intuited that my adrenal glands were swollen. He also told me my spine was "pushed up" into my head, so he did extensive cranial and neck work. Bottom line, the hypothalamus, which controls skin temperature, blood pressure and sex drive had been squashed, throwing my adrenals, pituitary, thyroid and all other glands out of balance. I started feeling better immediately. I also had some more acupuncture work by a beautiful M.D. I returned to better than normal within a month. Thank you, Jesus. I *know* you whopped me yourself.

I had been told by one of four medical doctors previously consulted that I was suffering from "chronic fatigue syndrome," a diagnosis with no cure and no specific meaning. Another had told me the diagnosis was "depression" and wanted to prescribe Prosac (which I declined).

Now, I have a close, almost constant relationship with Jesus and speak with him about any concern.

So you can see why I genuinely say, "It doesn't matter to me now if Jesus didn't say a lot of what he has been quoted as saying. It does not affect my current faith one bit, and I hope it doesn't affect yours, either. Jesus lives in spirit. Jesus cares. Jesus responds, fast."

Am I a Christian? I agree with some words from a pamphlet one of my fundamental Christian sons gave me, ". . . the Glorified Jesus is Available to Man. Call his name. Give him a task to do in your life."

My identical twin sons as mentioned, have fundamental beliefs, but do not belong to a denomination; they have become Self–realized, a term to be defined in Chapter 2, by devotion to the principles of Christianity gained from their intense eighteen years of study of the Holy Bible.

"Do you believe in **IMMACULATE CONCEPTION**?" I was among approximately one–hundred fifty persons listening to a metaphysical minister speak during the Christmas season, 1984. He said, "The immaculate conception is just symbolic. Joseph was the real biologi-cal father of Jesus." I heard a voice in my head which answered, "He is wrong." I trusted the voice.

Sai Baba was immaculately conceived. We have here the poignant description from Don Mario Mazzolen, Italian author of A CATHOLIC PRIEST MEETS SAI BABA, Leela Press Inc., Rt. 1, Box 339C, Faber, Virginia 22938, published in English in 1994. He tells us that one day Baba was surrounded by devotees. One asked, "Swami! Did you incarnate by entering the world directly . . . or through human conception?" Quoting Mazzolen:

> Baba turned to his Mother, so that she could answer the question herself. And his Mother said: 'I had had a dream in which an angel of God told me not to be afraid if something should happen to me which depended on the Will of God. That morning, while I was at the well to draw water, a great sphere of blue light came rolling toward me. I lost consciousness and fell to the ground, and I felt it slip inside me."
>
> Baba summed up, "There's your answer! I was not born through conception . . . I was born through a descent, not from human contact."

"Does having two Avatars in your life present any problems for you?" Not at all! When I am walking alone, I visualize Jesus on my right side and Sai Baba on my left. I am never alone. They also take drives with my husband and me. They are our most wonderful friends, terrific, loving energy. Not just us, many Christians visit Sai Baba in India.

I am sorry there is so much controversy *now* about Jesus. What happened as far as getting an accurate recording was inevitable. Jesus lived in a primitive, uneducated culture. The people lived in relatively small tribes. They didn't have stenographers. (A steno makes a verbatim transcript; a scribe attempts to get the ideas.) They didn't have audiotapes. They didn't have videotapes. The people did not have much formal education. Not many people knew how to write. The stories were carried as all news was, by word of mouth. The stories were not written down; some waited seventy years to get recorded.

In my past life regression when I was Peter, the therapist brought me into a time after Jesus' death. I was trying to help his followers keep in contact with one another. I felt very responsible and caring, but I was somewhat of an old fuddy duddy. The difficulties because of the heavy prosecution of the Essenes, Jesus' organized followers, were almost insurmountable, and I was aging rapidly. With no telephones or answering machines, no bikes, mopeds or cars, the devout did the best they could to secretly pass the information. Sometimes codes were used.

The miracle is that somehow, the general themes were canonized. In the imperfect process, nevertheless, *the Light went forward* and became the major messages: one God, love, forgiveness and service to your fellow humans.

It is hard for me to understand why the press doesn't report on our living Avatar and get the story right this time? Let Jesus do his current work out of body. If he should come again, he will come back when he deems the time to be exactly correct. Do the controversial details of Jesus' ancient life make a difference *now*? Let us get on with the ascension program! We are literally running out of time!

After I finished writing all this about Jesus, I broke into uncontrollable *spasms* of tears. This lady, me, raised by two scientists, had to get her this–life love for Jesus after ignoring him for fifty–plus years. Gut–level knowingness finally came from my past–life regression, from reading about him, from personal–miracle interventions (there are more I didn't write about), and studying the *extremely well-documented* and current life of Avatar Sai Baba. Since Baba does all the miracles he deems karmically correct if the person is spiritually receptive, I *know* Jesus did (and does) too.

Beloved ray of God, if you have not yet made your connection with the real Jesus and you have the desire, your way doesn't have to be as difficult as I have made mine. And once you make that connection, it doesn't have to be exclusive. You can enjoy all the Avatars, whether in or out of body; they want to serve you. As hard as it is to understand with your human mind, the Avatars, like God, are **omniscient**, have unlimited knowledge; they are **omnipresent**, present everywhere at the same time; and they are **omnipotent**, infinite in power. Amen.

CHAPTER 2

Close to Home

Start the day with love,
Fill the day with love,
Spend the day with love,
End the day with love,
That is the way to God.

— *Sathya Sai Baba*

TERMS AND PHILOSOPHY

Beloved Child of God, you have come with me a long way on our journey, one-third of the trip, and the basics of metaphysics have been covered. Congratulations for your tenacity!

If you would like to preview the concepts we will explore in Chapter 2, peruse Appendix I under the Chapter 2 heading.

We commence by taking a different kind of look at your physical body, your own temple of the Holy Spirit. "Where in the Bible are you quoting about our body being a temple?" I Corinthians 6:19 has this citation about the **PHYSICAL BODY**.

The body is a complex subject, and we have to talk about some particular divisions before we can truly understand. Remember, while you are in the body, the following protect the Being: (1) The body itself, (2) the emotions, the emotional "body," and (3) the mind, the mental "body."

You chose to take on a Planet-of-the-Cross body because it is a spiritual-evolvement mechanism. As said before, if you are the average old Soul, you have probably inhabited thousands of biodegradable or disposable bodies during your Soul's history. One spiritual teacher calls these bodies "costumes." Even though this is true, of course, you get just one costume this life.

Ideally, your this-life body, your vehicle also to enjoyment, should be an appreciated gift and not abused out of ignorance and/or laziness.

We have already talked about chakras – your spiritual energy centers, in, through and above your physical body. As you may recall, spiritual energy, lifetime after lifetime, works its way upward from the bottom of the spine. And in this Kali Yuga, the beginning of the seventh Golden Spiritual Age, it is being pulled extremely fast. We have also already spoken of the aural or Light body that interpenetrates your human body and radiates outside of it.

Now we will address other spiritual-evolvement parts of your body. *Notice as you read which aspects of each have to be overcome.* Your body as it works in third-dimensional consciousness is not yet the perfect spiritual-evolvement mechanism.

Doing some of the practices suggested in Cosmic Map is mandatory. However, I suppose you could conceivably evolve without the *realizations*, the mental concepts, although obviously I think learning the concepts will take you far. So realizations of how to overcome the blocks in the major divisions of your body will help your process.

First, we will explore the physical eyes and the physical heart. Then there is the physical brain, where the complicated functions of the mind occur.

"I have always been one of those 'I have to see it to believe it' people. Does this approach help in consciousness development, a total trust in what I see with my **PHYSICAL EYES?**" I wonder if you will be as shocked as I was when I first learned that what is seen with the eyes isn't at all like reality. Much of what you see is an optical illusion constructed by your mind for your convenience.

Here is why. Your occular mechanism, a pair of eyes, don't register the vibrations of things as vibrations. Instead, your eyes trick you into seeing these vibrations as solid objects! If you are like the average person, your eyes pick up only the surface, they don't see *into* things.

Visible Light gives the world shape and definition. The energy vibrations, which lead to nerve impulses do lead to information received by your mind. But what you see is not "real" because your mind fills in "the holes."

What gets added? Your mind instinctively gives you whole, finished "pictures." It works somewhat like newsprint pictures. (Check a picture in the newspaper with a magnifying lens and check out the dots.)

If you could look at the sub–atomic level, physical objects are just dots. At this level, there is *no separation* of yourself from the air, space, sand, fire or sunlight. It would be a lot easier to be spiritual if you saw reality in this way, yourself blending in with everything and everyone!

While round, your world looks flat. While spinning, the earth seems stationary. Each of God's embodied creatures has specialized sense perceptions. A bird of prey sees mainly movement, not scenery. No one has ever seen an object the way it really is. Your eyes do a visual, chemical dance. When Light hits the back of your brain, to complicate things, your emotions also color what you see.

What is out there is actually a mass of confusion of spots of Light like you see when you firmly press and rub your closed eye lids. Who knows what it would look like if you could see through the eyes of a whale or a dolphin? (By the way, Drunvalo also says that the dolphins and whales are inhabited or energized by the highest-level Beings on our planet, more evolved than we are. Another reason to immediately end all killing of these superior creatures!)

You continue to evolve as long as you realize the facts about visual limitation, and hold things lightly. You can use your eyes to drive the car to the prayer group, to the meditation group, to hear a speaker, to church, to friends' homes, and to work, grateful for the safety provided. You can use your eyes to read and gain realizations. You can use your eyes to keep your life in order. You can use your eyes to help create images to visualize what you want in your future. But you can't use your eyes to see what is really out there.

The physical eyes are only a tool to help in spiritual evolvement. However, as I told you before, the Soul has its own eyes. During my NDE, I saw myself approaching the Light Being and the Light Being approaching me; my physical eyes were still in my body on the operating table, closed.

"Okay, then, how does my **PHYSICAL HEART** work for my spiritual evolvement?" The human heart is a sending/receiving mechanism. *Your heart sends and receives God's love, the love vibration.* So your physical heart is the organ of Divine bliss.

Love is *not* an emotion. All love that comes through you is from God. When love comes to you from another fellow human and enters your energy field and heart, it is the same love that first came from God, is God.

Reread the prior paragraph and be sure you understand how important it is to know that originally, all love comes from God. *It is your*

job to let God's love through and to recycle it. Psalm 16:7: "Man looks on
the outward appearance, but God looks upon the heart." At the
same time, God's love is both magnetic *and* radiatory. It both
spreads itself out and has a draw to it. Love keeps all in ordered
sequence. God's love eventually perfects all that is. 1 Corinthians
13:13: "There are three things that remain, faith, hope and love – and
the greatest of these is love."

God's love has to come through a human heart before it has the
right earth–plane vibration. And once God's love comes through a
human heart, it stays on the earth plane and goes all over. It could
be conceptualized as a fine mist that creeps around. When you stop
to pet an adorable puppy and your heart gushes with that love, that
vibration eventually finds a place most needed. It may be outward
to another human Being, or it may stay with the puppy for awhile.
But you know how loving puppies are! That pup isn't going to
hoard it. Eventually, a human Being will feel that love but not
know why he or she is suddenly uplifted!

This is one of the processes that happens automatically in the
Universe, the sharing of this love. It goes automatically where it is
needed. This is the patterned intelligence working.

Additionally, new love coming through can be directed. One way to
do this is by just sitting quietly and thinking of someone you love.
To increase the love coming through, ask God to let the love flow
down through the top of your head, down through your throat, and
then down and out through your heart.

You can conceptualize that your heart has a lens, like a camera.
Visualize the lens opening and opening. Then picture the love pulsating through, and with the speed of Light, going to the person you
love. Isn't it wonderful? God's love gets there through you. It has
just the right vibration in it. That is why it is said that "God is love."

It helps you too. When you have enough love coming through, it
burns up your negative emotions such as anger and resentment.
Pope John Paul II said, "The worst prison would be a closed heart."

It is critically important that everyone find something or someone
they can love. Even loving your car or your couch helps (as long as

there is no attachment to the article – we will talk about the principles of non-attachment in Chapter 3). Loving another person a great deal brings forth to the earth masses of this marvelous energy. And once love comes into the earth plane, as already said, it never leaves. This love dances around, doing lovely things, of which we know not. That is why loving in general is so critically important to help raise the mass consciousness in time to save the planet and ourselves.

As I sit this day writing at an old metal table in a public park on the lovely lake where we live, scratched on the picnic table in a childish print is "Toni loves Marci." It is wonderful to know that even if the human attraction has been outgrown, the love vibration they brought in still resonates on the planet. Like them, loving you have done has never been wasted!

The love is coming down to us as never before. This heart vibration is coming back to save the planet. All we have to do is let it through. Shaman said that if we could just be open to one percent of it, we would explode. **Let's do it!**

Jesus, our Planet of the Cross's Ascended Masters, set up this love consciousness for us. And now at the beginning of the earth's Seventh Golden Spiritual Age, this love consciousness is slowly taking over the world. God's love vibration is now producing the consciousness shift, (the dimension change, ascension). All people who want to remain on this physical earth must be able to let it through in abundant amounts.

Years ago, I was attending a Brugh Joy seminar at the Asilomar Conference Grounds in Pacific Grove, California, near Carmel. Five hundred metaphysicians were in attendance when the speaker stood up and asked, "What are we going to do about Saddam Hussein?" Quickly, in unison, the group shouted back loudly, "Send him love."

That event stands out in my mind as the time I finally understood about love, God's love, unconditional. By loving our enemies as Jesus is quoted as saying in Luke 6:27 and 35, we can let the love through even when we cannot condone a person's human behavior, or really even like them, or enjoy spending time with them. Every Being deserves the love. And the love heals and creates a momentum toward Soul growth for sender and sendee.

Had Brugh Joy's students learned their lesson or what! Impressive!

Praying for God's love to come through us, to be sent to someone else, is a grand act when we cannot like that person, from the ego/personality level. We just disconnect our judgmental mind. As said before, if we only knew a person's complete Soul history, we would totally understand their actions. Souls get "stuck" in patterns, sometimes, lifetime after lifetime. These patterns get hardened and are sometimes slow to change. You know how hard it is to work on your own self-defeating behaviors!

This just-mentioned principle is still a difficult one for me on some days. I prayerfully send the love to new Souls or medium-age Souls, acting out, being their worst selves.

As the earth's terminal mess is getting turned around, the insistent time pressure means this Golden Spiritual Age demands a great deal. If we are resistant to opening our hearts, we are given predicaments, trials and tribulations, so that we will ultimately learn. More on this later in Chapter 3 under "dramas to grow our Soul" and "the path."

I have wondered if one way we get rewarded with good karma is by how much of God's love we allow through our physical human heart. Just how big is our "lens" and how consistent are we? Certainly, letting the love go through will give our Soul more pro-pellant energy that stays with us after physical death, giving us the Soul-energy for more choices after we leave.

In the middle of one night, unaware, shaman was apparently open to letting the love through. Remembering this, he said, "I thought some person was coming, only it wasn't somebody. All of a sudden this energy, just love, ran through me so powerfully, it was just immense. I had no want, no desire. I was just enveloped in this love."

Over lifetimes, God's love is impersonal. It has the potential to go to and through all of us equally. You are the one who holds it out.

Now, as for the limitations of the human heart. If you are really ready to have your heart opened totally, go back to the list of nega-tive-karma-producing behaviors. Go over it and honestly list for yourself which behaviors you have been engaged in during the past month. Your selection of negative behaviors is what you need to be working on now, to gain purity of heart. A total openness of heart. And besides your personal list, watch for the situations in your life that show you where you close your heart. Aware and sensitized as a highly conscious human being, you can actually feel it close down.

I consciously say to myself the following sentence when I feel my heart closing: "All that *really* matters is the love." Then almost always I can open up my lens again.

"If the human heart is a sending/receiving mechanism for God's love, tell us about the **PHYSICAL HUMAN BRAIN**." The human brain is also a sending/receiving mechanism. But it is much more complex because of the number of "channels." Of course, the nervous system is an integral part of the functioning of the brain.

The human brain is a sending/receiving mechanism that you can use to tune into the different "channels." I will talk about ten channels you can tune into. There are more channels that I don't yet know or understand.

To complicate matters, two or three of these channels may indeed be the same channels, but with different "access buttons." Here they are listed with a number in front just to help you keep track. After listing the ten, I will go into the details of each numbered channel. I take responsibility for the limitations and inaccuracies of this model.

Grandma Janis' Human-Mind-Channels Model

(1) Supreme Being mind (higher mind, measurable on biofeedback equipment as deep "alpha state or waves;"

(2) Ego-mind (lower mind);

(3) The akashic records, stored in the Supreme Being mind;

(4) Solution–finding mind, measurable on biofeedback as "beta state or waves;"

(5) A dreamy, but still–awake channel, measurable on biofeedback equipment as "theta state or waves;"

(6) The dream state;

(7) Sleep, measurable on biofeedback as "delta state or waves;"

(8) The astral plane;

(9) The subconscious mind, accessible through hypnosis; and

(10) The humor channel.

These "channels" are all *functions* within the physical *brain*. The physical brain houses the "fluid" functions. The fluid functions are the *mind*.

If you took just one "channel," let's say for example, alpha, or the deep meditative state, you will find many stages to alpha. When you first go in, you are in a shallow place. But as you are in longer and longer, you can go deeper and deeper. Each alpha phase, a consciousness mark–off spot, could have a name. Some Eastern religions differentiate many levels of deep meditation. It is as if when you tune in "on the dial," you can get closer and closer to the station. And there is less and less "static." Finally, for the very evolved Soul, the station comes in perfectly clear and is immediately accessible thereafter.

The physical brain is dense matter, and for most people the *left hemisphere* is time–sequenced, used mainly for analytical processes. The *right hemisphere*, again for most people, operates outside of linear time, and is used mainly for creative and intuitive processes. Then there is the *reptilian cortex* where survival instincts are initiated, including fear, pain and loss.

There are more complications. A great deal of chemistry is going on in our grey matter. For example, neuro peptides are chemicals which brain cells use to talk to other brain cells.

To make the subject even more challenging, in fifteen percent of us, the right and left brain functions are flipflopped or reversed. If you would like to know for yourself, some people can sense which side of their head gets deeply fatigued after studying or doing mental work for hours. If it is your left side, you are with the majority.

Both lower consciousness (ego–mind) and higher consciousness

(Supreme Being mind, superconsciousness) are *functions* within the physical brain. In order to function, this physical brain has to be connected with the rest of the human body. Thus it becomes a **system** within God, Goddess, all there is, The Universe, Existence, the God System, or your favorite name.

My *every* attitude, thought, or uttered word emitting out of my brain ripples through all the layers of ego, intellect, senses and matter, spreading out in wider and wider circles. I am a Light radiating consciousness for better – (or worse when I engage in the negative karma–producing thoughts and behaviors) throughout the universes. And so it is for you and everyone else.

To some extent, I am buffeted by other people's negativity or limitations and so are you. We can protect ourselves by having close relationships only with those of higher consciousness. We also protect ourself by meditation.

Psychological safety can also be had by mentally constructing a Lighted wall around yourself. Eleven years ago, when I first learned this principle I was working for the army. The creation I visualized was/is an eternal vibrating soft pink tank! I was told that using the white Light for shielding could have a boomerang effect because of its brightness, although I know many metaphysicians who do surround themselves with the white Light.

The following mind concepts are heavy, theoretical concepts. I am sorry they are not easy reading. But as of today, they are the best I can do. Although I own a simple, basic biofeedback machine, it doesn't help beyond what is offered. Advanced scientific procedures like MRIs (magnetic resonance imaging) and CAT scans (computerized axial tomography) are teaching us more about brain function. Already, subjects can be doing some mental exercise tuned into one of the brain "channels," and a three–dimensional, colored CAT scan picture is taken showing what section(s) is/are energized. Until more is known or until we all evolve into the next consciousness levels, here goes. Somebody has got to do it:

(1) The SUPREME BEING MIND

Infinite intelligence, sometimes called Higher mind, Big mind,

Superconsciousness, God's mind, the Godhead, or God. If you could
totally turn off the ego–mind/personality and turn into this super–
consciousness with your brain and never leave this consciousness,
you could do what Avatars do. But before that, your body would
have to be totally spiritualized. In other words, your totally open
physical heart would have to be at psychological purity level, and
your physical body and physical brain tuned up to a level where
you could be comfortable and totally functional within the incredible energy vibrations, as is Sai Baba; as was Jesus and Meher.

For those of us who can access the Supreme Being Mind in meditation, putting ourselves into this highest consciousness state, alpha,
God's mind, our own Soul's vibrations, we experience being in harmony with the collective messiah as children of the Light. In this
superconsciousness, we are in the pure present. On this channel, we
are totally aware of this great oneness with all things, since the
Supreme Being Mind also vibrates as the Holy Spirit in every atom
of everything in the universes.

The Supreme Being Mind is outside of the boundaries of time and
matter. I will say more on the concepts of "time" and "matter" soon.
But remember for now, that for most people, the right side of the
brain's functions are done without an awareness of time passing. Do
you remember drawing or painting, creating a block formation as a
child, imagining something creative to cook, composing some music?
And later realizing that hours had passed unnoticed? In some lucky
occupations, for example, being an architect, people get to be "out of
time." But later, the solution–finding function of the brain gets
accessed when building codes are addressed, and the architect
decides which lot to recommend buying to fit the current creation.

In the Superconscious, there is a "collective memory of human
beings," if you will, a storage space, but this place is not in our physical brains.

"Do these terms have something in common: ancestral memory,
archetypes, the collective unconscious, and morphogenic fields?"

Plato's **archetypes**, Carl Jung's **collective unconscious**,
Sheldrake's **morphogenic fields**, and the Indians' **ancestral
memory** contain all the positive patterns as well as the negative. I

suspect, that at the very least, all these ideas are the same *process*. As the human race rises in consciousness, this is reflected in "these ancestral memories" and creates positive change. All this is somehow recorded in the ethers.

"How does British Biologist Rupert Sheldrake explain morphogenic fields?" He says these fields are invisible templates that make possible the particular shapes that organisms take. For example, a cat has a "cat template" in the ethers. Using the cat example, when an individual member of the species learns a new behavior, it feeds back into the collective field to influence all other cats, either in the present or in the future. Sheldrake says, "Living organisms tune into these M-fields through a process called 'morphic resonance,' a resonance of like with like." Each cat that learns the new behavior makes it easier for all the other cats to learn it. At one point, a critical mass is reached. Then all cats, or *all of a species*, automatically demonstrate that behavior, a genetic component from then on.

Some people call this critical mass point the **"one hundredth monkey"** theory. Many metaphysicians apply this theory to the evolution of human consciousness, saying it will take 144,000 people holding the state of high Beingness, Christ Consciousness. Then everyone will automatically be pulled in. Others say the number is 300,000. This is where your help is needed. We have not been able to get that critical mass yet, enough people to "pop in" the whole human race.

Carl Jung's "collective" or "archetypes" is a similar idea. Jung, a Swiss psychiatrist who died in 1961, felt that at the conscious level, our individual minds are separated, but that our unconscious minds are merged, and linked to those who have lived before. In his model, there is, for example, positive "mothering" behavior available to the species. The negative, neurotic behaviors are stored in the collective archetypes also, for example, "beating children."

We will consider these ancestral memory theories again in Chapter 3 when we talk about getting rid of your "neuroses."

To sum up what we have talked about in the "Supreme Being Mind," we have a place in consciousness to go for peace and bliss, and it also has a mysterious collective memory that is unconsciously accessed, hence its other name, the **collective unconscious**.

(2) EGO-MIND

Every lifetime you develop a new ego. Let's face it, you are pretty fascinating, much more interesting than animals in the zoo. Each life you get a new body, basic intelligence, personality, material goods, friends. It's a blast. Even babies are aware early of their own enticing hands and feet. And later, are quite aware of "something better" and will crawl over to get "it" – and then something else – and something else, an endless process of wanting. It isn't any wonder that you compare what you have to others and develop defense mechanisms around weaknesses. And ego–mind doesn't realize that this–lifetime's traits and things and toys are transient.

Lower mind, little mind, the mind your ego operates out of, is an aspect of yourself that you will never get rid of totally – in this life. Indeed, it is a metaphysical mystery if the ideal would be to totally annihilate it. (Would we get so "Light" that we wouldn't care if a tree was falling toward us or never be concerned about eating right and doing our exercises? It seems to me that some self–interest is necessary.)

Anyway, with great work, you can loosen ego–mind's compacted-ness, so that you can access the Being Mind more often and for longer periods of time. You have to transcend your ego–mind to comprehend high–levels of reality. You have to gain the realization that it is not you who has to straighten out all situations. You do *nothing* without God's help; neither does an atheist.

Dear Being, this is usually a long–time process. You expand your consciousness, then go into a contracted time of feeling depressed or sad, then into another expansion – and then into another contraction – and another expansion – and so on until you break down the ego–mind and become "Self–realized" or "enlightened" in some life-time. In each life, your that–lifetime–developed ego didn't want to let go.

To be more specific, besides wanting things, ego–mind wants struc-ture, it wants order, and it wants to be in control. Ego–mind thinks up ways to outfox fellow humans; ego-mind is a schemer. Ego-mind keeps all the good stuff. Ego-mind is petty. Ego-mind feels superior. Ego-mind will not lend a helping hand. Ego-mind is overly concerned with making a good impression. Ego-mind doesn't like being wrong. Ego-mind likes to show off. Ego-mind has to be first, but if it can't make first, it needs to be second, and has lots of excuses if it doesn't. Ego-mind loves to defeat another. Ego-mind looks out for itself. Ego-mind is afraid of saying the truth for fear of being misunderstood. Ego-mind is "the judge;" it makes things simple, either "good" or "bad," "right" or "wrong." Ego-mind gets in the way of your relationship with your Being. Ego-mind is not interested in God. Ego-mind is an addict. Ego-mind perverts reality. Ego-mind fears both being alone and also being swallowed up. Ego-mind leads you to hold onto things that are harmful. Ego-mind has nearly destroyed the planet with its greed. Ego-mind expresses pride and vanity. Ego-mind is very, very dangerous.

Even more hazardous are two opposing ego-minds locked in battle!

Ego-mind just doesn't realize that you should not hold onto power, that it is a hook. Ego-mind doesn't know that whenever you try to become "somebody," you are lost. If it would just let go of its super-glue, superior-position hold, ego-mind could stay in a loose and subordinate position, and life would be much happier and more meaningful.

The encouraging thing is that once you identify your ego-mind's attitudes, thoughts, and behaviors, when you sense yourself having these attitudes or thoughts or find yourself doing an ego-mind behavior, you can just stop – and let go. If it is necessary to give an explanation to a person you are relating to, you can just say something like, "I just realized that my ego was hooked; I want very much to let this go."

Or if you seem to have bumped into someone else's ego-mind, you can ask in a soft and non-threatening way, "I don't want to offend, but did I just bump into your ego?"

We have a sign on our front door, "Please leave your ego and shoes outside."

Matthew 5:5: "Blessed are the meek for they shall inherit the earth." I suspect this means that those who have diminished their ego-mind and/or hold it subordinately will prevail.

A brain vibrating with alpha waves is an ego-less mind feeling connected with others. Ego-less mind feels connected to nature. Ego-less mind is spontaneous. Ego-less mind enjoys the moment. Ego-less mind doesn't judge people. Ego-less mind doesn't worry or have fears. Ego-less mind overflows with appreciation. Ego-less mind produces smiles and laughter. Ego-less mind extends love and kindness. Ego-less mind lets things happen, doesn't force. Ego-less mind loves for others to have fun. Ego-less mind revels in other people's successes. Ego-less mind doesn't strategize or protect. Ego-less mind loves God without reservation.

Soon, I will come back to ego-less mind to address the bridge subjects of "enlightenment," Self-realization, and how to meditate.

(3) AKASHIC RECORDS MIND

In the superconscious, there is a place with a file for each Being. In it are recorded each of the Being's lifetimes, and as Beings, everything the Being did, thought or said in its countless ages of existence.

The tiniest vibration was and is recorded in these ethers. As said before, you have been and are being watched all the time by these automatic processes, as well as your out-of-the-body helpers. (Remember, you are never, never alone.) From these experiences and the choices you made, character is formed. Out of this record flows your karma.

Someone who is both very psychic and very spiritually devout may access these records. Of course the psychic's human brain is used both in accessing, then receiving, the information. Now whether or not this access is through the same "channel" as the higher mind, superconsciousness, I don't know. I am calling the Akashic Records a different channel because historical information is stored there. When I am meditating, I have never had the experience of bumping into a bunch of historical information.

It is interesting that no matter in what language a portion of the

Soul's history was recorded, a high–level, devout psychic can access it in his or her own language, if access is allowed. The information vibrations somehow get translated!

It is my firm belief that not all Akashic Record information is available to you on the personal level and for good reasons. Called by Hebrew masters, "God's Book of Remembrance," you earn the right to know more about your own Soul's historical development as you move forward and more is released to you, either directly or by the psychics you consult.

Also on a group, state, national and world level, certain information is withheld until the timing is right. I feel sure there is an advanced Being (or Beings) guarding the Akashic records for the appropriate time.

There are so many advanced Beings working for you, if you only knew, you would rejoice.

In the book, *SAI BABA THE HOLY MAN AND THE PSYCHIATRIST,* (page 102) is an account of a man who had died, and was brought back to life by Sai Baba's grace. The Akashic Records of the man's Soul goodness were accessed and the man's consciousness was very awake and aware of his own judgement. The multiple–lifetimes information brought forth was stunning and an advanced Being, an ethereal judge, reviewed it!

(4) SOLUTION-FINDING MIND

This function continues after self–realization or enlightenment. I believe this function also works through the brain of Avatars, the totally God–realized saviors, while in their case, I don't even theorize how it works.

Even in our future, when everyone who stays on this physical planet is Self–realized and lives out of Christ consciousness or higher, we will still need to find answers, to do collaborative–solution finding. There will still be family discussions, business meetings and planning sessions.

In most people, this function probably occurs in the left side of the physical brain. It is logical, rational and non–emotional. (If you ever studied Transactional Analysis, the solution-finding function is exactly the same as the non-emotional "Adult .")

The solution-finding mind helps on a daily basis to remind you to pay the insurance, rent and the IRS. It tells you to do your grooming in the morning and awakens you to move out of the way of an on-coming train.

(5) THETA

The function of this channel, the dreamy but still awake state, may just be a corridor. It is the "channel" in meditation you want to avoid because it seems to be the *passageway* to and from sleep.

Later, I'll give you hints on how to stay out of this very pleasant consciousness state – when you don't want to be there.

(6) DREAM STATE

You enter dreams through delta, sleep. A right brain activity, out of linear time, only about twenty-five percent of sleep time is spent dreaming. A guesstimate of average dream time per calendar day is two hours. For most people, that is two hours of unconscious time.

During your dream state, if your Being is willing, higher Beings can educate you at the spiritual level you have reached.

When you are awake, you see objects by the Light of the sun, moon, stars or artificial light. In the dream state, the illumination is from your Soul. The colors and symbols as well as the Light itself, are your Soul speaking.

In the brilliant book, DREAM PRACTICE AND THE PRACTICE OF NATURAL LIGHT, author Namkhai Norby classifies types of dreams. The dreamer is doing one or more of the following:
    (1) Rehashing impressions of the day within the context of the personality [body intact].
    (2) Dealing with personal anxieties and concerns [body intact].
    (3) Accessing archetypical material from the collective unconscious, the rich and powerful repository of the

collective memory of the human race [body intact].

(4) Actually Soul traveling at a place in another dimension [probably the astral plane].

(5) Communicating with other dimensions of Beings.

(6) Using the dream to tell the future, a rare predictive dream [body intact]. This is considered to be a high class dream.

In some primitive cultures, it is imperative that a person seeking "enlightenment" master the dreamstate, learning to control the dreams so all danger is overcome, pleasure is had, and the dream has a positive outcome. This means you can consciously transform images (for example create dream "friends" by turning a stone into a puppy?), move things about, multiply or condense the dream's elements, turn things upside down, and change the sizes of the elements – sound like Sai Baba?

Norby thinks using dreams for spiritual transformation works at least partially in this way: By mastering total control over dreams, over a period of time, you can come to appreciate that ordinary reality is as unreal as the dream state and thus come to diminish tension in ordinary reality.

There is no doubt in my mind that these just-mentioned practices would create permanent Soul energy. I remember my shaman teacher's reply to a lady who bemoaned her husband's lack of spiritual practice. "Don't worry about him" he encouraged, "He does his practice in the dream state. He will be like me in the next life."

I also remember him saying to me, "Janis, you have a bombshelter over your dreamstate." He meant, not only was I not using my dreams to evolve, I couldn't even remember them. What a spiritual luxury he was, always telling me where I was stuck!

I was taught that the Being speaks to us in our dreams with symbols. Therefore, if I clearly remember a picture, color, or how many of a thing – for example three trees – I now use two different dream symbol books to check it out.

In THE DREAM BOOK: SYMBOLS FOR SELF-UNDERSTANDING,

Inner Light Foundation, Novato, California, 1983, Betty Bethards interprets, for example, a "cave" as "Unconscious mind; unexplored aspects of self. Great treasures lie within as you continue the adventure of self–discovery." In THE GYPSY DREAMBOOK, Samuel Weiser, Inc., Box 612, York Beach, Maine 03910, Sergius Golowin translates dreaming of a cave ". . . into meaning you withdraw from people too much as a consequence of exaggerated carefulness. You should overcome this and seek out good company."

After hearing about my dream, a gestalt psychotherapist might set me in a chair and say, "Be the cave and I will have a conversation with you. What are you trying to say, cave? What do you represent? What is it like to be a cave. What is in you?" Or the therapist might ask me to take both roles, alternately, sitting in one chair when I am "the cave" and then getting up to sit in the other chair to ask questions of "the cave."

One day, a woman whom I knew to be a medium–age Soul took great offense at something I was doing. She came to our house, and with three other people in the house within hearing distance, banged on the front door, and started shouting at me, calling me names, "witch," "bitch," "You call yourself a Reverend!" I thought I handled it pretty well. I didn't go into any retaliatory, or name–calling behavior. I just assertively and politely asked her to leave, stating that I didn't want her there. (I don't collude with anyone to treat me badly.)

Later, I reasoned that after all, what can I expect from a middle–aged Soul? She was doing the best she could. I asked my Angel Healing Group, "Could you send her some unconditional love?" I thought I had dropped it, but several nights later, I dreamed I was throwing alligators at her; but before I could toss each alligator, I had to get it unstuck from me.

The GYPSY DREAM BOOK didn't list a symbol for alligator, but Bethards' book indicates that alligator means "tremendous power for verbal expression, which must be watched carefully so as not to be used destructively" and "fear of misuse of verbal power." These indicated to me that although I didn't shout back names, there was at least an aspect of me that had wanted to. Rajneesh suggested that sometimes dreams are a way of helping us complete things that are not complete. It is interesting that after the dream, I could send her unconditional love myself.

(And if you want to hear something ironic, later she sent a letter to our house. The symbol on her first–class stamp? An alligator! How The Universe loves to play! Not only had I never seen an alligator stamp before – I haven't since!)

Some consider the method of processing dreams by looking up symbols in a book, a lazy habit, reneging on spiritual growth. Please do some reading on the subject of dreams. However, I often find an explanation of an archetypical symbol that resonates and offers help.

Some people find that keeping a dream journal is very helpful. Again, the task *is to be conscious* of everything exactly as if you were awake.

The beauty is that the more you pay attention to your dreams, the more you will remember them immediately upon awakening, which of course is the time to write them down. Tuning into dreams also seems to make the number increase and the clearness improve. Pray for the dreams that will aid your Self–realization efforts.

An aside, the symbols you see in everyday life can also be checked out in a dream book. (Not all symbol books on the market are authentic. Hold them in your hands against your heart; use your own intuition.)

Here is my own wide–awake story of using the dream book symbols: One very cold winter day, alone, I was sitting at my computer, writing. I was very ill (Jesus helped later) and wondering, discouraged, "Will anyone want to read Cosmic Map?"

The wind was blowing fiercely and the sky was grey. Then something caught my eye just outside the window. Our temple house nestles on a high cliff overlooking Clear Lake in Northern California. We are about a thousand feet above the water.

I could not believe my eyes. An eagle was heading into the wind with feathers ruffled, blown back against its body, and because of the headwind, was poised in space for a few seconds just one foot outside our window. I knew this event was a message. Quickly I left my work and headed for my dream symbol books. Golowin: "An eagle high up in the sky signifies success which will be known far and wide throughout the land . . . " Bethards: "Great power; spiritual self is soaring. Tremendous freedom to be used wisely . . ." Did that eagle make my day? You betcha! I also know from Golowin's book that odd numbers are lucky, one eagle!

Indeed, there are no accidents. The Universe is speaking to us all the time, if we could just decode the symbols and events, the "bumping into people," the strange "coincidences."

Not all dream symbol interpretations are happy ones. Here is an example. Golowin comments that seeing a "moth" in a dream means that "badly invested assets may soon dwindle as a result of unforeseen circumstances."

Now, back to mind channels.

(7) SLEEP

First, let us start with a comparison of frequencies of four of the states previously mentioned and measured during biofeedback. I am no expert, but as I understand it, clusters of brain waves are measured by the biofeedback machine in cycles per second.

Sleep, Delta	4 and below (three possible variations)
Dreamy but awake, Theta	5 – 7 (three possible variations)
Meditation, Alpha	8 – 13 (six possible variations)
Focused attention, Beta	14 – 30 (seventeen variations) Notice this broad band available for problem solving and collaborative–solution finding!

As you can see, brain frequencies are very, very slowed down in sleep. The ego–mind is off duty. In deep sleep, we connect with the automatically patterned processes of the superconscious mind in a way that re–creates our physical body/brain. This connection is done automatically, no intervention is needed.

During deep sleep, especially during the first two hours, the body is totally relaxed.

Historically, one of the ways prisoners have been badly treated is to deprive them of sleep. This method of torture is well documented to mess people up and totally alter their ability to function in the objective world. Sleep deprivation also sets the stage for enemy brainwashing.

Indeed, two of the harder practical tasks in life are (1) to determine just how much sleep you need for optimum day performance and enjoyment of life and (2) to design a lifestyle that consistently gets you that amount of sleep. Another benefit of mastering these two practical tasks is you won't fall asleep during meditation!

Involuntary astralprojection by the Light body into the astral plane is possible. For ordinary folks, in the case of this astralprojection, a temporary, total separation from the physical body may happen during the slightly higher cycles per second, (dream time). It is hard to tell. The biofeedback numbers are artificial lines drawn by experts. Who is to say exactly what is going on at 4.5 cycles per second? I have often wondered why my body sometimes jerks as I am falling asleep.

It is interesting that within a day of writing the prior paragraph, a friend dropped off an older <u>New</u> <u>Age</u> <u>Journal,</u> November/December 1988, containing an article titled Astral Travel. Author Jean Noel Bassior did an excellent job interviewing Robert Monroe who had written JOURNEYS OUT OF THE BODY published in 1971 by Doubleday & Company, Inc., documenting journeys he had taken starting in the early 1950s. (I had read Monroe's book in 1981. I thought he was extremely brave and his stories terrorized me so I forgot about them.) In the Bassior article, Monroe theorizes that the jerk is a separation from the physical body.

(8) ASTRAL PLANE

Here are some generalities. Do pursue this subject further elsewhere. It is fascinating.

The astral plane is a level of consciousness where Souls spend time between lives. The more spiritual energy you carry, the more evolved your Soul, the more you have lived life seeking truth and doing things for your fellow humans, the quicker you can move through the lower parts of this "region." After you die, your Soul moves through the astral plane; out–of–body teachers help you learn to perfect your vibration and disengage from elements of yourself that have traveled with you, so that you can move on.

The astral plane is a giant ethereal world not unlike our own, except it is not physical. Out–of–body Beings live in this immense consciousness. Some psychics see these Beings with ethereal clothes. There are schools and buildings. I received my first learning about the astral plane when shaman talked about the *lower* astral plane as a sort of **hell** and is probably the source of the stories of such a place.

Later I read Edgar Cayce's description of himself going into trance. Remember, I reported earlier that he perceived his essence as a dot. First he would see darkness, then a white beam of Light, then a path of Light. As he progressed he saw vague, horrible shapes, then mis-shapen forms of human beings, and then hooded dark figures.

Getting through that hell, Cayce saw figures in "outline" form: clothes, houses and trees, cities and towns, rumbling sounds and then music and birds. He was traveling (astralprojecting?) his essence toward the Hall of Records.

The lower astral plain hell is populated by both lost Beings (some with their physical bodies still alive here, a mystery to me – why?) and the ugly thought forms from planet earth that have taken on a life of their own, created by hate, resentment, jealousy and ill will. So not all malignant creatures there are Beings! You are partially responsible every time you have an ugly thought!

Some of our nightmares are trips to the lower astral plane.

Many of Monroe's real out–of–the–body journeys as he describes them in his original book, JOURNEY'S OUT OF THE BODY, were in the lower regions of the astral plane where he was sometimes attacked by monsters and ended up in hostile cities. Monroe, an atheist or agnostic, is brutally honest. In the 1988 article, at age 73, he still did not believe in God. The Light Beings that he occasionally encountered were just "beings of light."

I would say that, perhaps, he did not, at that time, have enough Soul energy to go to a higher place. I have not read his later books; I don't know if he has been able to climb higher; but if not now, he will in his Soul's future; it is guaranteed.

Monroe says there is an essential goodness to many Beings. In sharing his out–of–the–body journeys, it is clear when he feels the Beings he meets are acting in ways which cause him positive emotional response. (Note: These emotions are felt when his physical body is asleep on his bed at home!)

An **atheist** is a person who denies or disbelieves the existence of a supreme Being. An **agnostic** is a person who holds that the existence or the ultimate cause, as God, and the essential nature of things, are unknown and unknowable. An agnostic, therefore, is a person who doesn't know if there is a God or not.

Raymond Moody, M. D., investigator and writer about people's near–death experiences, indicated on a TV program that a person can no longer be an atheist or agnostic after a near–death experience. So we can be a bit confused: a brave, experienced astralprojector like Robert Monroe still does not believe in God, but a non–believer, an after–/NDEer, becomes a believer! These two processes, astralprojecting and leaving the earth plane after death are different.

Back to the astral plane. The Eckankar materials talk about the highly evolved Beings living at the top of the astral plane, some permanently. As described, it sounds like heaven. We are told that after reaching the top, we return to this physical, third–dimension earth only as a redeemer. Eckankar's Paul Twitchell describes golden palaces, canals of nectar, Beings living in incredible bliss, and miracles being performed in response to karmically correct earth prayers. But this is not the place where the Godhead lives.

The upper astral plane channel was accessed by devout psychic Edgar Cayce, a remarkable feat and extremely rare.

Apparently, higher forces see to it that the problems in the lower

astral plane get addressed periodically. And I know a psychic I trust
who told a devout friend of mine, "When you leave this life, you are
going to go to the lower astral plane and help clean it up." So we
might say that hell is not a place, but a "temporary" state of consciousness. One we can hope, at best, to have enough Soul energy
to move right through. When we die, we may not be going *to* hell,
but we may be going to move *through* hell!

A **saint** while living was described by shaman as someone able to
stay permanently in Alpha. After physical death, a saint uses the
Soul energy to go to a very high place. Having shed all bodies nec-
essary while on earth to protect it, according to Paul Twitchell, this
Soul now shines with the radiance of sixteen suns and moons!
You have this potential; we all have this evolutionary pattern.

Toward the beginning of Chapter 2, I told you that mind functioning
is a subject of some complexity. We are working now on brain concepts. We have covered eight channels of the brain. We still have
to address the subconscious mind "channel" and the humor
"channel."

(9) SUBCONSCIOUS MIND

This is a fascinating subject. We are related to the inner world
through the subconscious mind. I have been taught that it is the
passageway through which our consciousness rises to meet the
Superconscious. If this is true, it is a different "channel" from God's
mind, although some think they are the same.

If you can use the subconscious mind in a positive manner by keeping your conscious mind busy with expectations of the best, your
subconscious will faithfully reproduce your expectations. On the
conscious level, affirmations, creative visualizations and breakthrough thinking are systematic ways of putting this powerhouse to
work. So that we don't go too far afield here from the subject of the
physical human body/brain, I will wait and address these positive-
thinking tools as separate subjects toward the end of COSMIC MAP.

The subconscious mind's powers are simply amazing. I have seen a
performing hypnotist ask for a volunteer from the audience. The
woman he selected came up on the stage and he immediately put

her into a trance with several sentences of suggestion. He told her that her body was "a stiff board." He had her lay her head on a chair, and then he put her feet on another chair two feet away. Then the hypnotist got up and walked across her stiff–as–a–board body!

Now your doubting mind may have said to you that the performer had an assistant whom he had planted in the audience and perhaps she wore some kind of brace. However, in this instance, the hypnotist was performing at the community college where I was teaching, and the woman was a student known to me.

The subconscious mind is amenable to suggestion and is controlled by suggestion. *It accepts what you believe to be true.*

"You are going to get well," says the anesthetist to the drugged surgery patient. And on the average, these suggested–to patients get discharged two days earlier than patients given no positive affirmation.

Dr. Bennett Braun, a research psychiatrist and specialist in the field of multiple personality has seen warts, scars, rashes, hypertension and epilepsy appear and disappear the moment a patient changes from one personality to another.

In the placebo effect, a sugar pill believed by the patient to be the real thing heals thirty percent of the population. Again, we see the subconscious mind is more open to suggestion in some people. Not everyone would have become "stiff as a board" either. Obviously, some people are more suggestible than others.

Years ago when I was doing research for my doctorate, I read a report in a psychological journal of a woman who lost her lover when she was twenty–six. She went "crazy" from the grief and was put into an asylum. Not realizing time had passed, every day for forty years, she expected her lover to come in the door at any moment. At the age of sixty–six, she was reported to have still looked age twenty–six.

The subconscious mind disregards time. Hypnotism leaves a person free of current mental processes.

Besides programming good things to come, hypnotism is used to tune into memory accessible through the subconscious mind. In hypnotic trance, you are in a state of profound relaxation and heightened suggestibility, but are not asleep.

As a modern shaman healer trained in using hypnotic regression, I use hypnotism occasionally. (By the way, I consider a **modern shaman**, one who wants to give the knowledge away, and doesn't try to hold it to keep the considerable *power and status* of exclusive knowledge.)

With one middle-aged man, I gently took him back to the day his mother died when he was five years old because he couldn't remember anything about her death or *even what she looked like!*

When hypnotized, this beautiful man who so wanted to heal that wound, could see what his Mom looked like. He remembered every detail, including the green mint candy handed to him by a compassionate neighbor.

At the time of his mother's death, his father had insisted he not cry, but be a "big boy." Through play therapy and art, he and I processed the repressed memories. He needed to get mad, cry and express his anger. Then we were able to address the sadness and pain, still being felt as an adult, but unspecific.

So, besides its other functions, the subconscious mind has stored, unremembered, painful memories which can be brought forward and healed today. Interestingly, it is as easy to access a past-life and its unresolved traumas as it is events that have occurred in this life!

Thus the memory of the subconscious is permanent, while the physical brain is temporary.

The subconscious mind cannot speak without being spoken to. I so remember my hypnotherapist's phone ringing four or five times during a session. Although his secretary picked up the call from another room, I in the trance state, was startled by that ringing, but I literally couldn't say anything. Now, if when I was in trance, he would have asked me, "Janis, is that ringing phone bothering you," I would have been able to answer, "Yes." Then he would have had to say, "Shall I turn it off?" Then I could have answered, "Yes." However, I couldn't just volunteer, after it had startled me, "Please, would you mind turning off your phone."

(10) HUMOR

The way I arrived at knowing "humor as a different channel" was to realize that all the other channels had functions which were distinct, unique. And that when you are operating out of one of these channels, you are exclusively involved, at least for the moment, until you switch to another channel.

From personal experience, finding something really funny and/or having a good laugh leaves me feeling very uplifted, peaceful and happy. I am absolutely sure this consciousness produces beta endorphin, the happiness chemical, as does going into alpha in meditation. And anything that leaves me feeling so good in a natural way must be important.

The use of this channel, the use of humor, is an activity that almost didn't exist on the personal level during my grim-times childhood. I know that some of the early comedy shows, to be sure, had started in the 1930s. But it was an activity that started "out there." No one in my family was purposefully funny. No friends of mine laughed, giggled a lot, made jokes, told on-purpose funny stories, made light, laughed at themselves, or had thoughts that doubled them over with the hilarity of their own idea.

You can't be laughing and in deep meditation, alpha. You can't be giggling and ego-centered. (Ego is so serious, if ego is laughing, ego is faking it!)

You can't be exploring the Akashic records and chuckling because of a current thought or event. You can't be concentrating hard on solving a problem (solution-finding channel) and doubling over with laughter. You can't be falling asleep and chuckling. You can't be dreaming and silly unless the dream itself is funny. You can't be asleep and expressing mirth. You can't be accessing the astral plane and be amused. You can't be under hypnosis and laughing it up, unless something in the regression itself is funny.

Although, to be sure, some going back and forth, cross access, goes on between all of the channels. At some points of the day, we are flipping channels rather frequently. For example from the solution-finding channel to the humor channel when someone tells a good joke and then back to the solution–finding channel.

To me, humor is a saving grace, a developing Divine energy. It is my current learning playground – I am learning how to be humorous and to include it in my daily life. I am very fortunate because my impish, spontaneous husband is my human teacher. He loves making me laugh. And he always does it when I am least expecting it.

A master of the humor channel is Steve Bhaerman, alias Swami Beyondananda. His book is a must read for those on the spiritual path, WHEN YOU SEE A SACRED COW, MILK IT FOR ALL IT'S WORTH! published by Ashland Publishing, 1993, 3356 Coffey Lane, Santa Rosa CA 95403.

This "swami" advises a spiritual job seeker to get "hire conscious-ness," muses that marriage is the major cause of divorce, worries that the on–coming enlightenment will be slowed down by roving gangs of restless youths invading psychic space and defacing auras, rejoices that traditional customs are undergoing positive change in war–torn Eastern lands because "women are now encouraged to walk ahead of their husbands" (at least until all hidden land mines are discovered). Three chapters in his book are titled: "I Never Metaphysical Question I Didn't Like," "Achieving an Altared State: Swami's Tips on Dear–Hunting" and "Everything You Always Wanted to Know About Sects."

It is said that pain is a sign of too much seriousness. I like the advice of Tibetan Buddhist Long Chen Pa:

> Since everything is but an apparition
> Perfect in being what it is,
> Having nothing to do with good or bad.
> Acceptance or rejection,
> One may well burst out in laughter.

Now, that I have talked about all the listed channels, ten of them, please note something quite interesting: Seven of the mind–state channels operating through the human brain are of the **subjective world**, infinite, out of linear time, and require an *inner* journey: Supreme Being mind, akashic records, theta, dreams, sleep, the subconscious and the astral plane (the twilight zone that lies between matter and spirit).

Only three of the mind–state channels are of the **objective world**, finite, and time–sequenced, components of our *outer journey*: the ego–mind, the problem–solving or solution–finding mind and the humor channel. This is an eye–opener when we ask the question, "What is "real?""

Thus the different channels function in the brain. The term "**mind**" means that one of the channels is operational. Indeed, while we are alive, one of the channels is always operational, even if it is just the sleep channel. As we have seen, third dimensional consciousness has many different channels; we exist on many levels, and several of these levels are complicated by our awareness of time.

"What more can you tell us about **TIME**?" To start to answer this question, I used my computer's search feature to see what already had been said. It is amazing how many times I have used the word, "time!" Here goes.

As discussed, we are an exceedingly complex spiritual Being encased in a human body, our this–life costume, capable of existing on many different inner and outer "channels."

Only in the objective outer world, available on three "channels" is our existence time–sequenced; this is the realm of matter. Time and **matter** seem to go together.

Deepak Chopra said, "Time is a collective agreement;" indeed that is true in our society where racing against the clock is standard behavior.

As I have said, not all conscious dimensions are physical. In the inner dimensions, our consciousness is not aware of time passing. And there is no matter, as we know it here.

In trance, Edgar Cayce was able to bring in for us the knowledge

that *only a portion of the Soul* projects itself into the limited dimensions of time and matter. We alluded to this when we talked about
our individual guidance, our higher Self and higher Selves.

Jim Hurtak says that *we shall remember who we are at the end of time.* At
the end of time, we will be in **Soul time**. Only now am I beginning
to understand that I don't even know if time or the external world
exists or if these are figments of my Soul's "imagination," things that
it has invented to grow itself, akin to a dream. But I will remember
for sure when Christ Consciousness comes in. Until this ascension
into the 4th and perhaps higher dimension, I like most of my fellow
humans, have my mind calibrated through this time set with physical objects, including human bodies. And we have a consciousness
that projects linear time.

Remember the stories I shared about Sai Baba? In two of them, the
great Avatar disregarded time and matter: first, the man returning
through consciousness – instead of by plane – to Australia and second, the carload of devotees leaving much, much too late, but still
arriving early?

So time–sequenced "reality" operates in some dimensions but not in
others.

And time is encoded into our body's DNA.   We can predict how the
newborn is going to be acting and looking at one year of age,
although, of course, there are variations. And somewhat how he or
she will look when they are old.

Deepak Chopra says our DNA manipulates molecules into rhythms,
or vibrations, that we code into time. Other vibrations are decoded
by our brain and nervous system as light, sound, texture, smells, etc.

Brugh Joy, M.D., states that telepathy is our natural form of communication. When a whole idea is obtained at once by intuition, the
words do not come linearly, one at a time, following each other. He
says that as children we are *taught* to use words sequentially; our
brains learn to organize thoughts sequentially, and get used to *coding* the sequentialness into time.

Shaman said that within the next decade, 300,000 Beings will break out of this linear time into Soul time, the space behind the ego-mind. When this happens for all humans, earth will become our playpen, we will be gentle and loving. We will become radiant, real human beings at last.

Okay, so we are trying to outgrow linear time. But getting beyond time doesn't happen quickly for most people. We are so accustomed to being overinfluenced by our conditioning and emotions.

Sai Baba says that a person's ability to develop higher consciousness depends upon Soul growth in former lives. He says it is like a rock that has been hit so many times. That there comes a time when just one more blow is going to crack it.

A channeler and Master teacher named Lazaris said it this way: It is as if you went into a movie house that has different movies going in different rooms. All the movies are going at the same time. He said that is the way it is, all of your lives are going on at the same time.

Just when you thought you were getting it! In the foreword I mentioned that our finite mind cannot possibly understand the infinite mind!

So, I am one point of consciousness in a giant, intelligent sea. So are you. We can go on describing and labeling until we are blue in the face. Life isn't going to make sense. The only way is to experience the bliss, the joy behind the mind, out of time, where we can all go, be in the moment and speak the same language.

Nevertheless, since time is now part of your life, Sai Baba has something to say about the spending of your precious time, "Time waste is life waste." And further, "Take time for good companionship and good books."

"People ask if they can expand their consciousness by the use of **DRUGS**. What is your opinion?" Yes, you can. There *may have been* a period in the 1960s and 1970s when avant-garde Souls were unknowingly doing drugs for the collective consciousness, in order to break down the rigidity.

Here is why I am very much against drug intervention in consciousness *now*. Your Soul is protected partially by your human mind. The day and time of the ascension shift is unknown. *Having your Soul protection warped by drugs is asking to end up in God only knows for sure what dimension.* But my studied opinion is that your real Self with all its beautiful, shining potential is most likely, I am afraid, to end up in the lower astral plane.

Let's consider other dangers. First of all, how can you be sure this drug is the drug you meant to buy? How can you be sure that it is only the drug you meant to buy, and not mixed with other fillers like powdered soap, or crushed Draino. Even if it is the pure drug of your choice, how do you know it is going to enable you to tune into your desired channel? How can you get drugs right when you want them?

Many drug–taking folks, who say they "had a bad trip" got a preview, or maybe it was a review, of the lower astral plane.

If lower astral plane characters leak into your awareness, and this potentially frightening event occurs through natural mind expansion, you are still in charge. You can simply stand up, stamp your foot loudly, and/or noisily clap your hands. Tell the undesired creatures to go away and they will. If you get there on drugs, you may have to wait until the drug leaves your system and you may be trapped there. Robert Monroe, the lower astral plane mapper, says the astral bodies of the drugged and insane hang out and act out, often lurching about like zombies, while their bodies remain here.

These cautions about permanent mind expansion via drugs make it very problematical. Do you want to be making a powerful daily connection with God for the rest of your life? It is easier to do it the natural way. Then there are no drug residuals in your body and you don't have to rely on the drugs to do it.

Even drug takers who have eventually made it into Self–realization, or "enlightenment," have had to give up the drugs somewhere along the way. Most of them say that the drugs took them on a wasted–time–and–money side path and some, who became addicted, had the major obstacle of an addiction to overcome.

And if the person dies a drug addict (or any kind of addict), guess what learning task the Soul sets up for the next life? Right, drug addict or other addict – again!

It is well established by responsible research that long-term marijuana use negatively affects motivation, memory and sexual functioning. And I would like to add, common sense seems to go out the window.

Right now, I know three folks "on the path" who have been regularly using drugs. One of these people was put in prison five months ago after receiving a one-year sentence for growing too much of the stuff. From an incarceration spot with a very bad reputation, he wrote me about how clear he is now and how deep he is able to go in meditation, without drugs.

The other two are still users. One is on welfare and the other on disability. They both perceive a movement toward God. Their behavior, the choices they make and the predicaments they get themselves into, seem the opposite to me. Intoxicants alter perception so radically that a person truly cannot use discrimination in their actions.

After taking my stand, I was heartened when, two days before Cosmic Map went to the typesetter, some information came about the teachings of Meher Baba, the man I believe was Jesus reincarnated, our Avatar who has already come and gone. Meher gave clear directives against the use of drugs. Indeed you cannot even visit the Meher Spiritual Center in Myrtle Beach, South Carolina, if you have taken drugs in the prior six months and alcohol is not allowed at the center either.

"What can you tell me about my **EMOTIONS**?" They are triggered by a current event in your life, your recall of an event (memory), or your thinking about a problem. Emotions are also stimulated in dreams and in hypnotic trance. Processed through your physical brain, the emotion affects your bodily reactions; examples are your pulse rate, breathing rate, perspiration rate, skin temperature change, production of acid and adrenaline flow.

Your emotions are a physical spot on your brain which get energized. *On the brain, there is an anger spot, a sadness spot, a gladness spot, an optimistic spot and so forth.* As the energy drains out of that emotion's spot, your brain stops notifying your nerves. Unless, of course, you start thinking again about the event or begin to worry and regenerate the emotion(s).

Each emotion, both positive and negative, could be labeled as a channel of the mind. I just choose to leave emotions out of my model since there are so many of them! Grandma Janis' Human-Mind Channel Model is just a rough paradigm to help you analyze and get a feeling for a *very* complex subject.

Habitual negative thinking generates most negative emotions! Ideally, you can let your negative emotions stop on their own or get relief through calming the mind by meditation. If you get tired of feeling a certain way, you can access the Supreme Being mind and let your Being go home to God.

If your negative emotions keep coming back, they can also get processed quickly by talking them out with a trusted confidant, and then getting some kind of physical reassurance immediately, like a pat on the back or a hug. Then little damage occurs. This is a great method to use with little children who have just been psychologically, or physically, hurt.

Habitual sour emotions sour your body because they trigger your body chemistry, that pharmacy you have inside.

You need to *allow* the negative feelings to surface in order to know what you need to do; but you also need to heal them as quickly as possible. It is not too much different than touching a too-hot stove, feeling the pain, then removing your hand, and medicating if necessary. To stay angry at the stove would be pretty stupid; also it does not make sense to stay mad at yourself.

I have noticed that since I learned in meditation to access the joy at will, through the alpha state, my negative emotions still resonate, but they leave quite quickly most of the time. Being a long-time meditator has loosened the emotions up in some way, making them more transitory.

And just because I have a negative emotion, say violent anger at someone, I don't have to act upon that emotion.

Here is another example of how, ideally, negative emotions can pass quite quickly: I live in a rural area. Fairly frequently I see a dead deer or jack rabbit at the side of the road that has been hit by a car. When I see these loved, dead animals, I always have a powerful, sad feeling that runs down the front of my body. But to be perfectly honest, within five minutes I have totally forgotten that animal and my body is back in perfect shape. What good would come of my being sad all day about that animal whose Being has gone home?

If your negative-feeling emotion doesn't pass as hoped, or returns after meditation and/or talking it out with someone, concentrated processing on your own may help. If you have to, write out something like the following: "Right now I feel very angry at Alice. But I am going to let this go now. God bless Alice and her path." Or, "Right now I am feeling very lonely. But I am going to let this go now. Thank you, God, that I know to seek out company tomorrow." Or, "Right now I am feeling concerned about my finances. I have done everything I can for now; I am going to let this go." Psalms 23:1–6:

> The Lord is my shepherd, I shall not want. He maketh me to lie down in green pastures: he leadeth me beside the still waters. He restoreth my soul: he leadeth me in the paths of righteousness for his name's sake. Yea, though I walk through the valley of the shadow of death, I will fear no evil: for thou art with me; thy rod and thy staff they comfort me. Thou preparest a table before me in the presence of mine enemies: thou anointest my head with oil; my cup runneth over. Surely goodness and mercy shall follow me all the days of my life: and I will dwell in the house of the Lord forever.

Since worry, bitterness, hurtful remembrances and smoldering anger sentence you to a body that will get sick because of the chemicals released, it is important that you become sensitized as to what action to take quickly to get yourself out of the prison. Indeed, you may need to state your truth tactfully to the someone involved.

You are chained to everything you hate. You are the one who is suffering. And if you hate a person, event or material thing, you can bet that "it" will be drawn to you.

Here is an example. For many years, I hated black widow spiders and brown recluses after one had bitten my foot. I didn't know which type spider it had been, because I, feeling the pain, quickly squashed it with my other foot! The swelling right after the bite went clear up to my shin and the swollen itchy spot on my foot lasted a decade and still itches occasionally. During my "hating" years, I drew literally hundreds of these two types of hiding spiders into my living spaces. I had more of these spiders around me and in my environment than a hundred average "other people" put together! Now I have reduced that hate to a tolerance. These poisonous spiders still do get into my space, but rarely.

Let me say a word about other people's emotions. I am not responsible for them. *Their* negative emotions are *their* problem. If someone gets angry at me, let them process and release that anger. If they need to express it to me, they may. I may or may not alter my future behavior to please them. I may or may not apologize. I am still *not* responsible for their anger. They are.

Much of life is experienced through these emotionally volatile spots on the brain. *External* events are destined to keep you off balance, as well as your own *internal* anger, jealousy, fears, etc. Do you allow yourself to be immersed in this emotional washing machine of life?

I have already said that "love" is not an emotion. It is not a spot on the brain that gets activated. Love is a constantly flowing energy, vibration, coming through you from God.

This next one may be hard to take: Wonderful feelings gained from life events *are also* just energized spots on the brain and keep you away from Self-realization as much as the negative! When you are feeling joyous after a promotion, pleasantly surprised at a cherished invitation, excited about a new car – this is great. But, not if you don't do your spiritual practices. These good feelings derived from third-dimensional events are not helping your spiritual evolvement if you let them distract you.

A reminder, that while in a body your emotions are one of three components that protect your Soul. The other two are the mind and the body.

For further discussion, here, I would like to single out just two of the powerful unpleasant emotions: fear and anger.

"Why did you pick **FEAR**?" Fear is paralyzing psychologically and stunts your spiritual growth. Sure, there are people and events in your life where fear makes sense, for example a drunk person coming at you with a gun or an approaching, out-of-control forest fire.

And you are right if you know that only two fears are innate: fear of loud noise and fear of falling.

However, fear brought in from former lives or programmed into you by well-meaning parents or teachers petrify you and keep you from moving.

We are never afraid while we are in meditation in direct contact with the power behind the mind. Normal fears need facing. Shaman said, "Do what you fear to move toward enlightenment."

Fearful thoughts pile up fear-energy, creating just what is feared. "What you fear will come upon you." Instead, create by joyful thoughts, use reverse-thought forms. For example, if you are afraid of public speaking, picture yourself being extremely successful and confident while making speeches. If you fear riding in airplanes, picture yourself being the pilot, making decisions, in control, talking to the control tower, and talking with your co-pilot.

Well-trained psychotherapists and counselors have a mental tool called "systematic desensitization." If reverse-thought forms don't seem to be working on, say, your fear of flying, a therapist can help you, through suggestion, relaxing you deeply. Relaxed, the therapist starts your work of the therapy session by having you mentally leave your home on the way to the airport. Each session, the therapist deeply relaxes you, and gets you a little further toward the airport and the plane. Finally, you will be able to think through every step including boarding the plane, making the trip and deboarding without fear.

Then, hallelujah, you can make the trip in real life without fear.

"Why did you pick **ANGER** as the other negative emotion to talk about? Because it is so common. It is typical that the average person gets mad at work seven times each day.

Ephesians 4:26: "Be angry but do not sin; do not let the sun go down on your wrath."

To use a psychological model, anger results when you are prevented from reaching a goal – so there is a frustrating block between the current moment and what you want. Then you may be angry with yourself or angry with someone else. Notice I said, "with" and not "at." Just like with fear, you will draw to you the person you stay angry *with*. It puts you into an ugly dance *with* them.

As reported in the newspaper the day I was writing about anger, a wrathful, two-family feud which had been going on for over one hundred years culminated in three deaths. It was a real "Hatfields and McCoys" conflict: one man in each opposing clan dead, plus a deputy who was caught in the middle. Even the children of these families had been throwing rocks at each other. The children had been carefully taught to be angry and to act out their anger in violent ways.

Remember when we talked about Kirlian photography, the hands that were photographed as the owners exchanged angry remarks, and the spear-like sparks that came out of the hands? Recall that you actually throw psychic spears, psychic thought forms, directly at the person with whom you are angry! The negative karma, according to shaman, is greater for this type of warfare than physically doing harm, such as letting the air out of a person's tires.

Again, the goal is not to turn yourself into an emotionless, limp noodle. You are definitely better off when you don't repress your darker side. Feeling the negative emotion, saying your truth when necessary, as diplomatically and kindly as possible, and then letting the feelings totally disperse are the ideal way to *process* anger.

Besides going through the aforementioned clearing process or talking over your anger with someone you trust, you can also *shout your anger up to God*. There is no negative karma generated in doing this, and our Supreme Being can handle it.

This is an especially useful technique if it is **predicament anger**; some examples are anger at senseless wars that cripple and kill little children (not to mention the adults); politicians who say anything to get elected; a system which permits some rich people to pay little or no income tax; terrorists that plant bombs in planes and public places; nations that still allow the killing of dolphins and whales; nations that still test nuclear bombs; nations that yearly export twenty–five billion dollars worth of arms; nations that yearly spend two hundred sixty–five billion on defense; a nation with a post–office system that allows unsolicited junk mail to be processed and carried at significantly less cost than first–class mail, while raising first–class mail rates; a nation that cannot come to terms with what William J. Mahon, executive director of the National Health Care Anti–Fraud Association, estimates: Thirty billion dollars that were paid by us ordinary citizens to the IRS "were consumed by fraud and abuse" in our Medicare and Medicaid programs; dog owners that take their pooches for walks in public places and don't take along their pooper–scooper.

For dealing with anger, there is always the technique of pounding the pillow or using a sponge bat, a bataka. However, you need to say a prayer of protection for the person you are angry with before starting this type of catharsis or else your anger vibration will go directly to them.

Again, negative emotions don't have to be any big deal. They are an authentic human response. They *are* just a specific spot on the brain that is energized. When you have that spot energized, you cannot access your guidance, your higher Self.   Through the pain of nega–tive emotions, you have learned something about your journey, but you need to let your system clear and the sooner the better.

So negative emotions give you information about your stuck places and also alert you to decisions and moves you should be making. They are not to be avoided. We don't want to turn into a race of computer–like robots like the extraterrestrial "Greys" who have tor–mented our human race for decades.

Although it is a bit of a detour, let's talk more about those Greys. Linda Howe of the American Broadcasting Company, hosted a pro–gram called Strange Harvest. She documented the alteration of thousands of cattle all over the world. Without any evidence of the ground being walked on, the culprits left the carcasses totally devoid of red blood cells.

"They haven't been out to harm us," encourages Drunvalo, who attributes the cattle and human mutilations to the Greys. "They have given up now! They know they can't make it. They just wanted to understand emotions, then get them back into their race, because emotions are necessary to go to the highest places in consciousness. They really tried to understand the genetic code on our planet because they have lost their Divine DNA coding."

We can be hopeful the Greys *have* gone. A friend of mine suffered multiple abductions. She cannot speak of her experiences without crying. She believes they left monitoring devices surgically implant-ed within her head as well as having altered areas of her body.

I know there are metaphysicians who would say she gave her per-mission to the Greys. I would say, "Nonsense." Did I give my per-mission to my psychotherapist to let his phone ring during hypnotic trance? There are mental states where one's will is just not accessi-ble. And the bad guy extraterrestrials know that!

In Chapter 3, we will address other extraterrestrials, those that are our friends. Indeed Christ–consciousness Beings from the star Sirius along with others apparently saved our earth in 1972 and may be about to do another radical intervention, perhaps as early as 1995 or 1996.

"Getting back on track, so far in Chapter 2, you have talked about our physical body, our eyes and heart, God's love, mind channels, time, drugs and emotions.   Before we move on, could you review the ways and practices to build Soul energy? You told us this Soul energy gives us more choices either at death or at ascension time, and opens us up to paranormal experiences. You also teach that building Soul energy both raises our own consciousness and the col-lective consciousness."

Yes, a review would be worthwhile at this point. First, work on becoming a better person (the good karma list). Second, through thought and service, let God's love flow through you to your fellow humans. Third, become aware of your own ego–mind's narrow, self-centered pull, and let it loose; release it. Fourth, in prayer (Chapter 3), ask God, an Ascended Master, Avatar, or the angels (Chapter 3) for help. Fifth, discipline your thoughts. Sixth, quickly process and let go of your negative emotions.

Two more ways to build Soul energy are coming up: chanting or singing spiritual songs and meditating. Meditation will be covered in detail after the explanation of enlightenment and Self-realization.

"Please tell us more about **CHANTING** since it apparently builds Soul energy and awakens us to what we really are, spiritual Beings." Ethereal sounds like chants or enchanting spiritual songs and melodies actualize your astral/Being/Light body and the inner sound current carries you to the higher planes. You raise your vibrations via the sound frequencies. Hebrew and Sanskrit chants are in basic spiritual languages – sounds – and are especially powerful and more so if done with a group. The sounds of chanting tune up and expand your astral/Being/Light body, enabling it to carry more spiritual energy. This process also affects your physical body. Your atoms actually move further apart, over time, which is stressful and usually slow, but necessary for the enlightenment process to spiritualize the body.

Writing about sound, the late inventor and consciousness researcher, Itzhak Bentov points out:

> We could actually associate our whole reality with sound of one kind or another because our reality is a vibratory reality, and there is nothing static in it. Starting with the nucleus of an atom, which vibrates at enormous rates, the electrons and the molecules are all associated with characteristic vibratory rates. A most important aspect of matter is vibratory energy.

There are five languages of the Soul, seed syllables, composed of the vibrations of our Mother/Father, God's sound. These are the ancient languages, which can be somewhat different than the languages actually spoken today. Besides Hebrew and Sanskrit, are Chinese, Tibetan and Egyptian. These languages are actually composed of the Light projections from God and are the same vibration as the human Soul, since we are chips off the old block. When spiritual words are sung or chanted in these languages, the sounds serve as a common denominator to bring a diverse group of people into God's energy vibration.

Some American Indian tribes hold the model that chants bring energy down from the great spirit and up from Mother Earth into one's Being, thus enabling the partakers to give the best of themselves back to life. You may have seen film footage of prolonged chant dances when the dancers go into trance states.

We chant and sing at the Angel Healing Group before saying prayers or doing laying–on–of–hands healing. Not only does chanting set up a higher vibration for healing, it is also good as a prelude to meditation. Chanting one of the five languages of the Soul in the car while driving grants you protection and works wonders for your mental state, letting you arrive "Lighted."

Then there are special chants for special purposes. An organization that records and sells Hebrew chant tapes (and many other spiritual aids) is The Academy of Future Science, P. O. Box FE, Los Gatos, CA 95031. Send that SASE when inquiring.

A **bhajan** is the Indian word for singing praises to God; and when sung, it sounds like chanting. Sai Baba has been recorded singing bhajans alone and with devotees. You can inquire about these and other devotional aides from the Sathya Sai Book Center of America, 305 West First Street, Tustin, CA 92680, enclosing your SASE. If you live in a large city, you can check your white pages for "Sai Baba." There may be a Sai Baba group that includes bhajan singing in its programs.

A **mantra** can be a syllable, word, or series of words in any language that you use repetitively before and during meditation.

The very best, and easiest mantra I know is to *mentally* use the words "soft" on the intake breath *and* "slow" on the out breath. Do this slowly: Saw–ah–ta–f; sl–ooo–ooo. With your eyes closed as you enter meditation or just as a relaxation break at your desk, these words can have increasing meaning for your subconscious. There are a variety of ways you can use the mantra in the prior paragraph; that is, soft – slow: (1) breathe *out* and *in* just through your nose; (2) breathe both, using just your mouth; (3) breathe in through your nose and out through your mouth; (4) breathe in through your mouth and out through your nose.

When great spiritual teachers have used certain words for centuries, the mantra itself has been infused with powerful spiritual vibrations. An example is OM Namah Shivaya, used by the Siddha Yoga lineage. Phonetically, it is ah–o–mmm naw–maw she–vie–ya and means "I honor the Self within me."

Here are the Sanskrit words for the Gayatri Mantra, pronounced guy–a–tree. Sai Baba says to chant it three times a day for your own sake and for the sake of the humanity:

> Aum, Bhuh;
> Bhuvah Svah;
> Tat Savitur Varenium;
> Bhargo Devasya Dheemahe;
> Dhiyo Yo Nah Prachodayat. Aum.

Here is a phonetic version:

> Ah–o–mmm, Bur;
> Bur–vah su–va–ha;
> Tat sav–e–tur va–rain–e–um;
> Bar–go de–vas–ya dee–ma–he;
> De–yo yo–nah pra–co–day–yacht. Ah–o–mmm.

This is the English meaning of the Gayatri: "Om, Supreme Divine, you are the creator of this universe, of earth, space and heaven. We adore you, oh Supreme Light, source of all creation. We meditate upon your Divine radiance. Inspire all our thoughts, dispel our ignorance and illuminate our intelligence."

Most spiritual groups have their own songs and chants. When I get a chance, it is my absolute delight to teach the ones I know.

"Some of the groups I have been to, chant just one word, **OM**. What does it mean?" Ancient seers knew it as the cosmic hum containing all that is. Originally from the East, it is now used everywhere. It is pronounced more like "ah–o–mmm." Alternate spellings are "aum" and "ohm." To prove to yourself that sound, and singing, has vibrations, sing out "Om," while touching your hand over your throat, and feel the full range!

"Does **MUSIC** work like the chants and mantras?" Yes, if it res-onates with your Being. The vibration, pitch, chords, sequences of notes and timbres, help you to let loose of little mind. "Being" music takes a fragmented mental state and creates peace. However, what I consider "Being" music may not agree with your perception!

There is general agreement, though, that low decibel, high frequency sounds are more healing, like violins, bird songs, rain and running water. The more difficult vibrations are hard rock, the low hums of computers, fluorescent lights, microwave ovens, television and household appliances.

I have heard it said that God encouraged hard rock development in order to loosen and break down the old, rigid thought patterns of the 1950s, 60s and 70s.

There are also spiritual vibrations around certain songs that have been sung a lot; for example, "Amazing Grace."

Music is an effective instrument for international communication. It is a conveyer of higher consciousness far beyond words and lan-guage barriers. Indeed, sound exists in all universes.

Music is between the formed and the formless. It can take us to heaven. As described in the Eckankar materials, out of the body Beings in at least one dimension, the "bliss plane," use the sound current as their food! There is much use of sound and color fre-quencies in the higher dimensions.

"You have used a term you have not really described yet, **ENLIGHTENMENT**. I would really like to understand what it is and how to get it." Enlightenment, *as talked about in our third-dimen-sional reality* is becoming the way we are meant to be. Parmahansa Yogananda called the same thing, "**Self–realization**, . . . the know-ing in all parts of body, mind, and Soul that you are now in posses-sion of the kingdom of God; that you do not have to pray that it come to you; that God's omnipresence is your omnipresence . . ."

It is also the permanent letting loose of your ego-mind's control over your Being. This freedom enables you to operate from your Being and to answer to your Being and its higher Self aspect(s). The ego is still there, but it isn't in charge anymore and it doesn't take anything personally.

If you were third-dimensional enlightened, when your ego flares up, you would be as aware of it as if someone poked a red balloon in your face. Aware, you would put the ego aside and be totally present in the moment not concerned about the past or future. (That doesn't mean you would never use your third-dimension solution-finding mind to make your dental appointment for next week.)

Through meditation and the other spiritual practices, we progress by stages, able to hold the ego-mind out for longer and longer periods. One day, enough ego gets pushed out so that you are not bothered by it anymore. Neither is anyone else.

As said before, the ability to access the Being at any time is the definition of a **shaman**. Anyone who can access their Being at will can be a natural or trained healer. Those who hold this state permanently are called **saints**.

Actually, there is no such thing as real enlightenment for most of us, *now*. Because after we master the third dimension, there are other dimensions, planets and areas of the universes to master. That happens, after you become bored with the Planet of the Cross because there are no longer challenges here or ways that you want to serve mankind.

I believe that one day you may very well be a creator Being, very busy creating worlds. At that point, I would consider it genuine enlightenment. One day, I was mad at God. I shook my fist up to the sky and said, "What a way to run a universe!" Back came a voice, "You will get your chance." Humbling!

I am very grateful to a third-dimension, enlightened master, a German with the spiritual name of Devaprem. He had been in this country less than a year. When people meditated with this enlightened master during the short time he was in the United States in 1991 (he may have returned, I don't know, I lost contact), he used timed

music along with timed silence. I'll describe this next, under
"Meditation."

He noticed that I would shift my body during his group meditation.
I had not understood how totally relaxed I needed to be. I then had
some massage and chiropractic work done so that I *could* sit totally
still for an hour in comfort. Also, during his discourse, he had mentioned, "You set the stage for enlightenment to come to you if you
will meditate for sixteen days in a row." Now, I had never done that
either, so I made myself do it.

A friend took a commercial recording (I don't know who the artist
was that created this ethereal music) and made an audiotape for me
to use with what he guessed was Devaprem's timing.

With this tape, on the fifteenth day in a row of meditating for one
hour, my body left and so did my mind. The next morning, I told
an already Self–realized friend, "I know it doesn't make sense, but for
the last two days, I almost physically feel myself floating into a
'bubble' in the right side of my head. I have almost no awareness of
anything except my seemingly empty skull and this bubble."

My friend suggested, "That bubble might be your ego–mind. Why
don't you tell it to "Fuck off?" The next night when I was meditating, the same thing did happen. I was meditating alone. Wanting
to do it right, I did exactly as he had instructed. Knowing my
brother and his wife would not be disturbed as they were sleeping
in another wing of their house which I was visiting, I gave it my all.
I screamed out at the top of my voice, "ego–mind, *fuck off.*"

I remained in a bliss state for three or four months and was the
sleepiest person alive, sometimes snoozing for twelve or fourteen
hours a day. But being groggy passed. And I have been less bothered by my ego since then. Who knows at what stage I am at now.
I can access the bliss state, the joy behind the mind, every day, but
am not able to hold it all day long, every day.

There is no doubt that my Being is now in charge of my life, in
social, vocational and family connections. Among other things, I
don't worry, "stew," regret, try to control others, or calculate. And
when life is being difficult, the bliss always underlies my experience;

at that time it feels like "delicious cake, sour icing."

However, everyone has an entirely different story. Enlightenment is not information; for most people, it is transformation, slowly but surely.

Through the years, I have had at least three **satori** experiences, a sudden awakening, an expanded state where I was all–knowing and seeing lots of different colored lights, extreme bliss states, which were imitations of the real thing, enlightenment. The only difference is, this state fades in days or weeks. And of course, I didn't know at these times it wasn't the real thing. The satori experience is an initiation and is highly valued by spiritual seekers because at first it is believed it is the real thing. Even if it passes, one knows that progress is being made. "If I got there once, I can get there again!"

Rosamode Miller, a Fidel Castro prisoner in 1961, had a satori experience which was described in the <u>San Jose Mercury News</u>. Her experience occurred after she was beaten by prison guards. Her thoughts contained forgiveness as she realized that all humans have the potential for both love and hate:

> Suddenly I was overcome with a sense of connection to all people and things and a feeling of peace, almost like liquid, trickling, that sense of grace and an ointment, came over me. I could feel it in the roof of my mouth, on my head, in my throat, coming faster and faster, a physical thing.

During the afterglow of my own satori experiences, it was astounding how people rushed to help and serve me. Can you imagine simple events like pulling up to a gas station, and having three men rush out; one fills your tank, one cleans your windshield, and one checks under the hood, no charge and with beautiful smiles of gratitude because they were privileged to serve *you?* And then driving along, thinking of a needed summer dress, imagining what it would look like in some detail. You stop at a red light in a small town, look to the left and see *the exact dress* in a store window. You enter the store, and the clerk tells you that just twenty minutes ago, she had found the dress in a box and hung it. Life can be that easy when you are Self–realized!

Of course my goal is to be *there* permanently, delicious cake, delicious icing. In the meantime, no matter how stressful events are – and I have had some very hard knocks – there is that undercurrent of well-being. But the biggest thing for me is that although I experience the negative emotions, they just register and don't last. So my emotions tell me what I need to do for myself, but don't hang around to poison my days.

I can't believe it when I am so angry at someone one minute and the next minute I literally can't remember being angry, let alone remember what it was about. Liberating! Of course I still much prefer having life go all my way; I have definite preferences – but that isn't realistic.

"Please tell us more about **MEDITATION**." As just described, meditation has a transformative influence. You can tell by the number of pages I have written that I think this activity is important! I'll be interweaving what meditation is, why meditation is so useful and some hints on how to do it.

There are books on this subject. Most metaphysical groups and churches offer meditation courses. Meditating with a group of people who are learning together also helps your discipline and can be much more powerful. If you have a chance to learn from someone who is Self-realized, take it! If you have a chance to meditate with a group of people who are more advanced than you, they will pull you into their group vibration by the process of **entrainment** (different objects in the same physical location moving into a similar vibration) and help you along. Itzhak Bentov, expert on the entrainment process, said that in deep meditation the human being and the planet system start resonating and transferring energy.

"Are you an outer-directed "societal automaton"? Romans 12:2: "And be not conformed to this world: but be ye transformed by the renewing of your mind, that ye may prove what is that good, and acceptable, and perfect will of God."

If you are interested in raising your consciousness, you must become inner-directed and strong. The idea is to get your love directly from God and your guidance from your own Soul or Being.   Remember that your higher Self is an aspect of your Soul.

I can't say it too often: Behind the ego–mind there is joy. True meditation occurs when the concerns of the meditator's little mind, ego–mind, are shut down and awareness is in big mind, Supreme Being Mind. Meditation produces comfort, peace, bliss and know–ingness. You move from separateness from God/your own Being to union with God/your own Being. In this superconsciousness, you are in the pure present.

This joy is not the same feeling that you get from a positive life event. After you master connecting with your Being at will, you don't have to depend on the vagaries of life to treat you kindly in order to be happy.

Said another way, God is the ocean. Your Being is one drop in that ocean. Your ego–mind takes you out of the ocean. When letting loose of your ego–mind during meditation, you put your Being back into God and God permeates you. You realize your oneness with God.

Meditation opens you up to let love out and in.

It is also excellent for your health. In PERFECT HEALTH, Dr. Deepak Chopra, tells about the new research on long–term meditators. One study showed that for sixty–year olds who had been meditating for five years, their medical measurements showed "age forty–eight." And he said that adult meditators over forty go to the doctor seven-ty–four percent less often than non–meditators!

I predict that meditation will become the national past time as the long–sought–after–fountain of youth and springboard to health. Large group meditation in the United States will take place in ball–parks. Nearly all faiths will be represented. Meditators' hearts will beat as one. It will be so beautiful. God's love, the heart vibration, is coming to The Planet of the Cross to save us.

Now, let me assume you are just starting. If you are an experienced meditator, perhaps you can pick up a tip or two. Meditation is about relaxing. Even during your busy working day when you can't meditate, you can take deep breaths, slowing pulling air in through both your nose and mouth, slowly letting it out through your mouth, saying to yourself, "Relax, relax" and/or "let go, let go," and/or "soft/slow." It is a metaphysical principle that if you carry anxieties and worries, you will attract anxieties and worries.

Most meditation teachers have favorite breathing practices. There are all sorts of combinations. My favorite, and one for which you can record your own counting audiotape, is to breathe in through your nose with short breaths counting with each intake, one, two, three, four; and then out through your mouth one breath, two, three, four, five. Repeat in a series of ten inhaling/exhaling cycles.

Another is you can also visualize an ocean wave going out, counting as seems natural to you, and then counting as it comes back. Repeat ten times. This visualization sets you up to relax, to slow down and to loosen your thoughts.

Meditation is a skill, like ice skating. Someone can describe it to you but you just need practice, practice, practice. And with that practice over time, you get better, and better and better. However, I am surprised at how easily some people give up because at first, of course, they aren't good at it. Occasionally someone stays with it for two years; later, when they are good but not great meditators, they give up.

Devaprem's new technique of using timed music, and then timed silence, is exciting to me. It seems to relax and fool little mind, plus pull you back to the task at hand, meditating – not replaying the day's events, etc. Recently I used this technique teaching a small group of people who had never meditated.

I started the class with just ten minutes of meditation using timed music/silence, meeting once a week. They also practiced at home. In the nine months of the class, the meditation time expanded to forty-five minutes. All were accessing the Being Mind before the forty-five minutes were up; and they were also able to sit perfectly relaxed in bodily comfort for that time. With commitment, people can learn to meditate much faster than ever before.

The music, coming in after the silence, seems to bring the Soul in, and the mind back, into a cooperative awareness. Now, why do you need this periodic reminder during meditation? Studies of long-time meditators (connected to biofeedback equipment) show that sixty percent of the time they are asleep!

You will learn more about Devaprem and his timed music and timed silence technique shortly.

Techniques help, but because of ancestral memory, every person who has learned to meditate before you, has prepared the path to make it easier for you. You can learn to meditate much faster now than even a decade ago. If you tried it and gave it up, do try again.

Start with the longest time you can sit comfortably without moving. Choose a time either when interruptions don't occur or when you can ignore the interruptions. Do some meditating every day, *even though it is only for a few minutes.* One man I know reached Self–realization by a consistent twenty minutes both a.m. and p.m. However, if you are really serious, within six months, try to work up to forty-five minutes – and to one hour within a year.

Remember that you will make up this time because you will need forty-five minutes or one hour less sleep every night!

Here are my suggestions to get you started: Sit facing east or north. Sit upright in a comfortable, straight–chair. Sit on the floor only if you are very flexible and are totally comfortable there. Until you can get past the awareness of your body, you won't progress. So why try to pretzel yourself into a yoga position only to sit there and suffer? Sai Baba says "A perfectly straight body provides a conductor, so to speak, for Divine power to enter the temple of your body and give you the strength to accomplish your task and reach your goal."

Have on soft, comfortable clothes. Loosen ties about your waist; unbutton tight collars or sleeves. Don't meditate right after eating. And make the prior meal a relatively light one, but one that doesn't leave you hungry, either.

Close your eyes. (If you are an advanced meditator, it is okay to leave them open.) Sit with your hands relaxed in your lap. Rearrange seams that bind or clothes that pull. Sit perfectly still.

About this time in a meditation class, someone usually asks, "Can I lay down and meditate?" The answer is "No" if you want to get into the alpha state. If you just want to relax, get sleepy and drift off, that is relaxation or sleep, not meditation. Be honest with yourself. Center your energy at your heart. With eyes closed, raise your eyes to the area of your third eye. Imagine your favorite saint, Avatar, or Ascended Master as a picture whose essence astralprojects in through your third eye area and stays there inside your head. (More on the third eye in a few more pages.)

"Stinkin thinkin" will occur. Just let the words drift by as if on a screen in the back of your head. Don't be concerned. Don't judge your thoughts. As meditation is done more and more (I started in 1980), thinking gets looser. Relax. Relax. Take some deep breaths and then relax some more. Eventually, your mind will allow you to de-amplify its thoughts. In the first years, it may work like this analogy: It is as though your brain is a three-ring circus. But the spotlight is only on the alpha channel. *The other "rings" are there*, the thoughts, but they are not energized or lighted. The enlightened space is between the words (thoughts). As the words get slowed down, there is more space and the alpha state gets deeper.

It is a matter of letting go into what you already are, a ray of God.

It is fun if you don't criticize your progress. Whatever happens is okay. Interruptions occur from within and without. One day a construction worker used a jack hammer during my meditation to create a driveway out of a concrete curb next door. I had a good laugh. And today, a frog croaking disturbed our group meditation!

Several months ago, my husband and two friends hiked up to meditate at Spirit Rock in a local state park. As they settled in, they were overwhelmed with mosquitoes. Maybe these kinds of events are spiritual tests, I don't know. Maybe these kinds of noises and disturbances go on all the time and are exaggerated in an altered state.

Remember the soft/slow mantra mentioned a few pages back? The thinking stops or at the very least the words get further apart after many years of meditating. This means the ego-mind – the "pity pot" thoughts of the past and the "worry-wart" thoughts of the future – don't happen. The pure present is delicious. Ninety-nine percent of the time the present is just fine! Most of the emotional pain we experience comes from thinking about the dead past – or the always uncertain future.

This doesn't mean that emotional pain in life stops. Third–dimensional life *is* third–dimensional life. We have new Souls and medium–aged Souls to contend with. We even occasionally have old Souls doing contemptible behaviors (the very worst kind because they, as old Souls, have so much power.) Being able to quickly process and shift out of a negative emotion is very freeing.

Know that even several minutes of meditation produces beta endorphin (produces feelings of well being), lowers blood pressure, decreases blood cholesterol, lowers pulse, decreases lactic acid in the blood (fatigue producer), and improves vision. Twenty minutes a.m. and twenty minutes p.m. every single day can get you enlightened.

Together meditators create a "love soup," with great–feeling vibrations. If the young people could just know this, they would abandon their drugs, alcohol and other potentially addictive behaviors.

(One of my young editors, upon reading the prior paragraph, wrote: "*Old* people do drugs and alcohol, too!")

When you are separated from God, you feel pain. There is a temporary union using alcohol or drugs to get that altered state (casual sex may also work). But you feel more alienated than ever after the effects wear off. In striving for Self–realization, through meditation, you always get benefits.

When you have a group meditating together, the spiritual hierarchy uses your group energy to stimulate human progress by sending the right energy from the higher planes. Your body learns to integrate the gentle "bolts of electricity." The power cleanses your body.

And if you can get ten or more meditators, several advanced spiritual Beings will actually join you. (Psychically, some of you may witness this event.)

The dreamy–sounding music on the meditation tapes I use for a group of us serious meditators who get together at our house once a week plays for ten minutes, then there is five minutes of silence, then ten minutes of music, then fifteen minutes of silence, then five minutes of music – a total of forty–five minutes. You can make a tape like this with your favorite metaphysical music, wordless and dreamy sounding. (During silence, the tape keeps running so you don't have to get up and stop/start it.) If you or your group wants to meditate for one–half hour or sometimes for one hour, the music and silence can be staggered in–like ratio to ours.

When you finish meditating, if you come out gently, this will make it easier for you to go in the next time. When meditating with a group, the whole group needs to be extremely respectful of those who come out slowly. Don't talk or make noises until *everyone* is back. (If in doubt, watch a person's eyes; they will make eye contact when they are ready to be social.)

If you want to buy some wonderful commercial meditation tapes with the timed music and silence built in for various lengths of meditations, write to the publisher of COSMIC MAP for a brochure: Meadow Park Press, P. O. Box 14410, San Luis Obispo, CA 93406–4410 SASE. See if this isn't the best money you ever spent!

If you are meditating for less than half an hour, rather than stagger-ing music/silence, you can play soothing music for the first minutes, and then just turn it off. For example, if you are meditating for twenty minutes, try ten minutes of music and have an automatic switch, purchasable at a hardware store, turn it off to leave you ten minutes of silence. Edgar Cayce suggested using music to visit "The Holy of Holies."

I am very grateful to the German master, Devaprem, for teaching me this music/silence technique. Please see Appendix F, "Harvest, Devaprem Demystified Enlightenment." *For sure, this is one Appendix you'll want to read.*

He talks about how the mysterious process of entrainment works with groups of experienced meditators. Entrainment brings aspects of people into the same harmony vibration, like clocks in the same room that start "clicking" together. In meditation, the entrainment process works to help a *group* by bringing each member deeper into alpha.

In meditation, you visit with your Being between the words in your mind. Your goal is to be able to access your Being in a wordless mental state where linear time has stopped and you are in Soul time or Being time.

Meditation has the already-mentioned benefits of bliss states, know-ingness and health improvements. It is truly a talisman to your spirit.

Best sellers like THE RELAXATION RESPONSE, Herbert Benson, M.D.; PERFECT HEALTH, Deepak CHOPRA, M.D.; and PROGRAM FOR REVERSING HEART DISEASE, Dean Ornish, M.D., attest to the value of going into the silence to connect *directly* – nothing to get in the way there – with the flow of God's patterned intelligence which becomes our human body and controls it. Chopra says, "To change the printout of the body, you must learn to rewrite the software of the mind."

Long-time meditators (five to fifteen years) are breaking into Self-realization. Thousands are accessing the Divinity of their own Being in such a permanent way that they can't do anything from with-out of their Being. These enlightened people are getting in touch with their Being permanently and stay in that state a lot of the time. As said before, every person who is successful makes it easier for the next person, no matter if you are in England or Africa!

We may need as many as 300,000 people to become Self-realized, enlightened, to produce the evolution of homo sapiens. This higher level of vibration will permanently take the human race's energy from the lower chakras to the higher chakras. It will also enable our minds and bodies to go from this third dimension into the fourth dimension (and perhaps higher) on an individual basis, which is one of the basics for the evolution and the creation of heaven on earth.

In a book called PHILOSOPHIA PERENNIS, Bhagwan Shree Rajneesh said it poetically:

> If we can create a momentum in the world for meditation,
> for the inward journey, for tranquility, for stillness,
> for love, for God. . . If we can create a space . . .
> for God to happen to many, many people, humanity will
> have a new birth, a resurrection. A new man will be born.

As long as you are doing what you came to do, your spirit is powerful. Sit down for a visit with your Being today and every day. And you will come to know why you are here. How else will you know your **purpose and mission** if you don't listen through meditation? You had purpose when you came in. As you become more intuitive and your Being is guiding more and more, you are often lead to spontaneously say a certain thing, do a specific thing, call someone, etc. Or an idea may come to you that gives a shortcut to a goal.

You will also bring some of the Light and love you find behind the ego-mind into the world when you return to this awareness. Heaven is interactive.

Psalm 85:8: "I will listen to what God the Lord will say." Deep meditation is like sitting in God's lap.

Create a wonderful day for yourself. Start by centering your mind at your heart. Listen to wonderful sound, calm the mind with meditation, visit with your Being. If mornings are impossible, you can meditate any time that you aren't exhausted.

See also "biofeedback," coming up, for a more technical description of what happens when we slow the speed of brainwave activity.

"Zen" is a sanskrit term for bringing the mind to rest.

Since people shake off negative thought forms and neuroses when they meditate, it is necessary to use a smudge stick (could be a special incense or sage), to clean the space after meditating is done. Smudging or sage smoking an area transmutes these negative vibrations; they become harmless and disappear. Check a metaphysical bookstore or health food store for sage or the appropriate incense. Some psychics can see or feel these negative vibrational leftovers. Don't skip this process. Trust me, if you could see all the "yucky stuff" in the air, you would know this smudging is absolutely mandatory.

"Aren't you talking about relatively short periods of time for meditation?" Yes. There is also **samadhi**, a deep meditation done in the East for days or weeks at a time. The inner life is everything to the Sadhus, holy men. In this state, they observe existence in its purest form. These brilliant Souls have held the love energy for the race. However, unless you are totally drawn to meditate that long (receive intuitive information from your own Being), for most people in the West this kind of discipline is not required because you did not come to the Planet of the Cross to do that, this lifetime.

One *could* use the inner world as an escape. The idea is to go within for your Being's commands *and then* out into the world to honor them. Paul Twitchell, the Eckankar master – the religion of Light and Sound – said, "Harmony in the world within will be reflected in the world without by harmonious conditions, agreeable surroundings, the best of everything. It is the foundation of health, and a necessary essential to all greatness, all power, all achievement and God-union."

One of the most profound implications of metaphysical practice is that you don't have to chase beautiful things. They come to you *as a by-product.*

Through the years, as you meditate, little mind doesn't want to let go of the control of your life. It doesn't realize you would be more fulfilled with your Being in charge. As little mind's, ego-mind's, tenacious impactedness diminishes, this shriveling up may lead to pain, sadness and/or confusion. *These are transforming energies.* Your Soul is finding its balance within the cosmic forces, reconnecting with the deeper aspect of your Self, coming home apart from the ego-mind.

You can tell if the pain, sadness or confusion is caused by the shriveling of the ego mind: absolutely nothing has happened in your outer life to cause the depression or confusion. If the discomfort doesn't leave within a few weeks, talking about your pain with a trusted friend, counselor or spiritual teacher helps.

During alternate times when there is expansion and joy, it may be a temptation to give up on meditating. Don't, that would be a victory for your ego.

Sai Baba says, "God is seeking you." And "If you move one step closer to God, God moves one-hundred steps closer to you. Go in

and try to know the eternal flame ever shining inside." His prayer:
"Lord, take my Soul, let it merge in perfect oneness with thee."

In summation, regular meditation improves your health, expands
your intuition, smooths your path and is also good, essential now,
for the collective in this time of consciousness ascension.

Poet S. Kapp says it lyrically:

> I am determined to let myself be transformed by the sound
> arising out of the stillness of my Soul and to allow my heart
> to call the tune to which I dance my life.

"Can you tell us more about **BIOFEEDBACK TRAINING?**" Prior to
the 1960s, most Westerners thought that their blood pressure, pulse
rate, body temperature, muscle tension, and stomach acidity were
involuntary. Now it is known that by using a biofeedback machine,
most people can be trained to regulate these body processes.

To get a reading, the biofeedback counselor uses Velcro–type fasten-
ers to hook the machine's electrical wires to fingers, muscles or forehead. Biofeedback techniques are designed to help you learn to
relax, and relaxing brings the body into a healthier balance. A side
benefit is that biofeedback speeds the process of becoming a better
meditator, faster.

Hooked to fingers, the machine will tell skin temperature and skin
moistness. If you have cold hands while sitting in a comfortably
warm room, this indicates tension. This is also true of skin moisture.
Perhaps you have been aware while watching a cliff–hanger movie
how wet your hands get. However, if you notice habitual moistness
in your hands, this indicates deep–seated psychological pain from
something that was done to you. Habitual moisture usually indicates the need to root out neuroses (Chapter 3) which will probably
require some months of psychological counseling.

Biofeedback can be extremely useful in psychotherapy, especially if
as a child, your emotions "went numb" to protect you. This high-
tech technique can help you locate and heal "stuck spots." The
counselor talking to a client can watch the dials and know where to
probe/question as well as see what topics are neutral so as not to

waste time on them. Biofeedback shows specific sine wave signatures for each emotion. Every counselor needs a biofeedback machine in order to reduce client–billing hours.

Hooked to muscles, a reading can be obtained on muscle tension or lack of it.

Hooked to your forehead, the machine can indicate from brain waves which "channel" your consciousness is on. A brief review of the major brain patterns: **beta**, which is focused attention; **alpha**, which is a very relaxed state where we want to go in meditation, in which the speed of brain wave activity is slowed; **theta**, which is dreamy but awake; and **delta**, which is sleep.

Machines differ, but in biofeedback training, the client can hear either a noise, see a dial or see a changing light. As thought processes change, the indicator changes. (The noise raises with tension and lowers with relaxation, the dial points towards relaxation or tension, etc.) A client can alter consciousness intentionally after getting training and feedback in relaxation,"letting go." This skill increases over a number of training sessions. And people get so good at relaxing that eventually they don't need the noise, light or dial.

If you are interested in this kind of training, check the yellow pages under the listing "Biofeedback."

"I thought metaphysics was about being psychic or at the very least consulting psychics." The reason I have saved this topic is because it needs a broad foundation, which you have now.

In I Corinthians 12:27 we are told of the different spiritual gifts: "All of you together are the one body of Christ and each one of you is a separate and necessary part of it. Here is a list of some of the parts he has placed in his Church, which is his body: Apostles, Prophets – those who preach God's Word, Teachers, Those who do miracles, Those who have the gift of healing, those who can help others. . . " [No one has all the gifts, except an Avatar.]

So let's talk first about the third eye, then intuition, and then psychics – all aspects of metaphysics.

"What is the **THE THIRD EYE** ?" This is the mystical center of psychicness. It may be located at the back of a gland called the pineal
gland, and in front of the brain. Also called the spiritual eye, the
center may be the pineal gland itself. I have seen both places
reported. From the outside we can conceptualize the third eye at
the area on our foreheads between our eyes, up about an inch, the
approximate place that Hindu people wear a red powder dot.

Sai Baba has forged the energy of the human race up to the third
eye. That is one reason why so many people are getting more and
more psychic. I need to add "again." Spiritual teachers talk about
the fall of man as a time when we lost our psychicness. Drunvalo
says that this gland thirteen thousand years ago used to be the size
of a quarter but is now just the the size of a pea. I'll report more on
the human race's downfall in Chapter 3.

"Tell us about **INTUITION** and **PSYCHICNESS**." My first psychic-
predictive experience occurred shortly after my near–death experience. One of my young sons, then seventeen, came home with a
new girl friend, then nineteen. After he introduced the sweet young
woman, the first girl friend he had brought home, they sat down
about two feet apart on the living room sofa. As I gazed at them,
suddenly it was as if each of them was pictured in a separate slide
or transparency. Then the "slides" moved and superimposed one
upon the other. "My goodness," I thought "I'll bet the two of them
end up married." Well, four years later they did marry and have
enjoyed a strong and happy union. I wish I could always be that
accurate!

It was a decade ago that I took a psychic development course. I
remember specifically when the teacher asked a practice question,
"What is the name of the person who made our lunch?" The
answer came into my mind's eye in the form of a woman's hairdo,
pictured for me somewhat like a paper doll cutout/paste on. In
answer to the question, I answered the name of a woman who had
that hairdo. I was wrong. It was another woman with the identical
hairdo. At that point, I decided that I would attempt to get Self–
realized, and *if I was lucky, expanded psychicness would come to me as a
by-product*, I wasn't going to pursue just psychicness.

Spiritual masters warn us against becoming overenamored with our own psychicness, or someone else's. Only an advanced psychic has their body, mind and Soul's vibrations working in an integrated way. And even if tuned into the highest source, a misinterpretation of symbols or thought forms can occur.

Please don't interpret this to mean there is something wrong with psychic ability. Edgar Cayce said it is no different from other aspects of the creative forces: imagination, love and sexual energy.

You may be very drawn to becoming a professional psychic. Through your continued devotional activities you try to lift your spiritual consciousness until it encompasses *everything* you want to know.

Intuition is on a continuum. On the left side would be a brand new Soul to our planet earth. An Avatar would be on the right at the other extreme. Every Being in a body has some. Ideally, as we evolve over lifetimes, so does our intuition. It is *not* a left–side–of–the–brain function (as you may recall the analytical, time–sequenced side in most people). As we reincarnate, we move from a little to a lot and then into total psychicness eventually, some lifetime. So psychicness is for everyone to have.

Most spiritual teachers are saying that in fourth–dimensional consciousness and higher, we will all be extremely psychic.

As I just mentioned, Avatars have the total picture and can see your Soul–past, Soul–present and Soul–future. They are so evolved that not only do they see everything, they know what information to withhold from you at the current moment and what you need to see now for your spiritual evolvement.

Never before in human history on this planet has life been so complicated, interwoven, demanding at all levels, with so little that we can count on. The sign of the times is change, change and more change. Never has it been so important to know what we, as a Being, should or should not be doing to flow with this evolutionary change and take our constructive role in it.

Matthew 7:7–8: "Ask, and it shall be given you. Seek and ye shall

find; knock and it shall be opened unto you. For everyone that
asketh, receiveth; and he that seekest, findest. And to him that
knockest, it shall be opened."

And here are some additional suggestions for increasing your knowingness: Follow your natural inner knowing, highest thoughts and
overpowering hunches. Strong intuitive messages are ignored at
great peril.

If you are in a struggle or are confused, don't make a decision yet.
The right answer will come, and you will recognize it for its correct-
ness.

Every answer will eventually be helpful and uplifting to all involved,
although it may not seem so at the time.   Everyone gains when you
do what is right for your own Being and its higher–self(s) aspect.
(Your ego could easily change it, especially at first as you start to
work with your guidance.)

If a number of possibilities occur, the right one will become stronger
and stay. The others will drift and fade.

Peaceful feelings are a good clue that the decision is right for the
time. It may change though, so keep listening every single day.

Drunvalo says your higher self will never tell you to do something
morally wrong, but it might suggest something silly or even something downright stupid. Over time you may get a recognizable pattern like seeing lights, or your hand picking up pencil and paper
and writing or you may hear a voice.

Give thanks to God for the intuitive feelings right at the time you
get them. Act or don't act as intuited. If you follow your intuition,
it expands. If you ignore it, it contracts. The more you listen and
comply, the more you become in tune with the process of intuition,
i.e., your Being and its higher–self aspect(s) communicating through
your third eye.

The more you are in tune, the more you are supported by everything you need. The more you are in tune and the more you are
supported, the more strength you have to do your role in the cosmic

scheme of things, the master plan, with fun and enthusiasm.

You know you are "right on" when "**cosmic sync,**" **cosmic synchronicity**, happens. Conditions, situations and events work out beautifully with the proper timing and order. There is a flow. Just like in a satori expansion, it is almost as if there is a red carpet laid out for you as events and people fit effortlessly into place. You are able to help people, use your talents and training, and grow personally and spiritually all at once! I love it!

Cosmic sync may involve things *not* going well. I remember the day I that I had signed up for a book publication seminar. The leader forgot to tell me they would start at 7:30 a.m. in a little–known location. I arrived at her office at 8:30. In my confusion, frustration and anger, I did not connect with her and the class until 10:00 a.m. Now that did not seem like cosmic sync! But what flowed out definitely was. She was so embarrassed, she gave me a free, individual, one–hour consultation, which provided rich, personal advice.

In our efforts to build intuition and find Soul purpose fulfillment, few of us are meant to be a Mother Teresa. Perhaps you want to race cars, build natural–wood picnic tables, study the evolution of the panda bear, learn to do people's hair, check out the north pole, learn to plant and grow vegetables in organic fashion, take a leather tooling course, become a champion square dancer. There will be plenty of people with whom you can do dramas to grow your Being (Chapter 3). No matter what your chosen activities, there will be plenty of people to both learn from and to help.

Here are more hints about intuition. Most of the time, you are not getting any direction at all because it is not the time to act. My students have more trouble with my simple statement: If you don't have any intuitive hunches, *you don't have any intuitive hunches*!

You may get your best guidance about your concern when you aren't thinking about it. The solution–finding channel can block intuition.

Pay attention to very dramatic events. Information often comes dramatically. For example, a friend you haven't heard from for a year may call you and say she is bringing a book by for you to read.

Read that book! More specifically, follow what appear to be leads, but stay open. Maybe you are supposed to meet your friend's neighbor when you return the book.

Ideally, we would meditate a lot and get our own answers. However, what do we do during those years that we are expanding our intuition? We still need help when we get stuck; we would still like enlightened answers before making tough decisions when we don't appear to be getting insights. That is the time to get help from a devout psychic. Usually, you can find one by asking all of your metaphysical friends who they would recommend. The same name will start coming up when someone is good. Usually, the very best are *not* listed in the yellow pages because they live off referrals. There are exceptions to this rule, however. The 900 psychic number advertised in some magazines is problematical. I personally know two good psychics who work for that 900 number. But . . .

Psychic ability is not so hard to understand when you remember that everything from a thought to an event to a refrigerator is made of vibrations. Since "time" is a third–dimensional construct which the psychic gets past, all the psychic has to do is tune into vibrations. A rough analogy would be a train approaching a tunnel. Now, all common sense would tell you if you saw a train going in one end of the tunnel, it is a likely prediction that it will come out the other end.

As already mentioned, a study at Stanford University showed that even the best psychics are right only eighty–five percent of the time. Corroborating that statistic, Chinese psychic researchers at Beijing University testing psychic children say they scored correctly eighty-five percent of the time. So, since the best clairvoyants mis–read clues, when you are having a psychic reading, stay tuned to your *own intuition*. And psychics are notorious for being off on the timing of events. Hopefully, you can understand why, now.

Also, since your thoughts and actions have an impact on consciousness, you can actually change an event before it happens. Maybe that engineer in the train tunnel will stop the train and back up! But the psychic looking forward will interpret the most–likely event.

Poor psychics abound. Others will tell you what you want to hear.

Ask yourself, does the seer serve themself or God? Be careful. Those offering to be a medium to communicate with discarnate spirits using automatic writing, seances, table tipping and ouija boards may pick up a Being far less evolved than you. What you need to be after is spiritual growth, personal growth, and answers to practical life questions that help in service or work that benefits others.

When you have your reading, be sure to take your tape recorder and audiotape the session. It is easy to use the psychological defense of "denial" on information you don't want to hear. If it is taped so you can listen again later, you can't deny challenges.

If you have some "mad" money, having a psychic reading can be fun and absolutely fascinating. Hour–long sessions are commonly $60.

Devout psychics need no tools for reading. But they sometimes use tools because clients enjoy the fun and the technique or system provides a point of focus. Sometimes a person with a lot of intuition uses these tools to start reading, thus using the tool to expand intuition or psychic ability.

ASTROLOGY. On one's birth date and at the birth–time of day, the sun, moon, planets and stars were in a certain position. Around this fact, some clairvoyants use learned systems to give advice and council. I have seen this system used with great wisdom and contrarily with great deceit, depending upon the reader. I'll have to confess that totally computerized readings bother me as do the daily astrological advice columns in the newspaper.

There is no doubt, however, that a devout astrologer can be of assistance with your plans. Sai Baba says that "Timing is everything."

Constructed especially for Cosmic Map by a gracious former Universal Church of the Master minister, a Sai Baba devotee who now runs a Center in the United States, comes this interesting list of each birthsign's major spiritual task during the Soul's latter incarnations. You have chosen the Planet of the Cross again and again, plus chosen your time of birth, because you could get specific. As mentioned, your Soul knows your spiritual tasks.

My astronomer friend was telling me that Sai Baba says Souls are so

blessed to get to come to the Planet of the Cross because of the richness of the opportunities to learn love. Then I remembered what
shaman had said: "I can see Souls standing in line waiting to get a
body!"

The Baba devotee educated me: "Look at the signs of the zodiac as a
road map of the Soul's evolutionary journey:" You will find a few
overlap dates in the following brief treatise, for example, April 21. If
you were born on an overlap date, or close, read both months. You
will have some strivings of the previous sign. The Soul here appears
to be finishing learning from the opportunities of the previous sign
at the same time s/he is taking on new tasks.

I asked her if, "In our old-Soul lives, do we go from one, to the next,
to the next?" She answered, "I think many astrologers would say
'yes.' I think, however, that the Soul has free will."

The journey begins in **Aries**, March 21 to April 21. The Soul learns
Self-consciousness on an elemental level which enables it to discover oneness with God, the true meaning of "I."

In **Taurus**, April 21 to May 22, the Soul is reaching for stability and
contentment. Finding the meaning of true values leads one from
inner war into the peace that surpasses all.

The journey continues in **Gemini**, May 21 to June 21. Now is the
time to learn to be the messenger between the lower and higher
mind, gathering all the bits of knowledge that will someday be wisdom.

In **Cancer**, June 21 to July 21, the Soul encounters emotions which
build foundations to integrate and stabilize the personality so that it
is attuned to the needs of family and mankind.

The **Leo** incarnation, July 22 to August 22, is symbolized by the king
who is getting ready to abdicate his throne. His nature must
become impersonal and give warmth and love to all not just self, a
true gift of generosity to the world.

August 21 to September 22, as the Soul in **Virgo**, there is a constant
striving for purification and perfection in itself, the Soul is learning

the lesson of humble service and patience.

The journey is starting back to "the Father/Mother's house" in **Libra**, September 21 to October 21. This incarnation is evolving out of materialism into a deeper understanding of the meaning of life, with the realization that the second half of the journey involves other people.

In **Scorpio**, October 21 to November 21, the Soul and the personality must come into alignment. It is ultimately the death of the old and the birth of the new.

Sagittarius, November 21 to December 21, the restless journey continues as s/he searches for the way out of duality into unity.

True humility is learned as **Capricorn**, December 21 to January 21, courageously continues to climb to the heights of the spirit.

The Soul has now come to **Aquarius**, January 22 to February 19, the time of spiritual rebirth. One learns that true liberation can only come from within and freedom without responsibility is license not liberty.

The spiritual journey finishes in **Pisces**, February 19 to March 21. Here the Soul gathers all the pieces of karma to be completed and prepares to retreat from the world.

If you would like to learn astrology, a good place to start would be ASTROLOGY, A COSMIC SCIENCE, Isabel M. Hickley, Altieri Press, 1974, Bridgeport, Connecticut. Another possibility for beginners is A SPIRITUAL APPROACH TO ASTROLOGY, Myrna Lofthus, 1935, C. R. C. S. Publications, P. O. Box 20850, Reno, Nevada 89515.

Astrology is just one tool that psychics can use. Now we will continue with our overview of others.

CRYSTAL READING. A clairvoyant may ask a client to hold a cleansed crystal, then hold it themselves to read the client's vibrations. I have seen this done with great sensitivity and contrarily with great inaccuracy, depending upon the reader. (Among the ways crystals can be cleansed after a client has used it, are letting them sit in the sun, burying them in salt, or smudging them with sage smoke.)

PSYCHOMETRY. The clairvoyant holds an object worn frequently by the client (and only the client) such as jewelry. Vibrations are interpreted. My comment after "crystal readings" applies.

One lovely, very-psychic, devout friend told me half-jokingly, "I can even read from a person's socks."

NUMEROLOGY. A learned system, the cosmic vibrations of numbers add up to messages for the client. This system can be very helpful. As with the others, it depends upon the knowledge, psychic ability and devoutness of the reader.

PALMISTRY. A system of studying the hands, fingers and wrists, it takes meaning from texture, shape and lines. (And probably the vibrations of the person being read.) I have seen this system used "by guess and by gosh" and I have seen it work extremely well. Again, it depends.

PHONE READINGS. A clairvoyant does the reading over the phone. The psychic may or may not have ever met the client. The vibrations from the voice of the client enable the reading to start. I have had some of the sharpest readings over the phone, as hard to believe as it is at first. Again, it depends.

TAROT CARDS. Symbols on the cards and spreads are interpreted by the clairvoyant for client guidance and prophecy. These cards can be traced back to the 12th century. A Tarot reader told me she had been taught that they were designed by a group of enlightened men who spoke different languages. Together, the deck speaks a universal language because the cards communicate with the subconscious mind in a similar way in everyone. After development, the cards were given to gypsies to assure distribution all over Europe.

Paul Foster Case is the Tarot expert of the last century; his book is THE TAROT.

I have had some of my best-ever readings with Tarot. Again, it depends.

OTHER CARDS AND GAMES. You may want to research the **I Ching** and **Runes** for your own at-home use.

Much older than the Tarot, the I Ching originated in China before Christ. Here you need an I Ching book and three coins to toss. You ask your question and record the heads/tail's pattern of six throws. You match your recorded pattern of tosses with the I Ching book's matching hexagram patterns. Ancient, "sage" advice is received but for the modern person wanting clarity, you may not find an answer such as the following helpful: "Perseverance brings good fortune. Remorse disappears. The hedge opens; there is no entanglement. Power depends upon the axle of a big cart." However, a most respected psychic friend swears by the I Ching. It might really resonate with you.

New card decks and systems sometime attract clairvoyants. The good ones will stand the test of time. If you buy a deck for yourself, be sure to choose one that feels right in your hands and seems to you to be very pleasant looking.

The Viking Runes are stones with abstract symbols. Of mysterious origin, they date back over 2,000 years. The RuneCards (trademark) were created by the author of THE RUNE CARDS, SACRED PLAY FOR SELF-DISCOVERY, Ralph Blum. If you have the book, you can start working immediately with the stones and/or the cards. In this system, what is enjoyable is that even the difficult times have positive spiritual significance.

Practicing psychics get their information differently. Let's take a look at specific sensitivities:

CLAIRVOYANT. A person who sees without the physical eyes. The term is basically synonymous with the terms "sensitive" and "psychic." A clairvoyant person has extraordinary intuition.

A finer definition would say that a clairvoyant interacts with the material world and a higher dimension; a person using mental **telepathy** would get information from another person's mind.

CLAIRAUDIENT. A person hears without the ears. This type of psychic may hear angel choirs, other music, words, or sentences.

CLAIRSENTIENT. A person who feels with the whole body. This type of psychic gets information as "gut level" intuition and actually feels the emotions and feeling states of others. In looking backward or forward in time, the clairsentient may get feelings of danger or dread or joy and so forth.

X–RAY CLAIRVOYANT. A very rare talent, I have been privileged to watch three of these extraordinary psychics work (one a woman, two men). They can *see through the body*, check out organs and systems, pinpoint illnesses and psychological blocks. They also observe the aura and health of it and the spiritual energies.

PRE–COGNITION. This means getting information directly from the future. This is an element of intuition and psychicness.

Some psychics use a combination of these modalities for tuning into their own intuition.

"Is **CHANNELING** psychicness?" No, although some psychic people do channeling. A channel allows an out–of–body Being or extraterrestrial to speak through him or her.

The highest source coming through your own Being Mind is the intelligence of God, superconsciousness. Allowing out–of–body entities to enter your temple and use your human voice to speak to others raises these questions: (1) How highly evolved is the entity? (They do not necessarily offer good advice or accurate information). (2) What is s/he's purpose? (3) Why doesn't s/he stand in line for a human body so it can evolve? (4) Was Edgar Cayce right in trying not to allow out–of–body–Beings to speak through him? (This process, nevertheless, happened spontaneously fifteen times.) Cayce became physically ill on all of those occasions.) (5) Is allowing an entity to speak through you aiding your own Being development? (6) Does other–entity channeling puff up your own ego?

There may be another type of channeling, whereby the entity or entities communicate by telepathy or by a vibration that is in tune with a very evolved person's energy. I hope this is true, because some very evolved people I know are channeling. Another possibility is that at the Being level, they have agreed to shorten the length of their this–life body in order for certain urgent messages to come through.

It also probable that "now" is different because of the rapid rise in consciousness. Devout channelers are being used by the spiritual hierarchy to bring in much needed information.

As examples, here let me single out just three channelers who have gone public. First, is Annie Kirkwood who says she channels Ascended Master, Mary, mother of Jesus. Annie wrote MARY'S MES- SAGE TO THE WORLD. In 1993, I went to hear her speak; impressed by Annie's gold aura and her humbleness, I believe. You can order a newsletter which contains a new message from Mary every two months by writing Mary's Message/Newsletter, Route 1, Box 100, Bunch OK 74931, SASE.

Second, is Dr. Norma Milanovich who says she channels Beings from the star Arcturus as well as Ascended Masters. WE THE ARCTURI- ANS is channeled information from the extraterrestrial Beings that Cayce said are the highest in our galaxy. This book and her other publications can be had from Athena Publishing, Mossman Center STE 206, Albuquerque, NM 872109–1574, SASE. I have seen her talk on videotape and believe she is doing Divine work.

Third is Sheldon Nidle who says he channels extraterrestrial Beings from the star complex of Sirius. I'll talk about his incredible work in Chapter 3.

Now, we will leave the subjects of intuition, psychicness and chan- neling.

In Chapter 2, thus far, we have talked about how the design of your physical eyes does not let you see reality. We discussed in some detail the trickiness of the human mind, especially the "channels" of your ego–mind, your emotions, the wispy symbols of your dream channel trying to help, and the vagaries of intuition, whether yours or someone else's.

So your body/mind, your temple of the Holy Spirit, is not a rapid or sure spiritual evolvement mechanism. And, if you are like me, you don't feel like doing your spiritual practices if your body is sick.

"What can you tell us about the **HEALTH** and **HEALING** of the human body?" It is no accident that at this time of consciousness ascension, new healing "technologies" are being developed and old ones are being brought back from the ancient cultures.

And do we ever need this help! Besides the stress and pollution from modern life, your body is being asked, as you increase your consciousness, to accept more love energy as you change your carnal flesh into Divine flesh. As discussed, the love energy actually expands your atoms, pulling at the cells within your body, not to mention the push of getting new chakras and other invisible, potent evolvement mechanisms! Help!

Deepak Chopra, M. D., endocrinologist, the eloquently outspoken proponent of preventative medicine, says

> We create our bodies with our minds. If we don't relax our minds, we create sick bodies. Although we perceive our bodies as solid, in fact, they are more like rivers, constantly changing. We acquire new stomach linings every five days. Our skin is new every five weeks. Every year, fully ninety–eight percent of the total number of atoms in our bodies are replaced.

That old myth of your getting total body renewal every seven years made it seem as though *daily* bad habits weren't very important. Perhaps Chopra's words can motivate you to do the best you can each crucial day to healthfully recreate your body. You actually create almost 1/365th of your body each day!

More fluid flows inside your body in the invisible rivers of non-pulsing lymph than blood through the blood stream. Then there is your chi or life energy. Not to mention your mysterious glands, also being altered during this time of spiritual regeneration.

Modern traditional medicine was developed from corpses. Bodies without the Soul do not have "the rivers running," the chi flowing, or God's love vibrations pulsating between all the atoms. By the time a dead body gets to the medical school for the medical students to study, it has no aura or chakra action.

There is a reason the Universe lets this happen. New and creative approaches to healing have come from Western medicine, and they will continue. Examples are the care of complex-fractured bones, burns, a ruptured appendix, and acute pneumonia. However, most of our feelings of "being not up to par" could best be improved by other healing modalities that are gentle, non-intrusive, and cooperate with the body's natural energies, thus encouraging the body to self-correct. An ancient sage, the Yellow Emperor said, "The inferior doctor treats the man who is already ill."

An intervention in the body system at any spot will affect the entire body process. This fact is the reason that negative side effects result from anything that is harsh. Modern medicine's surgery and prescriptions are frequently garish. Unless my health problem is life threatening, or modern medicine has a unique answer – for an example – a wound that needs fourteen stitches, I first seek alternate types of health care.

It is common for those who have had a near-death experience to suffer poor health, and I have. Consequently, I for the last seventeen years, have experimented a great deal on myself, and in the process, learned a lot. I don't have the credentials to write at length on strictly health topics. So as a modern shaman – by my definition a shaman who wants to give away what she knows – here is my big chance to alert you to a few things you may not be aware of.

Grandma Janis' "Health Tips"

In this miscellaneous section, we will start off with three recipes:

The first recipe is a natural cold remedy.

SHAMAN'S NATURAL COLD REMEDY: 1 cup of hot water, juice from one-half lemon, one-half ounce whiskey or vodka, 1/4 tsp. cayenne (red) pepper, two capsules of Kyolic garlic (or crush your own to taste), and add some honey to taste. Use this to gargle or you can drink it.

The second recipe is a preventative.

SHAMAN'S UNNATURAL ANTI-INFECTIVE JUMPSTART:

Use this only a few times a year when you know you have been
infected with something or at the very first sign when you feel yourself coming down with anything. If *taken early enough*, it really works
and will not hurt you, if not abused.

Take 30,000 IUs of vitamin A (or beta carotene), one time. Take 2,000
mg of vitamin C – continue same dose of C for next two days.

The third recipe is a cookie recipe. One day when I was meditating,
suddenly, I started intuiting, of all things, a recipe. There was a
piece of paper and pen close by so I jotted down the information.
Here was the Universe playing. I have found that if I play with the
Universe, the Universe will play with me. Later I made and served
this recipe and called it Cosmic Cookies. My grandchildren, family
and friends say they are very good.

GRANDMA JANIS' COSMIC COOKIES

Mix these ingredients in a bowl
and let them soak one-half hour:

2 C. uncooked (oatmeal type) oats
2 well-beaten eggs
3/4 C. canola oil
1 1/2 C. *real* maple syrup
1/2 C. raisins
1 tsp. vanilla

Mix these ingredients in another
bowl:

1 tsp. baking soda
1 tsp. sea salt
1 tsp. cinnamon
2 generous C. whole wheat flour
(add more for the consistency you
want)

Pour first bowl into second and mix very well. Drop by teaspoon or
tablespoon onto Teflon–type cookie sheet. Bake at 275 degrees for
twenty minutes. Note that Cosmic Cookies, like our spiritual growth,
take awhile. The low temperature is like our three–D denseness.

Now we will continue with miscellaneous health tips. Did you
know that fluorescent lights "eat up" your aura? That is why you
feel hopelessly tired after working under them all day. Instead, boss
willing, you could be working under lights that actually have a
vibration similar to the sun. You are dreaming you say? No, these
are already available from Duro/Test Lighting, 9 Law Dr., Fairfield,

New Jersey 07004. Send a SASE when inquiring about their
"Vita/lite," which they say has the unique benefits of true, natural
sunlight; let's keep that company in business. These lights are
really wonderful.

The hum of a computer or photocopier in not at all good for you
either; any electronic machine vibrates at different rates than your
cells. So turn them off when you aren't using them! And keep the
periods of time you use them sensible. Take a break. Plan your
work so that you do some of it away from "the lovable monsters."

Do you know what causes cellulite (ugly fad pads)? If a needle is
inserted into your fat and a sample withdrawn, a laboratory can tell
what is the source of that fat; for example, butter, cheese, canola oil?
Any fat that hardens outside the body also hardens inside the body.
Cellulite? For starters, try butter, cheese and margarines that harden.

As a matter of fact, margarine and other products have a "no–no"
hydrogenated molecule that the body doesn't know what to do with.
Better avoid all hydrogenated–molecule products. "Oh," you say, "I
would never eat a hydrogenated molecule!" Wrong! Once you start
to read labels, you will realize how hard these are to avoid!

What do I eat on my baked potato? Walnut oil with garlic juice in
it. If your grocer doesn't carry it, ask the grocer to order it from Hain
Pure Food Co., Inc., P.O. Box 66967, St. Louis, MO 63166–6967. We
need a minimum of ten percent or our calories from oil. It is in the
oil that vitamins A, D, E and K are distributed to the body. (When I
first went low-fat in 1978, I got a good case of night blindness, defi-
ciency in vitamin A.) Don't used oils that have been heated. Use
expelled or cold pressed oils; they haven't been cooked.

What do I put on my toast? Tahini, which is mashed sesame seeds
(health food store or food co–op), or hummus, which is ground,
cooked garbanzo beans with onion, lemon juice and salt.

Do I think our alarming breast cancer rate is related to our population's high dairy, high animal fat diet? Yes, along with the psychological reasons. Shortly, I'll tell you the approach of master metaphysician, Louise L. Hay, who says breast problems are caused by
"overmothering, overprotection, overbearing attitudes." And for "can-

cer," although I had heard "refusal to change" from another source, Hay mentions "deep hurt; long–standing resentment; deep secret or grief eating away at the self; carrying hatreds; what's the use?"

Did you know that you need something fresh at *every* meal and snack, something that is not cooked or processed in order to get your enzymes. Live food, is an idea of the future based on the past: In cultures where the people live long and healthy lives, lots of *fresh* fruits and vegetables are consumed.

Another tip: An aide to the flowing of the lymph and chi in your body is a **skin brush**. You can get a "scrub–your–back–brush." Before bath or shower use your brush to firmly (1) brush around your abdomen in a clockwise motion (as you look down) five or six times and (2) brush over your limbs and extremities, making long strokes toward your heart.

This stimulates the lymph to excrete wastes through your skin, which is another excretionary organ like the kidneys and liver – and helps take the pressure off these vitals. If you have weaknesses in excretionary organs, doing this every day before your shower could significantly prolong your life.

My last health tip is aimed to those of you who feel you must let filthy flies, dangerous spiders and mosquitoes live because of reverence for life. Sai Baba says that it is okay to kill insects in your homes and offices. When the Dalai Lama was asked whether he kills insects he said, "First I ask them to leave. If they don't, I zap them."

I have finished with the recipes and health tips, now I will, as a senior lady, make a commentary on modern medicine.

When I was a little girl, when I was ill and my parents called the doctor, he came in shabby clothes, with a heart of gold, driving his old car right to our house. He attended me in my own bedroom. He healed me with the genuine caring coming from his persona, plus the fact I didn't have to be taken out; sick children are fragile.

What has happened in just fifty years is alarming. Tragically, big money came to medicine. In a greedy, sick, little–heart dance, the sometimes–reluctant partners are the following:

(1) the medical insurance companies (some with managed health care with many costly, and senseless bureaucratic procedures, policies and paperwork); some of these insurance companies think they can tell you what treatment you need or don't need. Others actually chose your physician for you. In some cases physicians have to pay a substantial sum of money in order to get on the "approved provider list."

(2) the traditional medical establishment who are philosophically unable to entertain new ideas because they have been taught in medical school that the only "scientific" ideas come from their own medical establishment;

(3) prescription drug companies that manufacture some drugs that are, over the long term, more harmful to mankind than are helpful, and

(4) physician–owned labs.

In the years to come, there will be many exposes about needless surgeries, harmful prescription drugs, and the dangers of going into a hospital as a patient.

"Anything that hasn't been shown with hard date to be an effective treatment is experimental. That would go for virtually eighty–five percent to ninety–five percent of all surgical procedures." Me talking? No, the quote is by Richard Greene, M.D., Agency for Health Care Policy and Research.

In a recent Ann Lander's column, she quotes an American Medical Association article which says the number of deaths by hospital-caused mistakes may be equivalent to "three jumbo–jet crashes every two days."

Am I bitter, angry. No, of course not. I have forgiven everyone! I know everyone has done the best they could under existing circumstances. However, it time for the changing of the guard.

Light workers, already inside the medical establishment, are remaking medicine. The greed will get taken out of it because the Light workers are already in place!

Let me tell you how this is working in India. Sai Baba, with the help of those he gathers about him, has built over two-hundred hospitals.

The most notable is the super speciality hospital at Puttaparthi, India, the Sri Sathya Sai Institute of Higher Medical Sciences. Isaact Tigret, former owner of the Hard Rock Cafes, was chosen by Sai Baba to be the general administrator in the conception, and development of the architecture and the building of the hospital.

The hospital itself was based on ancient, sacred geometry. They cleansed the land first. Then a mandala, sanskrit or mystic circle, was drawn on the selected property. This picture contained archetypical images. Then, the concerned planners were told that they couldn't start until an eagle had sat down upon the land. However, when those in charge went to visit the land, there were five eagles sitting in a circle in the center. The eagles didn't even fly away as they approached, just stayed and walked around with them!

The Hospital Corporation of America had drawn up the original plans. However, the best minds in India, when assigned to the project, changed these plans. When the final plans were presented to the World Health Organization, the physicians there were outraged at the deviations from accepted hospital planning. The last physician, arriving late, saved the day when he said, "Looks strange to me, too, but if Sai Baba is in charge, it will work."

And work it does. All admissions have their stay free of charge. The one-hundred acre site has forty buildings that house three-thousand, five-hundred staff members. Open heart surgeries and other complicated techniques predominate. Many are children with holes or other defects in their hearts.

Tigret said that they operate for three or four weeks, and then Sai Baba stops them. Those patients able to go, are sent home. Then the staff has group collaborative-solution-finding sessions to pinpoint weak areas and plan for improvements.

Sai Baba says this is a prototype hospital. The last I heard, October 1995, not a single patient had died there!

Now, although I have taken a compelling detour, I want to continuing on with the theme here of protecting yourself and taking care of your body.

You can find a pharmacist who will warn you about the dangers in your prescriptions, "Hey, are you sure you want to take this stuff, they are finding out that it . . . " If you haven't got a gutsy pharmacist, get the latest copy of THE PEOPLE'S PHARMACY by Joe Graedon, published by St. Martin's Press, New York. Joe's drug warnings are jewels.

There are already physicians who buck the craziness with their heart energy; for example, my physician, who has the arsenal of traditional medicine at his disposal along with acupuncture. A meditator, he is already Self-realized. Was he hard to find? You bet, it took me two and one-half years!

Medical doctors Chopra, Ornish, Joy and a physician not yet mentioned, Dr. John A. McDougall – who teaches vegan eating – are also wonderful examples of Light-worker physicians, *gone public*, who have gone against the grain of their profession – and people love them for it!

Ideally, medicine is revamping itself from within, but let some of us upstart metaphysicians give workshops to them on what *we know*. They don't have to incorporate these modalities, just refer when it is ethical and intelligent to do so.

On another subject, those of you who wear glasses and/or contacts, how would you like to follow a process over a year that will give you 20/20 vision? Something new from optometrists or ophthalmologists? No. Brian Severson had a passion. He wanted to be a pilot, but because of poor eye sight, he could not be one.

Over a ten-year period, he developed a method for himself to correct his vision. There is no surgery in his method. Now he is helping others.

It is interesting how often creative ideas come from outside a relatively closed field. It's not that I want to be knocking the establishment, it is just a metaphysical principle as we have already talked about, that relatively closed systems go into atrophy. (I believe I said it earlier this way: "Closed systems die.")

Severson? Now he flies! For information, write to Vision Freedom,
USA (soon to be the whole Planet of the Cross) 1665 Red Crow Road,
Victor, Montana 59875.

We have already mentioned in COSMIC MAP prevention and healing
modalities beyond traditional medicine: biofeedback training, meditation, having positive attitudes and thoughts, talking with a friend,
being in a spiritual support group, laying–on–of hands (intuitive
moving of the body energies and sometimes actual touch of the
skin), chanting, listening to soothing music, and psychotherapy.
Coming up shortly are nutrition (vegetarian lifestyle), yoga and aerobic exercise.

Coming in Chapter 3 to help in health are prayers, a prayer group,
using affirmations, and more on psychotherapy (to release your dark
side, your neuroses. Shaman talked about cleaning up "neuroses" as
casually as he did "cleaning his kitchen.")

The following have made their way into mainstream medicine: psychotherapy, biofeedback, acupuncture, and massage. Chiropractic
already gets the approval of some insurance companies, but some of
a chiropractor's most effective, non–intrusive work, using acupres-
sure and muscle testing may not get payment approval. I will elaborate later on the last two modalities in the following paragraphs,
iridology and colon cleaning. It would take a complete book to do
all of these gentle therapies justice – gentle compared to surgery and
synthetic medicines!

Homeopathy, herb and herb combinations – the Chinese medical
establishment has achieved mastery in the use of herbs. Their bare-
foot doctors take care of eighty–percent of problems right on the
farms – vitamin and mineral therapies, flower essences, all kinds of
body work including chakra balancing and Trager Work (stretching
and rocking), the latter developed by Milton Trager, M.D.

Further modalities are reflexology, both a specialized foot massage
and a diagnostic tool; water therapy (therapist "holds" floating,
relaxed client in different positions in a hot tub or heated swimming
pool, lasts about an hour); sound healing – finding out which vibra-

tions (notes) are missing from the body – then supplying them in the proper octave; using different kinds of stones (with different vibrations) laid on the appropriate part of the body; and healing with colors (doing art work or having the colors you need flashed in front of you). Practitioners of these and others can usually be found through referral by someone working at your metaphysical bookstore or health food store, and sometimes through the yellow pages. As a diagnostic tool, there is iridology as taught by chiropractor, Dr. Bernard Jensen. Dr. Jensen was born in 1908. Traveling the world, he has studied in more than fifty-five countries. He is one of the Planet of the Cross' most brilliant food scientists.

In iridology, an expert (this expert will have studied for more years than for a medical school education) uses a very bright light and a magnifying lens or a special iris camera (iriscope – costs about $5,000). What shows are genetic weaknesses, developing illnesses at four different levels of approach that have not yet showed symptoms, and areas that are probably causing current health symptoms. Also displayed in the iris are residuals of toxins, including medicinal and recreational drugs stuck in various organs and cavities. And to think that in some states it is illegal to practice iridology; iridologists are actually thrown in jail!

I know – there are some pseudo-iridologists, as in every profession, that botch things up. They have purchased a book, spent a weekend studying it and set up shop.

The developer of Iridology, Dr. Bernard Jensen, was originally a chiropractor. He is a vigorous old man now. He refined the science. Now someone needs to take over the licensing of iridologists. And I know just the lady – but I can't tell you who she is because someone might arrest her!

This lady, many years ago, rented a room from me. Typically, one morning at the breakfast table, she said, "You have a urinary infection, Janis." Sure enough, I had been having low-level symptoms of frequent urination and burning, but had been ignoring them.

On another occasion when she was giving a talk on iridology, before the talk, a medical doctor in the audience came up to her and said,

"I am going to discredit you!" Calmly, my friend looked into the physician's eyes and said, "Has your right shoulder been bothering you?" The physician gasped, "How did you know?"

In colonics, a purified, sterile water enema is given. Toxins and ancient, impacted waste are swept from your body's septic tank. This needs to be performed by a careful and highly trained specialist who uses disposable insert paraphernalia. The water goes into all three colon areas, first the descending colon somewhat like an enema. At the next session, water is carefully and gently worked higher, into the transverse colon. Then, in the final session, it is worked into the ascending colon. Again, I know the most fantastic colon educator in the world. But I can't tell you because someone might hurt her. Incidentally she is in her forties, looks fifteen years younger than she is. A beautiful woman, she walks her talk.

The first time I had a colonic, I had been feeling *very* tired and list-less. The improvement was *immediate* and *dramatic.*

Colon cleansing can also be done by yourself at home using colon cleaning products taken by mouth.

You cannot have a healthy body with a filthy colon. Everyone on the American diet who has not cleansed, if over thirty-five years of age, has a filthy colon. Anyone at any age who has a big gut is suspect.

I became a believer in colon cleansing when I saw what came out of me. Yuk. Talk about the dark side! And afterwards, my arthritis was gone. When my arthritis returns now after about a year, I know it is time to cleanse again. I can go for about a year because I am vege-tarian and eat few dairy products. Heavy meat and dairy product eaters usually need to cleanse every four months.

The guru of product colon cleansing is Rich Anderson who wrote a self-published book called CLEANSE AND PURIFY THYSELF, THE CLEAN-ME-OUT-PROGRAM. You can order a copy from Arise and Shine, 3225 North Los Altos, Tucson, Arizona 85705. Anderson doc-uments many other health benefits. He also mentions graphically what comes out; for example, one woman passed crayons that she had eaten as a child! Also ask about their colon cleaning products, but be aware that like all gurus, Anderson is a bit overzealous, God bless him.

If you decide to do a cleanse, after being amazed by Anderson's stories, forget them. Keep in touch with your own body. Back off for a day or two if you get muscles spasms (you need calcium/magnesium and potassium) or get to feeling very weak. In this case, Rich says you can eat a simple (he has specifics) meal.

Cost of the products to go along with the allowed fruit and vegetable juices will be close to $100, an excellent investment. Fasting is not a casual thing. Many people throw their body off when they ignorantly attempt this very radical procedure.

In any colon cleaning program, at a minimum you need the following products to do these specific chores: (1) herbs which loosen and dissolve intestinal mucoid, plaque material, (wouldn't it be sweet if the your diet only put plaque on your teeth!) (2) an absorbing agent which assists in detoxification, plus acts like a sponge, absorbing toxins, bacteria and parasites; (3) psyllium to soften and attract loosened mucoid layers and other debris; it is the "Ajax" for the colon, and "floats the dirt right down the drain!" (4) acidophillus–like replacement of the friendly bacteria swept away by the products (5) replacement minerals missed when not eating and (6) replacement vitamins, essential amino acids and digestive enzymes missed from having no food.

During the cleanse, it is also a good idea to take a calcium/magnesium supplement if your mineral supplement doesn't have the amount of calcium you need. Calcium needs are very individual. You'll have to research this. My–sixteen–year–old stepson needs sixteen hundred mg of calcium a day. He needs a lot because the meat he eats (concentrated protein) strips his body of calcium; and he is at an age where is he growing rapidly. Some of the tiredness and lethargy he feels is because of nutritional deficiencies. At my age, a vegetarian woman needs at least twelve hundred mg. A forty–year–old man, who has never had his colon cleansed, who eats lots of dairy and meat, by now has very poor intestinal absorption. God only knows how much calcium he needs.

I was shocked to see an off–the–counter, unabsorbed calcium supplement pill in my stool during a cleanse. It had gone all the way through! After that, I started ordering more expensive, but very absorbable, calcium and magnesium from Bernard Jenson, International, P. O. Box 8, Solana Beach, CA 02075. The ideal proportion of calcium to magnesium is being debated. You can watch the proportion of magnesium to calcium in off-the-shelf products for the time being. I suspect, though, the ideal may be an individual thing.

When taking calcium/magnesium supplements, take one product for three months. Then switch to another. Then in three months, switch to still another. Then in three more months, you can return to your original.

Back to cleansing, I eat several range eggs (chickens are free to roam) a day (five grams of protein each, way too many eggs for ordinary use) and a piece of tofu 2 1/2 by 2 3/4 by 1 inch. (I have been eating tofu so long, I can tolerate it right out of the waterless-pack carton) for an additional approximately ten grams of protein. That way my twenty protein grams, a minimum supply, is not interrupted. Rich Anderson *might* choke if he knew! I don't try to fast, exactly; I try to cleanse.

My husband does a cleanse in the pure way, just tolerates feeling weak on the second and third days, as Anderson says you will. David just drinks fruit and vegetable juice, no food, but he does take all the supplements.

Now, did I say to do a cleanse my way? Anderson's way? David's way? No way! What I am trying to do is to bluntly tell you, you have to take care of your body, now, yourself. Keep in tune with it and do it *your* way. But do it, nobody can do it for you. *We very well may get to keep these bodies for several hundred years or more! I am not promising, but I am not taking any chances.*

Right after the cleanse is a time to check your body's pH balance to see if you are too acid or too alkaline. This pH balance is a key indicator of health. Ideally, it should be about 6.8. You can check it by using a pH indicator strip dipped in your urine. You can get these Nitrazine paper strips at your pharmacy – if out of stock, the pharmacist can order them for you. Read the directions that come with the paper strips. If your pH is out of balance, then go to the library and research which foods you need to eat to self–correct. Food correction on pH is relatively easy and quick. And now that you have a supply of these papers, you can check pH at any time you want and then easily keep yourself balanced.

To get your body's electrolyte balance back, ask at the health food store for a product to help. If you get something off the grocery store shelf, it just may be loaded with salt and sugar, although it will take care of your electrolites balance.

If Elvis Presley had had a colon cleansing, he might still be alive today. The autopsy of "The King's" body showed his colon was terribly impacted, so clogged with the residuals of the multiple prescription and recreational drugs he had taken, there was no space left for his colon to do its job. Elvis died sitting on the toilet.

Many would disagree, but I do *not* believe in liver cleanses because some of the toxins overflow into your body. If you clean your colon, which is encased – the waste flows out of the body, then your liver – and gall bladder, too – will tend to self–clean, the ideal. Anyway, on liver cleaning, you really need to know what you are doing – I believe you could literally kill yourself.

I ignored my iridologist's pleas about colon cleansing for two years. Before we met, at my initial appointment with her, the very first thing she said after examining my irises was, "Janis, where in the world did all of that sulfa come from?"

As mentioned, she could see, by looking in my irises, that I had "gunk" in my colon! You see, I understand at a deep level why modern medicine was allowed to develop. It saved my life when I was ten, had pneumonia, and took those sulfa drugs. It saved it again by surgical intervention when I was hemorrhaging, followed by the NDE; however, it has been my belief that I would *not* have been bleeding excessively if it wasn't for the faulty design of my brand of birth control pills, which have now been taken off the market.

My message to you is, "When it comes to health, never give up. Talk with others. Your healers will come to you as do your teachers when you trod the spiritual path with concentrated intent to evolve."

What we are going to see in the coming years is not only the development and incorporation of alternative modalities, but also the reinterpretation of illness. For example, I all ready alluded to the fact that arthritis starts with a dirty colon. Overflowing toxins get into body joints. If you and arthritis are brand new, simply cleaning the colon will take away the arthritis. However, if you have had it a long time, then damage has been done to the joints themselves by the toxins. Even then, colon cleaning will drastically reduce your pain. And Bernard Jensen has products to stimulate bone re-growth. I would like to return to the subject of calcium because it is so essential, especially for adolescent boys and menopausal women.

The cure for osteoporosis, bone loss in late middle-age, is not new synthetic drugs or estrogen. (They tell us estrogen is natural, out of the urine of horses.) I say there aren't enough horses.

The cure for osteoporosis is to drastically reduce concentrated animal protein consumption, for example meat and cheese.

Only women who muscle test positive on estrogen should take it. Dr. John Diamond, another Light worker medical doctor, wrote BK, Behavioral Kinesiology, the New Science for Positive Health Through Muscle Testing, Harper and Row, New York, 1979. Dr. Diamond understands that all foods and medicines should be muscle tested before they are ingested, to see if the product strengthens you, or weakens you.

If you do not muscle test positive on estrogen, you can go to a health food store and muscle test wild Mexican yam for menopausal symptoms.

Colon cleaning, if you are really dirty, may lead to weight loss: plaque is heavy.

And speaking of weight loss, it is easy to lose weight (fat) and keep it off if you follow John A. McDougall, M. D. and his twin-ray-soul wife, Mary A. McDougall's plan. (What are twin-ray Souls? Coming up in Chapter 3.) The McDougall's have a number of excellent books. Start with THE McDOUGALL PLAN, Plume, Penguin Books

USA, Inc., 375 Hudson Street, New York, New York 10014.
Beautiful people, the McDougall's have simple, easy fix, dairy–free
recipes. (Dean Ornish, M. D. allows dairy in his program; his first-
book recipes are more time consuming.)

There will come a day when your medical insurance company will
pay for your colon–cleaning products. Grandma Janis' estimate? If
everyone had a clean colon, medical problems would drop by one-
half. Now, how would physicians support expensive lifestyles,
including the needed expensive office and staff, with half of their
income gone? Why should they support colon cleaning or other
modalities of prevention? The way their institution has evolved,
they have to deny the wholelistic approaches.

The body is the temple of the holy spirit. It is spiritually correct to
keep all temples clean!

If dirty colons are only causing half of the non–accident problems,
you might well ask, "What else makes me sick?" There is a school of
high–consciousness thought that says the reason is you are using the
wrong thought forms. Louise L. Hay wrote the masterful HEAL
YOUR BODY. In it is a chart with three columns: the specific health
problem, the probable cause, and suggested reverse-thought forms.
Let me give you several examples from her work. The probable
causes of constipation: refusing to release old ideas, being stuck in
the past and sometimes stinginess. Her suggested affirmation to say
until that problem disappears is, "As I release the past, the new and
fresh and vital enter. I allow life to flow through me with ease."

Another Hay example, trouble with kidneys: probable causes are
criticism, disappointment, failure, shame and reacting like a kid.
Her affirmation: Divine right action is always taking place in my
life. Only good comes from each experience. It is safe to grow up.

Indeed, health problems need to be addressed on many levels.

As a shaman healer, when it is right for me to work with someone,
the first thing I do with the presenting problem is to consult Hay's
book. That brave person totally committed to getting well, first has
to do some serious introspection. Hay realized that negative, hurtful
thoughts, bitterness and ill will clutter up and impede the free flow

of the life principle, the Holy Spirit in the body.

Besides negative thinking and attitudes though, my own personal belief is that karma may have its impact. For example, in a former life not pictured on my illustration, I was an Egyptian pharaoh. My mission was to protect the sphinx by seeing to it that a wall was built to keep out rapidly approaching invaders. Time was short. My soldiers had to work extremely fast and hard. I felt a tremendous responsibility but no love. If a man slowed down and did not work faster after being hit with a barbed pole, I had one of my officers throw him over the wall. In the hypnotic regression, I could see the perfect face of the sphinx which was not yet damaged, and I got the impression that the thrown men were left to die. Now, my illnesses in this life could logically be karmic from that life. Whether I was a good guy or a bad guy, men got hurt and died and my Soul had to resolve that karma.

So we are probably trying to overcome negative karma as well as negative thoughts and attitudes! It is no wonder we sometimes struggle for health.

By the way, I have not seen the research that says one cup of coffee or caffeinated tea a day is going to hurt you. What kind of hot drink can you have after you have had your caffeine quota? Try heating unsalted tomato or vegetable juice in a cup in the micro-wave oven or in a pan on the stove. (I think microwaving is okay; others don't.) Along with that, for your enzymes, have some unsalt-ed, unprocessed nuts.

Definite compensations to mute karma and wrong thinking, besides those already mentioned, include yoga stretches, eating nutritionally, doing aerobic exercise and coming to terms with what society has done to you.

What are you letting society do to you?

What do I mean by such a question? Do you watch TV daily? For more hours than one–half an hour? Do you ever mindlessly watch program after program? Is the TV on when you eat? Do you eat lots of dairy products? Do you eat lots of sweets? Do you eat refined flours? Do you eat meat? Think about it. Do you think our leaders mind if we citizens are slugged down, numb, complacent, "fat and happy." That way we don't have the energy to get uppity and demand right action. Now, let this modern shaman step off her lecture platform and get on with some good stuff, yoga.

"How did you get interested in **YOGA**?" It was in 1986 that a friend took me to a weekend seminar at the Mt. Madonna Center near Watsonville, California. As we drove up to the buildings, a group of volleyball players were having a vigorous game. Most of the players were males in their late teens or early twenties. However, there was one figure playing in a white robe with grey/white hair and beard. He was spiking the ball, jumping, springing, laughing, and running exactly like the young players. I thought, "Whatever he has got, I want it." It turned out he was Baba Hari Dass, author of the ASH-TANGA YOGA PRIMER. See Basic Books.

Yoga is an ancient discipline that combines breathing exercises with body stretches and postures, along with internal body cleanliness principles. It is a rare day that I skip my stretches that returned my youthful flexibility. And I am convinced that the physical agility also makes for more mental flexibility. I teach yoga with enthusiasm.

One former yoga student told me of a write-up she saw in a newspaper stating that eighty-year-old people with equal time devoted to yoga can make as much progress as a forty-year old! Another former student told me that on a talk show, she saw a one-hundred-year-old woman doing yoga stretches! Wow!

Yoga is included in Dr. Dean Ornish's program, the program that within two weeks of starting, actually begins clearing the plaque that blocks heart function. (Other segments of his program are aerobic exercise, vegetarian eating (low-fat), meditation, breathing exercises and other relaxation techniques, learning interpersonal communication skills, all done in a support group. His Reversing Heart Disease Program is being approved by a few insurance companies!

As practiced in India, yoga sometimes involves the yogi drastically lowering pulse and metabolism.

"What is **AEROBIC EXERCISE** and what are the benefits?" Aerobic exercise can be any type that gets your heart beating at its target

rate. Find your individualized target rate in an exercise book's aerobic pulse chart. The latest thinking is that we can benefit from
twenty-five minutes a day, six days a week. That *seventh day of rest* is
equally important. There is wonderful gym equipment to help, special classes, or you can just do rapid walking/arm swinging!

I can think of eighteen benefits of aerobic exercise, but there are
more: Your exercise: strengthens heart muscles; improves blood
circulation; normalizes blood pressure; increases the diameter and
elasticity of arteries; creates new feeder arteries; increases basal
metabolism (so you burn more calories as you sleep); slows down
the aging process; lowers stomach acidity; decreases constipation;
reduces tension and other stress symptoms; helps with weight control; helps cleanse skin; slows resting and working heart rate; lowers
bad cholesterol and increases good cholesterol; strengthens bones;
releases life energy for work and play; increases the accessibility of
sexual orgasm for women; improves sleep; adds to physical and
mental flexibility and moves toxins out of your body.

"Is it important to become a **VEGETARIAN**?" Sai Baba said years
ago,
> If you are keen on spiritual life, eating meat is not worth
> while; but if you are keen on worldly life, it is all right.
> There is another spiritual reason. When you kill an animal,
> you give him suffering, pain, harm. God is in every creature,
> so how can you give such pain?"

A friend who visited Baba in India recently, told me as I went to
press that lately Baba has intoned, "If you want to be called my
devotee, you will not smoke and you will be a vegetarian."

Once you make the commitment to a vegetarian lifestyle, you need
to select several vegetarian cookbooks. Look for those that have
good information on nutrition as well as recipes.

Among other things, you need to learn about protein grams, the
controversial combining of foods to form a complete protein, calci-
um/magnesium intake and pH balance. It is easy to become too
alkaline on a vegetarian diet.

You may want to subscribe to <u>Vegetarian</u> <u>Times</u> magazine, P. O. Box

446, Mount Morris, IL 61054-8081. If possible, join a group that has potlucks. Otherwise, it may take several years to master the extensive nutritional information and compile a recipe collection.

It is a jolt to your body to change suddenly. Decreasing your meat intake over a six month period may work best for you, especially if you have type "O" blood. "A" types seem more natural vegetarians. If you start feeling weak or bad, try a little meat, then see what happens. Thank the animal for dying prematurely for you. If you can't make it all the way, you can take it far by drastically reducing the amount of meat you eat. It took me six tries over a dozen years to finally make it. Now, I only feel deprived when I see fish or shellfish on the menu.

It was worth it. Long-term research on vegetarian Seventh-Day Adventists show significantly longer life expectancies: eight years for women and twelve years for men. Compared to the general population, Adventists have just fifty-five percent of the heart disease, fifty-three percent of the strokes, thirteen percent of the cirrhosis of the liver, fifty-five percent of diabetes, forty-two percent of the peptic ulcers and twenty percent of the lung cancers (also probably because fewer of them smoke.).

Vegetarianism is mentioned in the Bible. Here is Daniel 8 – 17 from THE LIVING BIBLE, Tyndale House Publishers, Inc., Wheaton, Illinois, 60189, my favorite translation for understanding, because it is paraphrased in our modern English. This long excerpt is used with permission.

> . . . Daniel made up his mind not to eat the food and wine given to them by the king. He asked the superintendent for permission to eat other things instead. Now as it happened, God had given the superintendent a special appreciation for Daniel, and sympathy for his predicament. But he was alarmed by Daniel's suggestion.

> I'm afraid you will become pale and thin compared with the other youths your age," he said, and then the king will behead me for neglecting my responsibilities.

> Daniel talked it over with the steward who was appointed

by the superintendent to look after Daniel, Hananiah, Misha–el and Azasriah, and suggested a ten–day diet of only vegetables and water; then at the end of this trial period the steward could see how they looked in comparison with the other fellows who ate the king's rich food, and decide whether or not to let them continue their diet.

The steward finally agreed to the test. Well, at the end of the ten days, Daniel and his three friends looked healthier and better nourished than the youths who had been eating the food supplied by the king! So after that the steward fed them only vegetables and water, without the rich foods and wines!

God gave these four youths great ability to learn and they soon mastered all the literature and science of the time, and God gave to Daniel special ability in understanding the meanings of dreams and visions.

Today, your food industry feeds you the equivalent to the ancient king's rich fare. It is not the industry's fault. They have given you what you wanted. Unfortunately, it has perverted your appetite with foods overabundant in fats and refined sugars.

All we citizens would have to do is stop eating the junk food. As it piles up in warehouses, the food industry would quickly get the message. As a matter of fact, this process of getting the love into our manufactured food has already started.

David and I buy pleasant–tasting soy milk and dry packaged tofu (soy bean curd) by the cartoon, our major food sources of protein and calcium.

For you, if you are just starting, bucking the established trend is not easy, especially when you are invited to someone's home, go out to eat in a restaurant or go on a trip. The hardest aspect, though, is fighting your own food addictions.

Even cockroaches and ants won't eat refined white sugar, Americans biggest addiction. Read the best–selling SUGAR BLUES by William Dufty, Warner Books, 1975, a classic.

Attention-deficit children need to be taken off sugar, not put on a synthetic drug. These children are so innocent, they don't know that those sugar cereals, sodas, candy bars, cookies, cakes and pies are the source of their problem.

And take a look at infant formulas in the grocery store. It is not unusual for them to contain twenty-one percent sugar plus over thirty percent corn syrup solids. Oh my God. If there is any doubt about nursing babies to give them the best chance at life, these facts should convince you. Don't tell me you don't have enough milk. I nursed the twins. None of my babies ever had a bottle in their mouth! You can do it! But get help from the La Leche League.

If you eat more than one hundred calories of refined sugar (four lumps or two scant tablespoons), your blood sugar level is affected, it rises and you feel great. Within a short time though, your blood sugar drops at the same ratio it rose. You feel down. If you are lucky, you can find something quick to eat. Not only does this affect you soon after the excessive sugar intake, these sweets affect your appetite for the next few days, increasing it. Gobble, gobble, almost uncontrollable "pseudo hunger." However, eating just a little sugar, several teaspoons, once a day, is not going to give you blood sugar or gobble, gobble problems. Also, you can use *real* maple syrup, as I do, sparingly, a couple teaspoons, when you need something sweet on your cereal or in your tea.

"Sugar makes appetite. Fat makes fat." Fat goes through the stomach and intestinal walls; it doesn't need digesting. If not used for fuel (if you ate too much that meal), the fat goes into an already made, partially filled fat cell. If all fat cells are filled, your body makes more fat cells. Unfortunately, when you lose weight, the nuclei of all already created fat cells remain, calling out in hunger for up to a year. That is a major reason why most people regain lost weight, rapidly. You have to keep it off for a year for those fat cells to "shut up."

Fat cells are very much like little jugs with a lid. If the cell has been defatted lately, the "lid" is like the mouth of a hungry baby bird. If one fat cell gets a refill it tells all the other fat cells to "Wake up, it is feeding time." What a grapevine! If a person can hold their weight loss for a year the lids finally shut all the way down.

An article in the September 18, 1995 Time, tells us that India is
protesting our importation of foods overly rich in sugars and fats.
This is not the only country that is complaining. What products?
Sodas and fried chicken.

The best educational video on health I have ever seen was produced
by John Robbins, Diet for a New America; and there is a book by
the same name. Not only does it specifically show the health reasons for a vegetarian lifestyle, John dramatically presents the envi-
ronmental arguments. If you are a teacher, ask your administration
to purchase a copy.   For under $25, you can order a copy from
KCET Video, Lifeguides, 4401 Sunset Blvd, Los Angeles, CA 90027.

Ultimately though, no matter how well you take care of yourself,
eventually your Being decides that the present physical vehicle has
served its usefulness. "Tell us about DEATH."

If the prior paragraph was an unpleasant jolt, then you have not
become comfortable with your own death. Read on.

Romans 14:8: "Whether we live or whether we die, we belong to the
Lord." What we know as death is but a trip to new cities in other
dimensions.

As we have said, there is no death of the Being, just the, this–life
body/personality. We have done it thousands of times. It is instinc-
tual, this crossing between the two worlds. It is definitely not be be
feared. If we live an intelligent and healthy life, thus avoiding a
slow, painful disintegration of the body, we slip out easily. It is a
relief to leave the denseness of this physical plane. Current–day
philosopher Ram Dass said, "It is like slipping out of shoes that are
too tight."

If we can become completely comfortable with the fact that we are
going to die (all that we don't know is the time), this leaves us free
to enjoy this precious life.

Ironically, when we are very comfortable with our death, we still
want to live!

If someone you know is suicidal, it is definitely not their Being that wants to leave. It is their ego–mind that is stuck. If suicide is cho–sen, the Being may spend some time in the lower astral plane, come to earth again, and butt up against the same problems. (Their Being, like yours and mine, will eventually progress; suicide is a detour.) If we have influence with that person, we should try to help them stay, giving them human support while they regain a more positive frame of mind.

It is common for a Being after death to stay around the earth plane for a few days. Long before my near–death experience, I remember a "non–religious" friend telling me about his father's death: "I got a call saying Dad was dying. I got on a plane right away, but he had slipped away before I arrived. At the family home, I bedded down for the night, had just relaxed. Suddenly, there was an exceptionally clear but transparent "image" of my Dad 'sitting' at the end of the bed. He communicated telepathically with me. 'Son, I am just fine.' Then he was gone."

What my relaxed friend saw was his father's astral or Light body; he had just passed from one state of visibility to another. There are many layers for us to lose before we are ready to come back in another body. Leaving our body is just the first heavy layer, gone. After death, the Being progressively discards its sheaths of outer bodies as it moves upwards.

Ideally, the Being itself and its remaining "bodies" know to leave through the top of the head. The astral shell or body has its own senses.

Depending on the needs of the Being, there is a "Being state" between lives varying from a few months to thousands of years. S/he doesn't have to come back. However, our Planet of the Cross has been one of the best schools in the universes to grow. And that is one major reason most of you have repeatedly decided to come here. Out of body, you know the potential. In body, you are blind–ed by the culture, your parents and friend's picture of life, your karma, and the animal body you inhabit. No wonder you forget, at least some of the time, that you are a spiritual Being having a human experience!

(Recall that "it" means something that is *neither* male nor female. My word, "s/he" means *both* male and female. Your Soul carries both potentials, as does God.)

When a Being is completely purified after its journeys and has lived in God only knows how many inner and outer dimensions, only then can it get into the highest heaven and receive a glorious welcome back by the Godhead. Many Beings have chosen to stay permanently in wonderful other areas of heaven. But because of their high Soul energy, they might make a different decision tomorrow to seek the highest place.
There were eight years between Sai Baba's last incarnation and his current life.

By the way if you are *God-realized*, like Sai Baba, you may chose to have a **conscious death**. That is when the Being does not create a terminal accident or illness, but just permanently leaves the body of s/he's own accord. It is my belief that, perhaps, those of us who survive the ascension will have this choice, too.

All Beings need to go home after each incarnation to get "recalibrated," attend more celestial schools, and visit a planet or two and prepare for another life, if desired by the Being. Family and friends who have lost a loved one often hold them to the earth plane by their thoughts and longings. If we hold them, we are inhibiting the loved one's Being growth. Opinions vary, but two years to grieve is the max.

No need to hold on, we see everyone again on the other side. Even those from past lives, whom we will recognize – even our "enemies," whom there, we will love!

What do we get to take with us? Our Soul's energy, our capacity for love, and according to one teacher, our knowledge.   (I don't think he meant intellectual facts, probably just our knowingness, but I am not sure.)

If someone you love crosses over, your grieving will be made easier if you have acquired metaphysical realizations. Nevertheless, even though the loss may not take the usual two years to grieve, you will still need to healthfully loop and reloop through these healing phases before you are at peace: shock, denial, panic, anxiety, depression, sorrow, anger, powerlessness, guilt, disorganization, hope, healing, and reinvestment.

Dearly beloved Being, eternally a ray of God, as we end Chapter 2 on our COSMIC MAP journey, here is a reminder of the main realization about death, in lines from a poem by an anonymous author: "Do not stand at my grave and cry. I am not there, I did not die."

CHAPTER 3

You Have Traveled in the Dark and the Light

To every thing there is a season, and a time
for every purpose under the heaven:
A time to be born, and a time to die;
a time to plant,
and a time to pluck up that which is planted;
a time to kill, and a time to heal;
a time to break down, and a time to build up;
a time to weep, and a time to laugh;
a time to mourn, and a time to dance;
a time to cast away stones,
and a time to gather stones together;
a time to embrace,
and a time to refrain from embracing;
a time to get, and a time to lose;
a time to keep, and a time to cast away;
a time to rend, and a time to sow;
a time to keep silent, and a time to speak;
a time to love, and a time to hate;
a time of war, and a time of peace.

— *Ecclesiastes 3:1-8*

This book of the Bible was compiled
by the person(s) occupying the office
of the "keeper of proverbs" about the
end of the 3rd century, B.C.

TERMS AND PHILOSOPHY

Dearly beloved, we have completed two-thirds of our journey.   I hope you have an increasing excitement about the study of meta-physics, whether you are new or have been on the path for a long time.

I consider myself a successful teacher only when my students con-tinue studying the subject after a class is over.   If you feel you have a fair mastery of the material you have read, a good place to go after **COSMIC MAP** would be a book listed under "Advanced Books;" specifically, the one by Godfrey Ray King, THE MAGIC PRESENCE.

If you would like to get a preview of the concepts in the last one-third of our Cosmic Map journey, see Appendix I under the heading of Chapter 3.   We will start with some ancient history of the Planet of the Cross.   We will end our journey with a summary of the old and new prophesies plus a sum-up of the spiritual practices to grow your Soul.   And before you finish reading, you will have a pretty good idea of what the extraterrestrials are up to.   Let's get started by taking a look way, way back into time, a time that did not get recorded in our history books – yet.

"What can you tell us about the ancient history of planet **EARTH?**" Dearly beloved child of God, this is quite a story!   We will have to address the answer in two segments: (1) the history of the physical earth and (2) the history of our physical bodies along with the histo-ry of the consciousness within the physical body.

After I had written what follows, my husband, David, was reading DIVINE MEMORIES OF SATHYA SAI BABA by Diana Baskin, Birth Day Publishing Company, P. O. Box 7722, San Diego, California 92107.   Baskin, with different members of her family, was invited to live at the ashram in Puttaparthi, India, during the 1970s.   They were privileged to spend time being close to Baba.

Baskin tells about a Baba-appointed devotee in the 1970s reading from an *unpublished* book written by Sai Baba himself.   It was not published, he had said, because the world was not yet ready for the information.   The readings talked about "the creation, the solar sys-tem and planet, and the decline of humanity among other topics."

I have to wonder what his book says. Would it be anything like the following I have put together for you?

Do you remember that I mentioned earlier you might need to con-sider COSMIC MAP as science fiction. Well, here goes. Just keep what resonates with you. Obviously, everything I put here resonated with me.

Although it seems like a detour, we are learning this history in unusual ways from special Beings. What follows comes from Jim J. Hurtak, PhD, Sheldon Nidle, Drunvalo Melchizedek, the Edgar Cayce readings and Dr. Norma Milanovich. And there are others; these are just those I have read or heard.

Hurtak is an earth human, the reincarnation of Jacob, who was taken by **Metatron** into God's presence and returned here to write and teach. Metatron is the incredible, higher–level spiritual Being who is responsible for supplying the pure and unmixed Light to our outer world and is the inventor of the electron. Earlier, I told you about Hurtak's book, THE KEYS OF ENOCH, listed in the back of COSMIC MAP under Advanced Books.

Sheldon Nidle is a channeler, not yet mentioned. He and his sister have been visited since they were children by extraterrestrial Beings from the star complex of Sirius. (If you haven't studied astronomy, the Sirian complex is in our sky.) Nidle came close to earning a PhD; however, his distracting contacters became more urgent. Nidle worked with writer–devout channeler, Virginia Essene, to produce in 1994 perhaps the most amazing book I have ever read. It is extremely clear and thorough: YOU ARE BECOMING A GALACTIC HUMAN, Spiritual Education Endeavors Publishing Company, 1556 Halford Avenue #288, Santa Clara, CA 95051. Nidle was the chan-neler; Essene was the scribe and also asked and had answered many astute questions. Through their book, we are introduced to **Washta**.

Washta is an incredibly evolved Being who lives on Sirius. He is currently head of a six–Being interplanetary council, The Sirian Council, operating under the spiritual hierarchy. (One of this com-mittee's members serves on another committee headed by Metatron.) The Sirian Counsel and its work set into action the incredible events of August 7, 1972 which saved the body of the Planet of the Cross

and all its inhabitants; this true story is coming up as soon as I finish with the ground work. As mentioned before, this intervention
for the Planet of the Cross had been okayed by the Galactic
Federation.

The Galactic Federation was formed four and a half million years
ago to prevent the powerful interdimensional dark forces from dom-
inating the galaxy. Today there are almost 200,000 members. Will
our planet soon become a member?

Drunvalo Melchizedek is a **walk–in** arriving April 10, 1972. A walk–
in is an extraordinary Being who, under an agreement from the spiritual hierarchy, agrees to come here for a special assignment in this
way: A living person, who has already completed its Being's work
this lifetime, agrees and is rewarded for walking out of his or her
body at the prime of life. The walk–in takes over the body, life, education and karma. There is a long period of adjustment before the
walk–in's work can begin; no wonder, her earth body felt like concrete to one walk–in, who was familiar with a much–less dense
body! (This getting up to spiritual speed method is faster, though,
than going through the wait in line, pick a body, get born, go
through the third grade – again – method!)

Advanced Being Drunvalo from the thirteenth dimension, had a
very bumpy, approximately million earth–year trip in and out of his
Light body and other bodies. He even spent a year attached to a
Sirian whale (who telepathed earth history to him). At one time, he
was given an adult male Sirian body and had many other experiences. Drunvalo tells his stories in his Flower of Life workshops, but
you can get some of them beautifully organized in Bob Frissell's
NOTHING IN THIS BOOK IS TRUE, BUT IT'S EXACTLY HOW THINGS
ARE, North Atlantic Books, P. O. Box 12327, Berkeley, CA 94712.

Author Bob Frissell is a conscious human, a former teacher, a very
clear thinker, a rebirther who attended Drunvalo's workshop as a
student, then he both went to work for Drunvalo and managed to
quickly get our walk–in's remarkable stories into print. In fact, reading these last two books plus the one in the next paragraph is highly, highly recommended; they will quickly bring you up to date.

Dr. Norma Milanovich channels Beings who identify themselves as

Ascended Masters and Celestials from the Galactic Command. She is responsible for seeing that WE THE ARCTURIANS (A TRUE STORY) was published: Athena Publishing, Mossman Center Ste. 206, 7410 Montgomery Blvd., N. E., Albuquerque, NM 87109–1574.

To sum up, we are getting our history from contemporary earth humans: one who traveled in his Light body to the highest heaven, another who hears telepathically from the head of the Sirian Counsel, an advanced–dimension walk–in, a trance psychic (Edgar Cayce), a hypnotherapist, a former college teacher who channels advanced Beings from the star Arcturus, and an anonymous Mt. View woman you will hear from later. And there is another, a Being who used to live under the earth!

Our physical planet is extremely old, perhaps as old as five hundred million years. Pole shifts have occurred every twelve thousand, five hundred to thirteen thousand years. At least two continents have been destroyed and totally submerged by Being wars. Extraterrestrials have come from all over the Milky Way Galaxy, combining with each other through genetic experiments, sexual, and asexual means, producing bodies for Beings. Physically, it has been tough for Mother Earth, who according to profound seers, is the body for a Being of a different ilk than we. (Other planets and stars house this type of Being.)

This type of information has not been available to us because the Akashic Records were either sealed or broken five and and a half million years ago, which according to Dr. Hurtak is the real age of the sphinx. Cayce readings indicate civilized man has a ten and one–half million year history.

In more "recent" times, the Arcturians had the first space colony here. Later, enlightened Beings, Hyborneas, came a million years before their civilization was destroyed, one million years before Jesus.

Our current–day seers have seen two past continents that present–day scientists deny: **Lemuria** (900,000 B.C. to 25,000 B. C.) and **Atlantis** (500,000 B. C. to 15,000 B.C.). Both larger than any current continent, they were eventually destroyed as was the biosphere, two separate globe–shaped filaments of ice, held in place by crystals around the world strategically placed, that kept the earth atmosphere perfect (with no weather variations). These destructions, (including the destruction of a second moon), done on a horrible scale, partially with nuclear weapons, caused the great rains and the Noah flood.

After the flood, Atlantians rebuilt. They developed huge, reflective crystals to supply energy which powered all sorts of flying and land vehicles. They invented among other wonders, laser beams, long-distance photography and electronics.

Lemuria, a fully conscious civilization, sat roughly where the Hawaiian Islands are today; Atlantis was centralized (colonies in later years) on a large continent that, if still there on today's globe, would sit in the Atlantic Ocean between North America, South America and Africa.

That was a very rough summation of our physical earth and some of the Beings that have been attracted here. Now the physical bodies: They have varied from gross/physical bodies like our own third-dimensional vehicle in different heights up to twelve feet tall. The different skins may have been like Reptoids and Dinoids, scaly. Plus the Edgar Cayce readings reported feathers, tails, claws and hooves. Different noses from none at all to huge, with different eye structures. A variety of head shapes, the most evolved, intelligent and enlightened, had a long, rounded "cone head."

At some time, God intervened and gave *each skin color* a perfect "Adam and Eve."

Washta has channeled that part of the **fall of man** was the outcome of the inter-galactic and intercontinental wars: our human body was genetically reduced, a mutant! A mutant with a muted ability to achieve higher consciousness! He says soon, this mutant, we ourselves, will become something quite different, excitingly improved with a semi-etheric body and heightened psychic ability. Like Sai Baba, we humans will be able to rejuvenate our own bodies, be virtually ageless, and able to change our bodies with thoughts (thought forms). From homo sapiens, we will become **homo novas**.

Drunvalo was told by the whale about advanced Beings from a

planet with an elliptical orbit taking three thousand, six hundred years to make one complete circle of their sun. Called the Nefilim, they came here for gold and created earth bodies to work in the gold mines in Africa. Their earth body crossed with Homo erectus to form the specie body we inhabit today, another reason for the fall of man and our dense consciousness. Thus our bodies are extraterrestrial bodies. The wars and the great flood wiped out most physical evidence.

Besides the Arcturians, Hyborneas and the Nefilim, the Lemurians, highly conscious, were a **starseed** civilization. The larger Atlantian nation was mixed; the dark forces going there from other areas of the galaxy eventually caused it to go amuck. Edgar Cayce said that one reason Atlantis was finally submitted to earthquakes and overwhelmed by the sea was that it became so wicked.

Before the destructions, the most highly conscious Beings migrated all over the earth. There are speculations that the cultures that flowered overnight, ancient Greece, the Inca Empire, and the Mayan civilization as examples, were started either by newly arrived extraterrestrials or by migrating Lemurians and Atlantians of high consciousness.

During this time, all evolved humans were psychic through the pituitary gland. The sub-humans, the Biblical sons of Belial, which crossed with humans for the fall of man, were not evolved in this way. That is when our specie body lost it.

Besides migrating to other continents, millions of descendants of the enlightened earth Beings live under the earth today in enclosed ecosystems! Three sources cite this: Saint Germain in the MAGIC PRESENCE, Hurtak and Cayce.

The reason our scientists cannot see current civilizations on planets and stars such as Venus, Sirius, Arcturus – now the most advanced race in our galaxy – the Pleiades, Orion and others – is that they are looking from a limited third-dimension mind, with limited third-dimension eyes, with third-dimension technology into fourth-, fifth- and higher-dimension consciousnesses. They probably have to go to a bit of trouble to intentionally reveal themselves to us. Or it may be as simple as turning on a light switch?

Indeed, we are going to need a new science! That is probably the reason our very own brother and sister underground Beings haven't been discovered in mass, they are fourth- and higher dimensional Beings.

Washta tells us that *the fourth-dimension is a time portal through which the third-dimension passes into the fifth.* In the fifth, sixth and the seventh dimensions, the laws of Earth science and physics don't apply.

Another newsletter, World Ascension Network, attempted to keep abreast of our consciousness evolution. The Spring/Summer 1993 edition had a lengthy article listing subterranean cities in Brazil, the Himalayas, India, Mt. Shasta in California, and on the border of Mongolia and China. Descriptions of some of the inhabitants' Beingness, their appearances, and lifestyles make for interesting reading. The information mostly comes from two hundred eighty-two-year-old Sharula, a former underground inhabitant, appointed by her people to be one of the ambassadors for a future uniting with the outside world. She says the gentle, loving Beings will stop being secretive when we have no more wars or even judgmental thoughts! A most devout friend of mine who has been in Sharula's presence says she looks to be in her thirties. She underwent temporary cellular change to trim her twelve-feet high frame down to an average female human height.

Besides extraterrestrials and Beings like Sharula who go to a lot of trouble to communicate with us, we can be so grateful for the egoless, sweet, happy Drunvalo, *our* walk-in, for bringing knowledge. It would be like you or me going back to an insect existence to help them. (He says memory of his home is blocked; it would be too painful to remember, but he does *know* he liked it better than here.) We have to honor them; these extraordinary Beings are the subject of much scorn and criticism from those stuck in closed-minded systems.

Drunvalo's story which I promised you of why the earth is not a crisp, burned-dead planet follows: *This is the major reason why psychic predictions made after this date have not been accurate:*

Some of our scientists and a few in government had seen it coming. They didn't tell us because they didn't know what to do. On August

7, 1972, our sun produced four massive solar flares with two and one-half million mile-an-hour winds. Lucky for us, the Galactic Command had seen it coming, too. However, unlike our truly helpless government, they decided they had better try to do something, even though they didn't know if it would work.

Our Milky Way Galaxy's hierarchy, with Jesus in command, leaves the Souls on the Planet of the Cross with free will as long as events are not destroying the chance for life. They intervene reluctantly, with great care if something is destroying that chance.

With permission from the spiritual hierarchy and from their advanced consciousness friends, with the Sirians in the lead, the Pleiadians, the Aldebarans [I know nothing about the Aldebarans], the Arcturians and others set up space ships around our earth. From a higher dimension, they shot laser light from ship to ship, billions of tiny refracting light beams connected to all humans and animals. They placed a protective hologram around the earth which was later expanded to take in our entire solar system, our sun and its planets. I am sure we will learn more details of how this historic intervention worked soon.

And other friendly interventions: they have just started to repair our ozone layer and to work on the planetary dimensional grids damaged by nuclear activity, both bombs and power plants. They are also working so our planet will not have to undergo another pole shift. "Why?" Because some of our specie genetics come from them, and they love us very much. They consider us their "children."

The major reason why our wonderful consciousness heroes and heroines are able to do their work is that timewise, we are at the beginning of a Kali Yuga. A **Kali Yuga** is a period of time when the earth and all planets move closer to the center of the galaxy. There is a twenty-six-thousand-year cycle. (When earth and inhabitants move away from the center of the galaxy, they fall spiritually asleep. If our solar system maintains its present system of rotations, this Kali Yuga will end in the year 3127.)

Beings from advanced dimensions can shift down their vibrations to come here. Great mystery civilizations like Sumeria, Babylonia and Egypt were created by advanced Beings from other planets representing the **Light brotherhood**.

Drunvalo tells us the great pyramid was built in a day, using a space vehicle starting from top down, mastering gravity. Cayce said the builders took one hundred years, although, to my knowledge, he didn't refer to them as extraterrestrials. The stones were floated in air.

(The time difference building the great pyramid is one example of an inconsistency. There are others which you will find when you read the suggested books. But the similarities vastly predominate. And my interpretation undoubtedly has some holes in it. Plus each dimension's inhabitants may interpret "time" differently.)

"Are these ancient past patterns, the dark forces warring against the Light forces, ignorance against knowledge, destined to be replayed over and over and over?" Perhaps for a few more years, but in the cosmic scheme of things, Drunvalo says Lucifer and his **dark brotherhood** are giving up!

In March, 1994, at the spring equinox, Drunvalo spoke before a conference of spiritual seekers at Banff Spring Hotel, Canada. He enlightened us about Lucifer, the powerful angel who decided to use the holy spirit and be better than God.

"Is this proud, rebellious archangel responsible for every negative thing that has happened on the planet?" I don't know. Here is a brief summary of Drunvalo's enlightening explanation.

God hasn't stopped this **duality** or **polarity** consciousness but instead has made use of it to make everything work together for love: *the Light uses the dark. This is done when the Light transmutes darkness to produce an even more incredible Light!* Since early 1991, *if the dark force resists, it is actually giving energy to the Light.* There are infinite combinations and connections of Light.

The forces of these two brotherhoods, the dark and the Light, have tended to balance each other out so that our evolution takes place at exactly the right pace! Once our consciousness has reached a certain level, the problems will heal themselves. Now is the time to work on yourself to get your individualization of the collective in shape for the evolutionary leap.

Drunvalo has asked us to pray for a way for the dark forces, too.

In the Flower of Life Workshop videotapes, Drunvalo speaks of the time Lucifer actually visited him. Basically, all that happened was that Lucifer wanted to know why Drunvalo was here and what he was up to. He has left Drunvalo alone, proof to me that he doesn't want to give the Light force any energy by resisting it.

You can inquire about the Flower of Life Workshops by writing Bob Frissell, North Atlantic Books, P. O. Box 12327, Berkeley, CA 94712. They teach a special, advanced meditation to be used to help through the "birth canal" into the next dimension or dimensions once the shift starts.

Some extraterrestrial Beings have had advanced technological civilizations but still serve the dark brotherhood. *So technological advancement is not synonymous with spiritual advancement.*

A Mt. View, California, hypnotherapist, whom I promised could remain anonymous, says she was taken into an extraterrestrial vehicle in 1994. She was there to be the witness to the signing of a treaty with a physically ugly form of extraterrestrial named the Insectoids (I have seen drawings of them produced after abductions). Acting on our behalf were some friendly extraterrestrials representing the Galactic Federation. It seems that for millions of years, the Insectoids have lived off the vibrations of our negativism here, particularly fear. In the treaty, they have promised not to instill fear anymore in order to get the by–product, their "food;" but they can, as long as we go on producing bad vibes, continue to live off the vibrations of our human–produced negativism, including that fear!

We need to continue to be cautious. These Reptoids would not be the first Beings to break a peace treaty. And even though Drunvalo says the Greys left in 1992, they were very secretive and could conceivably come back.

Some negative extraterrestrials *are* still around. One of my best women friends in Lake County called me in November of 1993. With great excitement and worry, she said, "My seventeen–year–old daughter and her girl friend were driving down a country road. A strange "space vehicle" appeared over their heads. They raced home, and it followed them. They felt an ominous energy coming from it. It terrorized them. – What would you suggest we do?"

I told my friend, "Drop everything and bring your daughter out to see me." They arrived quickly. What I did was to teach them some Hebrew chants. They in turn taught the chants to the daughter's friend.

One of the chants proclaims: Holy, Holy, Holy is the Lord God of Hosts. Another calls upon God's power and Light. If *you* are ever accosted, use words like these, and tell the Being "If you don't serve the Light, leave." Stamp your foot hard. They may use tricks to make you think you are doing with your free will *what they want you to do.*

The girls started chanting when walking or driving alone and when home alone. My friend's daughter was visited again the next night, this time in her room. She started to sing the chants and the Beings left. They did not bother her again.

If you have been meditating awhile, you will intuitively know from the vibration whether the Being is here to serve *or* here for some negative reason.

So I have painted a very, very sketchy picture of extraterrestrial activity from the beginning of Planet of the Cross history until the end of 1995.

At the end of this book, I will talk about the various theories and prophesies of when and how the shift, the birth, is expected to occur.

So we have been just one of probably billions of planets in the Universes where Beings can go to school (**do dramas to grow the Soul**). However, there is admiration by extraterrestrial Beings for those schooled on the Planet of the Cross. The atmosphere here has been dense and Being growth is relatively fast. We live a life that is a series of dramas that, hopefully, grow our Soul.

The dramas are spiritual hurdles, challenges that stretch us and give us compassion.

Chapter 3 continues the foundation work for building a metaphysical philosophy which helps in the *conscious use of the dramas* for spiritual growth and preparation for whatever the Seventh Golden Spiritual Age brings.

"From the foreword, plus Appendices A through C, it seems as if you have a wonderful family and have had a rich and varied professional life. Has it been all 'peaches and cream?'" My life has been extremely blessed. But believe me, before I understood what was going on, I was intensely involved in many, many dramas.

I gained much insight into what the dramas really are when I took that class on developing intuition from the devout psychic. She told her true story:

> I was at a PTA meeting. The people there were arguing and backbiting. The general atmosphere was tense; each talked for their favorite project, not listening to anyone else.
>
> I became bored and astralprojected out of my body. From my higher self, I looked down upon the meeting. Then I became aware that the higher selves of everyone were up there with me, and *we were all having a great time, laughing and playing.*

I didn't want this book to be my crying rag. But briefly, here are some of my own dramas, that if told in detail would make one of those delightful boo–and–hiss melodramas. First, in 1983, my then-previously devoted husband decided to move in with a woman he had just met six weeks earlier. He divorced me as he was going out the door. In 1984, my GS–12 graduate school teaching job and career disappeared because I was betrayed by some colluding colleagues, including several powerful military officers. But the most difficult years lay ahead.

Indeed, about that time, one of my identical twin sons spontaneously came up with a new nickname for his mom, "Mama Drama!"

One situation involved a con man who took my life savings of $280,000, signed my name to legal papers, and then initiated law suits against me.

In 1989, I entered psychotherapy to try to cope with what I allowed the years of drama to do to my mind and body. By that time, I was extremely frustrated and angry at the con. He wouldn't show up in court to facilitate the law suits he had initiated; the many delays were infuriating!

The psychotherapist, a psychiatrist, board certified and profoundly psychic, hypnotized me and skillfully took my consciousness to a higher dimension to meet the higher self of the con man. At that level of consciousness, on that "channel," I *just loved* the con. Unconditional love energy was flowing out of my chest. I came out of the hypnotic regression in a loving haze, totally amazed!

Incidentally, since that time, I have, on the street, seen several men whom I thought were the "con." Both times, I excitedly started to run after the man like he was an old buddy – before I realized it wasn't him!

I have been told that when we are out of body in one of the higher dimensions, we love everybody unconditionally. And these two stories of reality on a higher vibration verified this must-learn principle. Isaiah 42:16: "I will lead them in paths that they have not known; I will make darkness light before them, and crooked things straight."

Indeed, problems teach humility and reverence! I can't change the world much, but I can change my approach to it! Someone said that our lives are a creative ordeal! Trust that the shattering that life gives you is exactly what you need to make you let go of everything so that enlightenment or Self-realization can happen for you.

I wish I could say that I never get hooked into new dramas after these realizations. But I am much better at recognizing them. At the very least, I know I am allowing myself to be engaged in a drama dance.

The Universe will go on presenting us dramas until we learn to love everything for what it is. We master some realizations and go into a spiritual expansion. Then we attract to us the person who will teach us the missing elements in our learning. Then we hit another spiritual contraction, and the inevitable depression, **the dark night of the Soul.** Philosopher Alan Watts said, "You have to go off to know when you are on." Contractions are not a backward step; they are an integration.

In John 15:2 Jesus is quoted as saying, "I am the true Vine, and my Father is the Gardener. He lops off every branch that doesn't produce. And he prunes those branches that bear fruit for even larger crops. He has already tended you by pruning you back for greater strength and usefulness . . ."

The incoming newer consciousness is in a violent stage of labor. The spiritual path demands much of us. Drunvalo says that one year in the 1990s is like three-hundred *other* years!

There is oh so much more going on than we can understand. One example: Cayce said that the militant blacks are the reincarnation of former slave owners of earlier America.

Whatever our own dramas, they test us and teach us. We can keep saying positively, "I am doing this for a reason. I pray to know what is really going on." Be assured that you will never experience anything that at your Soul level, you have not accepted. And always assume you are moving. Don't compare your progress with anyone else's experiences or progress. Your path and its dramas are uniquely yours.

I wear a jewelry cross to indicate that I am from this dense Planet of the Cross. By the way, I also wear the cross to indicate I am trying to "cross out" my ego.

I just loved it the day a visiting spiritual friend said his goodbye in this way: "So long, Janis. I have to leave now and go do another drama!"

"Is that what **THE SPIRITUAL PATH** is then, just what we attract and master?

This is true, and of course, the path includes our formal teachers, events, people and friends that both support and challenge us.

Are there times of discouragement? Sure. The Dalai Lama, the current chief monk of Tibet, was asked "Do you ever get off the path?" His answer, "Yes." Question, "What do you do?" His quick answer, "Get back on!"

It isn't all struggle. Our efforts do get affirmed. I asked in prayer one day, "Lord, is my heart pure enough to withstand the love energy that is on its way in?" My answer came a few weeks later in a Mother's Day card picked by one of my fundamental Christian daughters–in–law. It said, "Purer than gold, softer than a flower petal . . . is your heart!"

We are tried, stretched until we master the lessons our Soul has committed itself to learn, this time around.

"A monumental dark–sided event that has mystified people is **WAR**. What is going on metaphysically?" When the collective unconscious gets heavy with the totality of people's unresolved anger, fear, hate, resentment, bitterness, greed, uncaringness, feelings of revenge, and other bombastic emotions, a war will explode somewhere.

"Behind the scene," here is an example of how it works. Years ago, before the Berlin Wall blockade came down, Sai Baba left his body one day, astralprojecting, taking two earth humans with him. All were astralprojecting in their Light bodies. One of them was the founder and former owner of the Hard Rock Cafes, Isaac Tigret.

Tigret shared his experience: Out of their physical bodies, the three of them headed toward Russia. Baba pointed out a black mass over *all* of the Soviet Union. The gigantic mass was dark and menacing, with lighting bolts running through it. Baba told his two travelers that this was the accumulation of thought forms from Russia's history back to before the czars. This huge, amorphous, ugly mass was mostly composed of the people's *fears!* Sai Baba showed the two how to stick holes in this terrifying form; it eventually dissipated and disappeared.

So individual's spiritual growth is connected to planetary peace. Better educated, can we expect an Avatar to go around cleaning up after us?

The old saying, "If everyone swept their own doorstep, the whole world would be clean" applies here. Karmic dissolution is *our* job. If everyone had known to clean up their own part of the collective unconscious, there would be no war.

Collective thoughts have great power for evil or good.

"So is **PEACE** just the absence of negative thought forms?" Sai Baba is more specific, "Peace can only be won the hard way, by eliminating violence and greed from the hearts of individuals."

The other consideration is that peace is formed or constructed in the collective consciousness as individuals and groups say prayers for peace, meditate, and chant with energy focused at the human heart. Remember, thoughts seek compatible energy or vibrations because all energy is in a state of motion and seeks similar energy.

"You have repeatedly quoted from the **HOLY BIBLE** and yet have never really addressed this book?" I had an early passion for the Bible. At one point in the few years that as a young child I was allowed to go to Methodist Sunday School, the Sunday school teachers had a contest. I intuitively knew the Bible had Light, and I badly wanted my very own copy. All I had to do was memorize the names of the old testament plus new testament books in order; then I would be rewarded by receiving a free copy.

Just at the time I was getting close, I suffered a serious sunburn over most of my body. Unable to tolerate heavy clothing because of the pain, I begged and received permission to go for another try – wearing my own practically designed costume, just panties and a gossamer cape! Determined, I ignored those kids making fun of me. I wasn't successful that Sunday; however, within several weeks I had my very own Bible! I kept it into high school, but atheist relatives pressed upon me to throw it away, and I did. I still remember my sharp sadness as it hit the bottom of an empty metal wastebasket.

I believe the Bible is the word of God. However, every living human is a chip off the old block. So technically, what anyone says is the word of God. It was the best that could be gotten through the level of consciousness at that time. It does contain Light but is often difficult because of lack of knowledge of the history, culture and religious tradition the writing comes from. And truly, now is not that much different. Books like COSMIC MAP are just the best effort of a human or humans.

Both the Bhagavad–gita, and of course the Bible, are not single books, but a collection of many authors' writings over perhaps a thousand–year period.

The Bible is also tarnished by denominational interpretations, mis-translations, latent remembrances, and human egos (most who recorded were not of Avatar level, God–realized or even Self–real-ized). And language was a stumbling block. Was Elijah fed by ravens or Arabs in Kings 1:17? Ancient Hebrew was written in con-sonants without vowel sounds; the meaning was left to oral tradi-tion.

In 1991, an almost 200–member group of Bible scholars met in Sonoma, California. After six years of voting, they ruled out *almost eighty percent of the words attributed to Jesus in the Gospels* and "emerged with a picture of a prophet–sage who "told parables and made pithy comments."

I now own six Bibles, the notable ones being: (1) the King James Version (2) the HOLY BIBLE FROM ANCIENT EASTERN MANU-SCRIPTS, by George M. Lamsa; Lamsa knew the ancient languages and did his own translation and (3) THE LIVING BIBLE, Tyndale Publishers, Wheaton, Illinois, 1971, paraphrased for easy reading in our modern English. The latter is the one I would recommend if you are going to own only one Bible. But I will soon own seven. My lovely, visiting Jehovah Witnesses just talked me into their ver-sion, which they say, has replaced the word "God" back into over seven thousand places where it has been left out by translators.

It is fun to compare the verses. Here is one example, St. Matthew, 20:23–24 in the King James version: "Then Jesus said unto his disci-ples, Verily I say unto you, That a rich man shall hardly enter into the kingdom of heaven. And again I say unto you, It is easier for a camel to go through the eye of a needle, than for a rich man to enter into the kingdom of God."

In the Holy Bible from Ancient Eastern Manuscripts, "Jesus then said to his disciples, Truly I say to you, It is difficult for a rich man to enter into the kingdom of heaven. Again I say to you, It is easier for a rope to go through the eye of a needle, than for a rich man to enter into the kingdom of God."

The Living Bible version, "Then Jesus said to his disciples, "It is almost impossible for a rich man to get into the Kingdom of Heaven. I say it again – it is easier for a camel to go through the eye of a needle than for a rich man to enter the Kingdom of God."

By the way, Hinduism teaches that there is nothing ungodly about becoming very wealthy. However, remember first that the wealth is held in trust from God; and secondly, it must be used rightly, returning part to help fellow humans.

Many of the concepts found in both the Old and New Testaments stem directly from Zoroastrianism (Persia), although that religion is never mentioned.

The thousand–plus paged ILLUSTRATED DICTIONARY AND CON-CORDANCE OF THE BIBLE, 1986, published by The Jerusalem Publishing House, Ltd., Jerusalem, reprinted in the United States by The Reader's Digest Association, objectively explains each book of the Bible. To explain and defend the Bible, I would have to do it Book by Book. This immense task has already been done!

Secular groups sometime produce a revision; for example in 1750 A. D., the Catholic and British Bishop Challoner oversaw one effort.

Some of my metaphysical friends, as seriously committed as I am in trying to max their level of spiritual evolvement (maturing and energizing their Being) in their current body/minds, have completely given up on the Bible. One example they believe: The concept of reincarnation, a tenet of Hindu and Buddhist religions, was by a small vote, taken out of the Bible at the Council of Constantinople, in 534 A.D. (My view on this as given earlier still stands, "Reincarnation was so taken for granted, nothing needed to be said.") However, undoubtedly, other material was deleted at that conference. And perhaps added?

There are schools of thought around the Bible being written in codes. If you want to pursue the ideas for word codes, contact the Unity School of Christianity, Unity Village, Missouri. For number codes, try the Academy of Future Science.

We can and do get bogged down in dogmatic arguments. The life of the spirit is alive, energetic and charged. Get the life of the spirit into you through practices. Use the Bible for its abundant wisdom, poetry, comfort and historical references. Although not pure because of third–dimension limitations, the more devout we become, the more certain citations will resonate.

In Appendix G is a list of verses with metaphysical interpretations, Scriptural References for Mystical Phenomena. Using this list to become a fundamentalist's adversary would be destructive. People behave badly once they become adversaries.

Rather use this list for inspiration. Another list for comfort, Appendix H, is Scriptural References for Troubled Times.

It is impossible for me to believe that our God would go silent after the Christian Bible was put together in its current form. I cannot believe we would not be given new information as the spiritual climate changes. That is why I read, attend workshops, listen to visionaries, constantly ask God questions, and listen to my own Being and its higher–self aspect(s).

In the primitive Christian church, teachers and preachers were filled with the power of spirit, doing many of the things that Jesus had done, healing the sick, prophesying, seeing visions, communicating from on high. But some of the formal churches have discouraged these practices, relying more and more on dogma.

I believe our God is alive and communicating to us – as parents do to children – watching us and giving us instructions. And among what we still have today is the Holy Bible, an esoteric book, a sym-bolic book, with its poetry, wisdom and inspiration.

"Do you have anything to say about **RELIGIOUS INSTITUTIONS**?"

I would like to quote Sai Baba here:

> All religions exhort man to cleanse the heart of malice,
> greed, hate and anger. All religions hold out the gift of
> Grace as the prize for success in this cleansing process.
> Ideas of superiority and inferiority arise only in a heart
> corrupted by egotism. If someone argues that he is higher,
> or that his religion is holier, it is proof that he has missed
> the very core of his faith.

As far as sheer number of participants, Buddhism is the largest religion in the world, then comes Christianity, Mohammedanism (Islam:
Muslim), Hinduism, Confucianism and Taoism.

Although almost–closed systems and strong ties between people
produce and maintain conformity, they can still produce Soul matu-
ration. However, young people intuitively seek the spiritual energy
with its aliveness and will go where they find it.

The churches have carried the messages for two thousand years:
One God, love, brotherhood and forgiveness. I visit, anonymously,
all types of churches and always enjoy my time there, even if the
preacher is of a "sin and damnation" mold. I just mentally change
the word "sin" to "limitation." The Rev. is right, we have been limited!

"What is a **CULT** and are they dangerous?" A misunderstood word,
the word "cult" just means a particular system of religious worship
with its own rites and rituals.

However, they do become dangerous when the leader demands that
participants not only give up their connections with friends of other
beliefs but to also stop communicating with their families. Usually
in this case, the participant is asked to give heavy financial support
to the organization and its leader.

And even potentially more dangerous is when the cult is isolated
and armed.

And now let's take a look at some brighter subjects, for example,
angels.

"What can you tell us about **ANGELS**?" God's messengers, another dimension of etheric intelligence, they don't ever live a life, like we do, in a human body. Superior in consciousness to mortals, subordinate to God, they are here to aid humanity. They enlighten us with ideas that lead to our protection or healing and awaken us to helpful or creative ideas. They can occasionally speak through a human Being in a body, if that Being will allow.

They can temporarily create a human-looking body from which to operate, if necessary, in emergencies, but this is extremely rare.

You have at least one angel in attendance, always, your guardian angel. Children have more; I have been told seven up to the age of seven. Angels can be seen, if the angel allows.

About twelve years ago, at an Angel Workshop I learned that we can ask our guardian angel to let us know its name and to let us physically see it. What I didn't know, was that it takes the angel a great deal of energy to break into the third-dimensional consciousness and allow a viewing. I would not have asked if I had known.

My first attempt at communicating with my guardian angel was instantly rewarded. After meditating alone, I asked, "Guardian angel, what is your name?" I heard a voice with one clear word, "Nausha," a name I had never heard. Pronounced "naw-sha" I later learned that it is a Guatemalan woman's name.

Since then, I have referred to my guardian angel as a "she," although I know she is not! Actually, since the voice I hear frequently is a man's voice, always a different voice, maybe I had better take a look at why I call my guardian angel a "she!" But then the voices may, at different time, be my higher self(s), spirit guide(s), or an Ascended Master passing through!

Sometime later, after again meditating alone, I asked, "Nausha, may I see what you look like?" Imagine my surprise when she revealed herself as that "irregular, many-variations-of-blue crystalline vortex about one-foot high and one-foot wide, not anything like drawings of angels," that I spoke of at the beginning of this book. (She had expanded herself for me. Later, spontaneous sightings have shown me that she can make herself the size of a dot or expand herself to any size necessary for the job.)

When I told shaman excitedly, "I saw my guardian angel," doubting, he asked for a description. When I told him, he broke into a grin and said, "Yes, you *did* see it."

Nausha has been an appreciated companion who sits above my right shoulder. I frequently ask her to go ahead of me and make arrangements for some expected event. I also often send her to the higher self of some other person, seeing if she can make "peace" between us by helping to create an understanding of some past situation or event. Perhaps the following specific examples will motivate you to become acquainted with your guardian angel and put it into more service for you, the reason for it being with you. A loss certainly, if you don't become acquainted!

Here is one example: "Nausha, we are going on a trip to Lake Tahoe tomorrow. Could you make our way Lighted and safe?" Then after the wonderful and safe trip, I say "Thank you dear Nausha for your help in the safe and wonderful trip to Lake Tahoe."

Here is another example: "Nausha, could you go and visit my special friend's higher self and see if there is a way of resolving our disparity in beliefs about reincarnation, which is currently causing bad vibes between us? If there is something I need to do, please communicate your answer to me through my higher self." A few days later when my friend telephones and says, " I love you anyway, even though we will never see eye to eye on some subjects," I thank Nausha for restoring the good will between us, even though the friend is clear he doesn't want to talk about my subject – I am grateful for Nausha's intervention, since I valued the friendship and didn't want to lose it. We don't have to have carbon copy spiritual beliefs! None of us is *all* right! That is a given.

Here is another example of how an angel, this time unseen by me and unknown, worked: During a workshop with shaman, an angel entered a man sitting slumped, close to us workshoppers who were lunching together. In my generation, because of his appearance, he would have been called a "tramp." He was listless and speechless. Suddenly, the man became animated, stood up, walked up to me and delivered a passionate anti-war speech, then went limp again and slouched down, looking like he was in a drunken stupor. On this occasion, shaman had seen the angel and immediately interpreted the stunning event. My teacher said I was the one to speak to because I was doing some writing in which the words could be included.

The Angel through the down–and–out man said, "If there wasn't any money in wars, there wouldn't be any." And "If you could just get the men who plan the wars to fight the wars, there wouldn't be any." Which prompted shaman to add: Many men who died early in the Vietnam war are back to help prevent future wars.

This event can make you wonder how often angels are speaking through others to you. My sense is that not just angels, but all higher Beings and servants of the kingdom are able to get through to you often and easy if you loosen up your consciousness by meditating.

I am told that in two–hundred, forty–eight different places, the Bible mentions angels ministering to man.

To find out the public's awareness of Angels, CBS News conducted a poll to be used on the program Eye–to Eye with Connie Chung: Random telephone calls to one thousand, one–hundred seventeen adults found that sixty–seven percent think angels exist; fifty–four percent believe they have a guardian angel; and twelve percent say they have communicated with them through real–world encounters and internal realizations.

Here is another tiny example of how an angel can work: Another time I saw my guardian angel when I was in a dark hall with a key trying to open a door that was really stuck. Just as I thought, "Oh, oh, what will I do now," I saw her blue crystalline light pass over the lock and at that very instant, the door opened.

After we cover the subject of "prayer," if the idea appeals to you, I will tell you how to form an Angel Healing Group and describe one way to make it work.

"Do angels sing?" I have heard celestial–sounding music twice. Whether on these occasions it was **ANGEL CHOIRS** or **THE MUSIC**

OF THE SPHERES, I don't know. Perhaps they are one and the same. Heavenly sounds of harmony that can drift into a person's awareness are unexplainable. There is nothing in the "real world" that is an explanation for this music. Of course, it may just be the movement of some type of atoms moving through space. On both occasions, even though I had never heard sounds like it, I, at first, thought there was a radio broadcasting never–before–heard ethereal harmonies.

"Are **SPIRIT GUIDES** the same as angels?" No. You have in atten-dance at least two spirit guides at all times, sometimes more, and sometimes there is a changing of the guard. Spirit guides are intelli-gent Light ethereals who seek to enlighten you through accessing your intuition. If you are open to them and they choose to reveal themselves to you, they often "clothe" themselves in an image that you trust, a long gown or Indian garments; then they let you have a brief glimpse of them. Or you can just sense the presence, see a flicker of light, or hear them going through walls or ceilings.

Three guides in spiritual–looking garments did a dance around me in a swirl to indicate I should buy a house a friend was previewing. Having just gone along for the entertainment of viewing new hous-es, single, it made no sense for me to buy a house priced at $240,000 to live alone in its three thousand and ten square feet. Both my brother and the realtor advised me not to; but I made a ridiculously low offer of $190,000; the seller countered with $192,000. I had a breathtaking house and I wasn't even in the market for one! I had won out over the con in court and gotten enough back to make the downpayment!

This became the Temple house and a gathering spot for many spiri-tual happenings and many beautiful Beings who are my best friends.

"Were the three spirit guides a **SPIRIT BAND**?" Perhaps, I don't know what they would have called themselves. I know Spirit guides can travel in a group. The band I *know* was a *spirit band,* looked very much like a wreath of clouds. I might have thought I was see-ing things, except this cloudlike wreath was there every night over my bed near the ceiling for ten nights after, those many years ago, when my then–husband very suddenly fell in love with his lady and left so suddenly. (They are still happily together. I am now so glad he left. My spiritual growth would have been thwarted if he had stayed!) I felt such compassion, companionship, and great love vibrations coming from this mystical presence, the spirit band.

Perhaps they found me like a "search and rescue team" in my time of acute distress. I hadn't asked or prayed for their presence. And I guess they stayed until they were sure I could make it.

Sometime later I was sharing this experience with a friend, a very evolved metaphysician. She told me that it took a great deal of energy for them to reveal themselves to me, especially for so many evenings in a row. At such a devastating time, I appreciate what they did to give me comfort.

This brings up an important point. Whenever we are communicating in any way with any entity that does not have a form recognizable to us, if there is any doubt whatsoever, we can state: "I do not believe you serve the Light. Go back to the Light, go back to progression." This includes extraterrestrial Beings as I said before, whom we intuit are not yet serving the Light. *Dark cannot exist where there is pure Light; even the word "Light" is so intimidating, the dark Being will leave!*

"Are **ELEMENTAL SPIRITS** and **NATURE SPIRITS** two names for the same spirits? And what about **FAIRIES**?" An advanced course in metaphysics could probably draw distinctions for you. Just think, when we can really see and sense all that is really going on, life will be so much different!

I believe the three are the same. They are composed of the elements in which they live and of which they are in charge, for example tree elemental spirits and rock elemental spirits. They put the whole thing together. In latter years, the elemental spirits started leaving, pretty discouraged with what humankind was doing to the planet. But the latest word is, they are coming back!

Toward the end of this book before I try to give you a perspective on the prophecies of what is to come, I am going to review all our out–of–body helpers of which I am aware. It is good to know that besides Ascended Masters, friendly extraterrestrials, angels, guardian angels, spirit guides, spirit bands, elemental spirits (nature spirits), and the archangels we have spoken of already, there are even more for me to introduce you to. They all can cooperate in getting your prayers answered.

"Is there much to say about **PRAYER**? Isn't it pretty straight forward?" If you have the conception I had as a child, of saying a prayer and having it heard by God, sort of like calling the neighbor next door on the phone, you may be jolted by what I have to say.

Taken instantly by heavenly messengers, angels and Light Beings *to the highest necessary power*, prayers are always answered if karmically correct and if the intent is very clear and positive, although the timing may seem slow to us.

However, rarely does a prayer get to the Godhead. Usually it is handled by the hierarchy!

I don't know about you, but at first I didn't like this idea of not getting through to God; but the more I thought about this, the more comfort I took. I used to dislike bothering God about small matters – and didn't. Now, I can say a prayer about the most mundane change needed, confident that my prayer will go up God's hierarchy just as far as it needs to go, and it will be taken care of at that level.

Mark 11:24: "What things soever ye desire, when ye pray, believe that ye will receive them, and ye shall have them."

Why worry when you can pray? If you have been up all night praying, all you have been doing is worrying. A prayer doesn't take *that* long.

It has been scientifically proven that prayer works. DR. DEAN ORNISH'S PROGRAM FOR REVERSING HEART DISEASE quotes a study done by Dr. Randy Byrd at San Francisco General Hospital: Byrd arranged for people to pray for one hundred ninety-two of the patients but not two-hundred and one others that were admitted to the coronary care unit during a ten-month period. Comparable in ages and the severity of their disease, the prayed-for patients suffered significantly fewer complications and had significantly less fluid in their lungs. None of the prayed-for required artificial respiration – while twelve not-prayed for had to have it. However, twenty–three other measurements did not respond.

The prayer sayers had been recruited from around the country. They were asked to personalize their prayers in their own style, to pray once a day, and were told the person's name, whom they did not know.

Just think of what we could heal, if we would just get started!

It is important that greed be left out of prayers. It is vital that what we want does not take advantage of anyone, hurt them, or try to control for our benefit what they do.

A good prayer, silently or out loud using words (1) Gives recognition to God as the absolute reality (2) Unifies the prayer–sayer's consciousness with God's kingdom (3) Realizes that the prayer–for–changed circumstance will be accomplished through this system of vibrations (4) States what needs to be done or changed (5) Makes a statement about the prayer having to be okayed by the prayed–for person's higher self and *having the prayer automatically negated if it is not okay with the higher self.* (6) Gives thanks for the change, if okayed by the person's higher self and (7) Releases the words, (no worrying or ruminating because these additional thoughts create more thought forms, the wrong kind). (8) Says goodbye. "Amen" at the end is wonderful. Literally translated amen means, "And that is the truth!"

I would like to elaborate on number (5). Let's say one of my friends has a medical problem for which he is seeing a physician. There is a reason he is ill. Perhaps he is paying off some karma. Perhaps he needs to make some changes in his life because of attitudes, diet or exercise. etc. Perhaps he has a past–life pattern he keeps repeating, which he needs to see and address.

Now, his higher self knows the purpose of the illness. If I bungle in and pray for his recovery and he gets well, I may have interfered where I have no business. Maybe next time his learning will have to come in an even severer form.

Here is a prayer for him that can be answered if appropriate. Before starting, I center my energy at my heart.

Thank you glorious God that we are all included in your incredible
kingdom, which is all there is. [This includes the (1), (2) and (3) just
discussed.] This evening, my beautiful friend, John Doe, has bronchi-
tis and is running a temperature. If it is okay with his higher self
and he does not need this illness for spiritual growth, I ask that he
be immediately relieved of this affliction. If this condition has sur-
faced because there is something he needs to learn or change, I ask
that he be given this information. [(4) and (5)] It is with extreme
gratitude that I place this prayer into the consciousness knowing it
will be answered as appropriate. [(6) and (7)] Amen.

Prayers said for a person *actually create loving energy* around the person. An evolved psychic can see it arriving! And as incredible as
that is, it is *every bit as powerful to pray from a distance as it is to be in a
person's presence!*

"Seeing" in our mind's eye the change(s), makes for a more powerful
prayer. We are thus using symbols, our Being's language – creative
visualization.

A recent Gallup Poll found eighty–seven percent of Americans praying at least once a week. [italics mine]. The headline said, "U. S.
Spiritual Fervor Simmers." Not in my book! There is a certain type
of prayer that needs *saying all the time*, prayers of appreciation and
gratitude. The Universe just loves to give to you if you notice what
you are receiving: tree bark, the breeze, the ocean's fragrance, the
wonder of the stars.

Also, prayers need to be said before digestive intakes. Prayers have
essential, complementary vibrations to correct the vibration of food,
water, ice water, juices, food supplements and medicines. If whomever prepared your concoction was a new Soul or angry, your suste-
nance needs to be spiritualized. Even if an Avatar prepared it, however, a prayer of gratitude is in order.

Remember that at the Soul level, you are innocent, pure and worthy.
You are valued. But you are inhabiting an animal body. You must
do the work; use your thoughts and words! The more you pray,
the easier it gets. Heaven is interactive. The Universe is prepared to
give you all you are prepared to receive. It doesn't have to be done
in the lockstep increments just mentioned if you understand the

basic principles.

If you don't want to pray because you feel separated from the God system, who moved?

When things get muddled, you don't have to pray softly. You can rant and rave and state your confusion or feelings of separateness. An earnest, honest, heart-felt prayer is oh so much better than a rote one with all the proper ingredients.

When you have an emergency or a critical situation in which you are personally sympathetic, or if you are very upset, worried and/or fearful about a prayer's outcome, your prayer has the wrong vibration. At this time, immediately get someone else, or a spiritual group, to say your prayer.

When timing is critical and there is earnest need coupled with pure intent, a prayer does go all the way to the Godhead.

"You told us earlier about an **ANGEL HEALING GROUP.** Could you tell us how this works?" Yes, it works on two levels. There is a group of human Beings who gather regularly to say prayers and do healings. Then there is the group of angels that come regularly to start the working of the prayers and healings. Some of us can see and hear the angels arriving.

We humans work as a group because *prayers with group energy on them have enormous power for good.*

World peace prayers and meditations that rotate around the world are incredible, because they focus the collective intent. There are two methods for Peace Prayers: One is where everyone involved is saying the prayer at the same time (different hours! around the Planet of the Cross), and the other is a rotating prayer. In this second method, the prayer starts in one place, and then, hour by hour, travels around the world. When someone initiates these types of prayers, I gratefully join in. I consider this sacred opportunity the most important item on my calendar for that day.

One reason an Angel Healing Group works so well are the group dynamics. In college, I have both taken and taught whole courses in the principles of group dynamics. For our purposes here, though, let me just quote Abraham Zalenik, who was when quoted, a professor of management at the Harvard Business School:

> Civilizations, governments and institutions come and go, but the small group has remained as the persistent form of social organization. The fact that small groups satisfy important human needs assures their survival as a form of organization.

At the Temple house, once a week, we hold a prayer circle called the Angel Healing Group. Soliciting the angels' help, we pray for the concerns of ourselves, our friends and families, our community, national, international, intergalactic and consciousness–heightening matters.

Our group also has a **prayer chain**: when someone in the group has an urgent problem between meetings, usually an emergency, each of us has three people to telephone. These three in turn call three more, etc. Anyone can organize a similar prayer chain. It doesn't have to be part of a prayer group.

When my Mom had a stroke which paralyzed one–half of her body in 1992, prayer chain action was immediately started. Within a week, the paralysis left. Within a year, her slurred speech returned to normal. She doesn't even recall having had a stroke – "Why, Janis, I didn't have a stroke – did I?"   Metaphysical knowledge is beautiful to have and so practical for every day.

In saying prayers for another person there are three important principles:

The first principle, **the prayer-sayer cannot intrude selfish wishes.**

We will say prayers for the healing of the body, mind, or spirit of someone, *asking for whatever is in harmony with their Being and her or his higher self.* We won't say prayers that try to control another person. Thus we would *not* say any of these prayers:

> Wife: "Please pray that my husband will come back to me."
> Husband: "Please pray that my wife will go on a diet and

lose 50 pounds."
Mother: "Please pray that my son will start college in the
fall."
Adolescent: "Please pray that my mother will stop taking
business trips and stay home with us."
Grandmother: "Please pray that my grandchild will be raised
in the same faith in which I raised my daughter."

In the aforementioned prayer requests, the requester has undoubtedly already asked and even nagged the other party to do his or her
bidding.

The second principle is that **for successful prayers, the prayed-for
person must be spiritually receptive; his or her Being and higher
self(s) must be in harmony with the prayer.**

The third principle is equally important: **It is God through the Holy
Spirit and the hierarchy, the God system, that answers the prayer.
The prayer-sayer is just a volunteer channel.** In other words, I, as
prayer sayer, don't do it.

Here is how I found out about working with angels.

After my then–husband departed and my cherished career abruptly
ended, taking it all personally, not realizing these were just dramas
to grow my Soul, I became very ill.

A friend told me about an Angel Healing Group that met once a
week at the Sunset Center in Carmel, California. I attended that
group for four years. It had been hosted by Universal Church of the
Master minister, Rev. Dorrie D'Angelo, "The Angel Lady of Carmel,"
before she crossed to the other side. After her death, her husband,
Rev. Andre D'Angelo (UCM) lead the group until just three years
ago, when I understand, it stopped functioning. Attendance had
varied from five to thirty people, with eight or nine being the norm.

Procedurally, the one that has been meeting for two and one-half
years in our home follows a similar format as did the Carmel Group.

Here are things for you to think about to get a group started:
The meeting usually lasts about an hour and a half. We always start

on time even if we know someone has to arrive late. It gets sloppy if this isn't done. You can meet anytime your group decides. In Carmel during the years I attended, The Angel Healing Group gathered at 3:00 p.m. on Fridays. The Temple-house Angel Healing Group in Clear Lake Riviera meets at 8:15 a.m. on Wednesday mornings.

Once a time is selected, stick with it. The time of the meeting is a very, very important decision. The angels know to come and so do the humans!

If a person can't make the hour chosen, ask that person if they would start another group with different people. There can't be too many Angel Healing Groups. Angels are coming to the Planet of the Cross and its upward-evolving consciousness by the billions in this Kali Yuga.

To set the stage for the group to be aware of ego intrusion, when participants walk in the door, there is *that* sign: "Leave your egos and shoes outside."

To start, about ten committed people are needed who are happy with the chosen meeting time and place. That leaves room for people to be absent when they have urgent personal business or are ill. One person is deemed responsible to keep the group going. The one that meets in our home has me as the responsible person. In that role, I became the head of the prayer chain and the one called when someone has a prayer for Angel Healing Group work; or if urgent, prayer chain telephone calls. We accept correct prayers from anyone, not just those in our group.

Discuss the pros and cons of meeting in a private home versus a rented facility.

The facilitator rotates each week. After a person has attended four times (so they can get a sense of the purpose and how to raise the energetic vibration in the room), they can take their turn at leading.

We have the following order of service written boldly on a piece of butcher paper, backed with stiff cardboard. This sign is stood up against a wall every week before the meeting so everyone can see it. The atmosphere is light and happy, with lots of giggles and laughs.

It is *hard to keep an earthly focus*; that is the reason for the sign, to keep us on track.

Between meetings, the sign can be hidden behind a piece of furniture at the meeting spot. Following this list are more details about each suggested inclusion.

ORDER OF SERVICE, ANGEL HEALING GROUP

(1) History of the group.
(2) Confidentiality rules.
(3) Volunteer clean-up "angels."
(4) Your name and town.
(5) Join hands and let the love energy flow.
(6) Prayer to call in the angels.
(7) Song or chant.
(8) Angel stories.
(9) Healings:
      A. Those present – if okay with the person, laying-on-of-hands
      B. Those absent.
      C. Common causes.
(10) Song or chant.
(11) Closing prayer to thank the angels, and ask them back next week.
(12) Basket passed to pay for facility, newspaper advertising of group, flowers, candles, and snacks afterwards (if any).
(13) Prayer chain business and announcements of coming events.

Now, by number, let me elaborate on this procedural list:

(1) The history of the group is repeated *every* week – what was the exact date it started? Who was in attendance? And where did it meet? Thus your group builds your very-own unique angel culture.

(2) Every week the facilitator of the day reminds regulars and newcomers, "What is spoken plus the names and concerns of those prayed for, stay in the group – confidentiality. Unless it is public

knowledge; for example, a terrible automobile accident that was written up in the newspaper.

(3) The volunteer clean–up "angels" are the people who will, this day, put everything away. It is important that this activity be done with volunteer "love;" also so that one person doesn't get "stuck" every week.

(4) Even if there isn't anyone new, this is another ritual which serves to join the group together: One at a time, go around the circle. Say your name and what town you live in. By this time, only five minutes have passed, well spent for group cohesion.

The regulars often bring visitors, family, friends and out–of–towners. Children over ten can be allowed once; then if they dig it, the group can invite that particular child back. Younger children, brought for healing, can arrive with their parent(s) at a suggested hour; thereby not having to sit through the whole group process.

(5) At the facilitator–of–the week's direction, join hands, bow your heads and consciously open yourselves to God's incredible love energy. Visualize bringing it in through the top of your heads and out through your human hearts. First visualize filling the room, then the country, then the state, then the United States, then the world, then the universe, and finally all the universes.

(6) The facilitator selects someone to say a prayer to call in the angels.

(7) Sing or chant for the angels. The song and chant words have been photocopied at the inception of the group by the regulars, who brought their favorites. The facilitator can choose the song or chant or ask one person "Nancy, do you have a favorite today?"

Always be open to new songs and chants.

Just sing or chant from the heart. This doesn't have to be professional music you create. One person used to joke that we sang so bad, the angels left for a few minutes!

(8) The facilitator presides over the telling of angel stories. Usually

everyone partakes in turn, but skip those who don't want to share at the moment, or want to have more time to think of a story, and then come back to that person. Most participants will have an occasional week when they just can't think of anything to share. No problem.

These are possibilities, which usually have occurred in the last week, but may be some mind-boggling spiritual event from the past: something pleasant; mystical; an event where cosmic sync was apparent, perhaps orchestrated by angels; a miraculous healing; an answer to a prayer; something lovely in nature; a happy surprise, a family get-together, etc. Occasionally, someone will have more than one wonderful, uplifting story to share.

(9A.) An ordinary chair without arms placed in the center of the group houses, one at a time, those present who want a prayer said for themselves. The facilitator asks, "Who wants to sit in the chair and place their order?" Everyone is encouraged to sit. Thus, week in and week out, The Angel Healing Group becomes a vital support group for those regulars on the path.

The person getting prayed for in that chair can ask one specific person by name to say the prayer after they have "placed their order." Or, the sitting person can just ask for "anyone who feels moved" to say the prayer request. If the sitting person desires, the group moves to the chair space and all place hands on the sitting person. Usually the prayer-sayer stands behind and places both hands on the person's shoulders. The other group members, as they individually feel moved to do so, go and place hands on the sitting person's arm, hand, knee, foot, or a prayed-for physical "ouchie," if there is one. Everyone centers his or her energy at the heart before the prayer-sayer starts.

Occasionally, it will seem correct for everyone present to say a few words of prayer, a rotating prayer around the sitting-person. (This takes too long to be included as an every-time ritual.)

After the prayer is over, any attendee can ask the sitter "Would you like my perspective on your prayer request?" Maybe they had a similar situation, know a metaphysical principle that fits, can actually offer a helping hand, know of an herbal combination that might be worth trying, etc. Any insight needs to be offered with love, not a preachie dialogue and *not a dogmatic statement of theories.* This is not the time to show off how much you know nor to have a discussion group.

If offense might be taken, suggestions can go privately to the person after the meeting is over. Error on the side of caution on this one until you get to know a person's interest in feedback.

Not metaphysical preachie dogma time!

(9B.) Prayer requests are then taken for those absent and a volunteer or asked-for person says the prayer.

However, if there are a lot of people in attendance, and/or you are running late, names of the prayed-for, one at a time, can just be put on small pieces of paper. (A nice lady made us papers with the pictures of angels on them, photocopies.) The person with the request writes out the first and last name of the person, the reason for the prayer (compound fracture, left arm), and the town where the absent person lives.

We have a black box as part of our stereo system where we put the prayer requests. A black box is a mystical place to write and place prayer requests. If no black box is available, these pieces of paper can be put in a sacred basket or carried home by participants for further prayer saying. Or a crystal bowl might work even better.

The requesters, one at a time at the direction of the facilitator, read out loud all that is on his or her piece of paper, before it is distributed, laid in the sacred prayer "basket," or put in the black box.

(9C.) Common cause prayer requests are attended to that involve what the group can think of from the past week: a war somewhere, the starving children of the world, a developing nation that was highlighted in the newspaper, giving thanks to the Ascended Masters or anyone or thing common to all, the world's leaders, the people that work for the IRS (lots of anger directed that way), a community concern – anything anyone wants to mention.

We often call on "angel specialists." Examples might be angels who specialize in helping children with broken bones, in helping world leaders, in giving comfort after the loss of a loved one. This list would be endless.

It is up to the facilitator to watch the meeting time and keep the process moving. Sometimes, if time is short and concerns are many, heads are simply bowed while a lot of people and/or things are mentioned.

(11) The facilitator asks someone to choose a closing song or chant. Then the facilitator either says the closing prayer or asks someone to say it. Last, if anyone knows of metaphysical meetings, musical events, plays, etc. in which someone might be interested, this knowl– edge is shared.

(12) At the basket passing, no pressure is made to give. All gifts need to have the right love energy on them. Someone dropping in her or his last dollar resentfully, knowing they are going to have to skip lunch, is an example of money not having the right vibration on it! Also, someone may drop in a ten dollar bill one week and then not contribute for three weeks.

The money is used in service of the group. No one person keeps it.

(13) If anyone is new, the prayer chain needs to be explained, and if that person desires, their name and phone number can be added. (Many people who feel they can't come every week still like to be on the prayer chain, as it only takes a few minutes during the week to say a prayer for a person or cause. And if you have an answering machine, you don't have to be at home to get the call.)

One more comfort is offered as appropriate during the proceedings, a blessed angel stone to take home or keep in one's pocket. Inexpensive, polished stones are purchased by the group, put in a container, and that stone–filled container passed around each week as you are saying prayers, each participant briefly holding the con- tainer up to his or her heart before passing it on. Anyone new to the group or anyone in a painful situation will receive comfort from a self–selected angel stone; the stone can be put in a pocket, purse, or by the bedside, as a reminder of being loved by God and the angels.

Little children love to have an angel stone sitting on the table beside their bed!

Stones can be any that are attractive and relatively inexpensive; they can be purchased at a rock shop. About the size of a quarter, jasper is nice if available. Or if someone is an expert on the healing vibrations of different stones, she or he may want to make this stone contribution to the group instead of giving money.

After the meeting, there is usually lots of joviality, with hugs, and if the group desires, light refreshments and visiting. Most leave on a high, having been reminded that we are spiritual Beings with a lot of prayer power, power to change our lives for the better and to help those around us, when it is in harmony with the Being and higher self(s).

Many miracles have happened as a result of the prayers. I will mention just two. We said a prayer for the stopping of the Malibu, California fire (if it was okay with everyone's higher self that was involved). Some of the prayer was done with us using creative visualization, putting walls around the fire – we essentially created a box to snuff it out. The prayer was said at 8:55 a.m. one Wednesday. One of our regulars listening to her car radio on the way home heard the announcement: "At 9:00 this morning, the wind suddenly died down and firemen were unexpectedly able to control the Malibu fire."

One of the members in the group had a pregnant daughter-in-law, whose baby boy – a sonogram had revealed the sex – was in the wrong position for birth, which was imminent. The daughter-in-law had been admitted to a hospital and placed under sedation so that the baby could be turned, but the medical intervention turned out to be one-hundred percent unsuccessful; the baby boy could not be budged.

Our Angel Healing Group, aided by a picture from a health book of how a baby is supposed to be positioned for birth, slowly did a guided visualization (one person talked us through) gently turning the baby into proper birth position. The baby's actual turning followed the prayer by about twelve hours. A normal birth ensued!

Your doubting mind could well say that these examples are just coincidences. And maybe they are, except these types of things happen week after week, month after month, and year after year! I chose these two particular examples because I felt you, as a reader, could identify with them.

We often send the Angel Blimp, our invention, for situations that cry for help – but we don't know specifically what to pray for. For example a family where both parents are drug addicts, the children are acting out and the father has just lost his job.

In alignment with everyone involved's higher self, we visualize sending a huge blimp filled with violet light over the house (business, town, country, whatever). The blimp in our mind then opens up holes and lets the violet light flow down, rain down, upon the situation. Usually, we just leave the blimp in place to continue flowing. Some beautiful and amazing things happen because violet is the "fix everything" mystical color.

The group does get creative!

James 5:16: "The prayer of a good person has a powerful effect." Get your friends to say your ethical prayers for you.

After six and one-half years of working with the angels, I guess it is not too surprising, but the following two events pleased me: two psychics, on different occasions, both in different, far-away towns who didn't know I worked with angels, volunteered to me that I was "surrounded with a *lot* of angels!"

Now we will leave the subject of helping entities and turn to aspects of human relationships.

Look back and notice that the way you get your karma is mostly from the way you interact in your human relationships – and with God – your daily behaviors! It is not your accomplishments that count, or your degrees or your title!

Now in order to take a look at relationships, we will touch upon the subjects of truth; listening; non-attachment and letting go; giving and receiving; service; pleasure; desires; being in the moment; judg-

ment; forgiveness; sex; soul mate; twin flame, twin-ray soul; relationships themselves; marriage; divorce; and raising children.

"What is the truth about **TRUTH**?" You can't help but love someone if they are real.

If someone says their truth to you (hopefully tactfully and lovingly),
revealing a fault, really appreciate that person! Sometimes the truth
hurts: so what! You are tough! If you decide they are right, you
have something to work on!

People have to tell the truth, if they want the friendship or love relationship to last. It takes energy to be forthright. This is an essential
part of the work of the relationship.

Over the long haul, if you evade or suppress feelings or facts, the
energy in a relationship gets restricted. If non-truth telling is a pattern, eventually the relationship falls apart because of the stifled
energy.

The energy deteriorates even more rapidly when there is frequent
deceit or habitual lying. Only a spiritually immature person will use
these protections. Saying truth takes a spiritual warrior.

There is a fine line between expressing what you think or feel honestly, saying how your friend's or lover's behavior is affecting you
versus trying to change that person. Even saying your truth from
your heart, the listener may not be willing to alter behavior. We
can't change another adult. We can only work on ourselves.

If you say your truth from the heart, and it hurts a person's feelings,
it isn't karmic. You can't take responsibility for their feelings. If you
become a constant people pleaser, you will be become a cosmic
noodle gone astray from your Soul's purposes.

On the other hand, if you are constantly dissatisfied and "bitchy,"
these vibrations destroy your intimate's and colleague's well being.
Here are attitudes, if you will, that will do this: the habitual attitude
of being hateful, having self-hate, habitual blaming (responsibility
shifting), feeling cheated, not having enough, constant worrying,
looking with a critical eye and so forth.

Contrarily, looking for things to appreciate, praise, love and take joy from, creates a heavenly vibration, a heaven on earth in which to live.

When a person is truthful with you, thank them for the information. *Always remember that hidden information and/or feelings plug the relationship.*

We have to be a good listener to really hear and understand someone's truth. **Listening** is a skill like bicycle riding is a skill. I have written instructional materials on "How to Listen." But from many years of doing human relations training, I know that only *practice* in listening makes a good listener along with an attitude of really wanting to understand *both facts and feelings*. Paraphrasing what you think you heard *and* sensed is a good way to start.

Then let both have their complete say on the subject at hand before any collaborative-solution finding gets generated. Taking a time out is good if one or the other gets overwhelmed, angry or exhausted.

It works very well if each of you can "lay your viewpoint" on a table. Then the other person or side "lays their viewpoint" on the table. That way, you aren't directing comments at the person. This is a technique that defuses negative emotions and sets the stage for collaborative-solution finding.

Indeed, in practice, the two basics of good human relationships, saying one's truth plus being a good listener, are not simple behaviors. It bothers me greatly that basic human relations skills are not taught, as part of every school curriculum. Tell me someone, why do we need algebra in elementary school? In spite of what educators say about "no room in the curriculum for additions," there is room in the elementary, middle-school and high-school curriculums for using role playing for learning good human relations skills. And the use of drama in this way is an excellent, experiential-learning tool. And kids and adults love it!

"What do the principles of metaphysics say about **NON-ATTACHMENT**?" Whenever you hold very tightly to something, it is called "attachment." Whenever you are attached, you will get "bumped." If it is a person, they will leave you or stay away from you. If it is an article, you will lose it or break it. If it is a car, it will get scratched, dented or destroyed. If it is money, you will lose it. The way to "hold" something is to appreciate it, take care of it and enjoy it. With a light touch, you can be *very* interested and productively involved. That is quite a different attitude than hoarding, grasping and using power to control.

Ken Keyes' HANDBOOK TO HIGHER CONSCIOUSNESS, Living Love Publications, St. Mary, KY 40063 contains a masterpiece of explanation of this principle. He says that with addictive programming, life will continually provide you with the experiences needed to become a more conscious human being. In other words, trials and tribulations.

Keyes talks about your lower chakra motivations, tied in with your ego–mind, making you hold onto something you do have, pushing you to try to get something you don't have, or urging you to avoid something you don't want to do.

Eventually, you have to let go of everything except your Being. Remember that you are spiritual Beings having a human experience. The physical realm is not your origin. Passionate holding onto anything or anyone is futile.

What Keyes teaches is, over a period of time, consciously for each chakra, turning your additions into *preferences*. "Preferences let you stay in touch with the here and now in your life. They enable your mind to become calmer and calmer – until it functions as a powerful, quiet, one–pointed, peaceful, effective servant of your consciousness." He points out that out of the billions of people on earth, not one has experienced enough security, delightful sensations, or power to be continually happy or fulfilled from these.

Keyes calls the chakras from the bottom up, The Security Center, The Sensation Center, The Power Center, The Love Center, The Cornucopia Center (what you communicate), The Conscious-Awareness Center (you have become a witness to your own dramas, accepting of the ups and downs), and The Cosmic Consciousness Center.

Sai Baba explains simply, "As long as you are filled with egotism and attachment, you will not be able to free yourself from grief and sorrow."

The Universe put my husband and I to the attachment test. Cosmic Map was in final rough draft form, when giving us six days notice, my husband's company transferred us to the Central Coast of California, six hours from my stepchildren –my husband's twelve-year old daughter and sixteen–year–old son – our beloved metaphysical friends, the multiple rainbows, the deer, rabbits and eagles. We left behind three thousand and ten square feet of awesome two-story–high rooms, windows all around with lake views on three sides and a golf course on the fourth. These windows were the ones from which David and I had seen ten rainbows, a redtailed hawk and an eagle the day we had made the commitment to spend the rest of our lives together.

This cliff Temple house, situated on a high–energy vortex used by ancient Indian tribes for sacred ceremonies, has Cathedral ceilings, an incredible raised–hearth fireplace, with a mantle long enough for pictures of fourteen gurus.

Ironically, I had been thinking that the voice had been wrong this time. Six months earlier, the voice had said, "You will be moving from this place."

We have rented and are settled in an eight–hundred and twenty-three square foot house, and just love it. We still keep in touch with family and friends via the telephone, Fax, letters and visits. But the Temple house and the idyllic lifestyle? We never think about them. Our realtor is rather discouraged that the Temple house has-n't sold, but the Angel Healing Group said the prayer for "house sale" for us. It will sell at a fair price – just as soon as the house angels find some-one who will really appreciate it. We sincerely don't worry even though my husband is putting in long hours to pay for both rent, here, and house payment, there.

Within ten days of moving, we had found a number of vegetarian restau-rants, a Sai Baba sanskrit chanting group and two meditation groups. The vibration of the love energy coming through these new people is the same, of course, that came through our familiar groups. We are very con-tent. The new location brought a special friend for Janis, who would affirm her current work and start to teach her of the higher planes, Janis' next learning task. I'll talk of this incredible lady, Jean Martin, in the Afterword.

The Angel Healing Group and meditation group continue to meet, but not at the Temple house.

How did I get "jerked" on the attachment principle? – My close friends will tell you that I do not lend my metaphysical books, even to them, because I don't want to lose these references. So what was the only thing that got lost in the move? Indeed! A box of metaphysical books! I had a good laugh about this. I might as well have loaned and lost them!

"What are the principles of **GIVING AND RECEIVING?**" Contrary to what you may think, it is *not* more blessed to give than receive. In your ideal state, you would do both equally. It is God's love in one form or another that you are letting enter your space (receiving) and passing through you (giving). This is such an important principle.

You get your spiritual expansion through letting things go, and then something better comes into its place. You cannot receive if you cling to what you have.

If you have any doubts as to which process you are overemphasizing, ask a half a dozen friends and family.

This is an easy one to change, unless you are a scrooge or conversely want to impress people with your generosity or you give because you want someone to be beholden to you.

If feedback says you make it hard for people to give to you, here is your homework assignment: For the next two weeks, pray for "gifts." Accept everything that is offered to you with a "Thank you." (You can always give the material things away.)

On the other hand, if feedback says you don't give enough, here is your homework assignment: For the next two weeks, keep asking yourself, "What might _____ (my mother, father, sister, brother, children, etc.) need that I want to give?"

Truly, it is just a matter of paying attention to giving and receiving.

Another principle is, "Deeds, not results." This means I had better not be giving with the attitude that this gift of time, money, love, or thing is going to get me something. This is not pure giving. Doing good deeds is great, but not if you are looking for a return.

Another important principle is "Do not give gifts you can't afford to give." When you resent what you are giving to someone or what you are doing for them, it is a tainted gift, not purely given. It will not have the right energy on it. Don't give it.

"But don't the great teachers say that **SERVICE** is ultra important?" Yes, it is part of the plan to give back the blessings you have received.

As you grow spiritually, you *naturally* want to be more helpful, kind, thoughtful, and responsible. Your deep and daily meditation will keep you in tune with what your Being is desiring to express.

For some people, this will be obvious service; for example, work in a soup kitchen for homeless people, joining a group that picks up trash alongside the road on Saturday mornings or volunteer work on the suicide hot line.

For others, this will be the service that: the housewife gives to her husband and young children; the husband gives to the customers at the tire shop where he works; or the teen gives in his part-time job at the car wash.

The idea is, whatever you are drawn to do, you flow with an attitude of love and service. Do you know anyone with the opposite attitude? "Take care of me, wait on me, pick up after me, do my errands. I dare you, try to make me happy. When you are not looking, I am going to do something sneaky."

You are not to be someone's slave.

The right service for *your* Being makes you feel so good! Contrarily, doing service just to make a good appearance is just going to make you tired, and is not going to earn you good karma.

Do we have a contradiction in the following two pieces of advice from Sai Baba? I don't think so. He tells us that *service to our fellow humans is service to God*. And – he also says to stay at a great distance from the wicked. Apparently we serve the wicked best by *not* giving them, or their cause, our energy. Your intuition will help you decide.

I have given a beggar $10 when I felt the urge to do so; I have walked past some and not even acknowledged the person; I have lectured others kindly, "You could do another job better than you are doing this job" and not given them money.

As far as service to your fellow humans, remember that Edgar Cayce suggested three times a day asking, "Lord, what would you have me do?"

Ken Keyes says, "As you become more conscious, your energy will increase . . . less of it will be drained by your own [lower chakra] security, sensation and power addictions. You will then liberate a continuous stream of energy which will flow in loving and serving people around you [in a way that is natural and easy for you]."

Just being here at this time, you are a channel through which the love enters the earth plane, a real service you came to do for the Planet of the Cross! Thank you!

"Do we need to grit our teeth and let go of **PLEASURES**?" No! "You will be called to account for all the permitted pleasures you have failed to enjoy." This is a quotation from the Talmud, an old book on Jewish law and fundamental principles.

But the pleasure can never be *taken* at someone's expense, cost or pain. That of course brings negative karma and drains your Soul's energy.

It would be fun to have a group brainstorm on what pleasures are "permitted pleasures." Here are a few I can think of without much effort: Laying outside in the sun; taking a hike in the mountains; enjoying a lunch with your best friend; the family praying together at Thanksgiving; a stroll with your spouse or significant other around the block; watching the sunset; going square dancing;

watching a baby grow into a toddler; and taking a drive out to see the wildflowers.

With growing mindfulness, it is easy to increase pleasure in life.

"Well, if permitted pleasures are okay, what about the gurus who tell us we must let go of our **DESIRES**? It really comes down to what your desires are. If you are desiring the possession of material things, if that is what you work for, plan for, think about, envy other people for, if the pursuit and owning of these material things is what compulsively occupies your time, then indeed you are hooked.

It is not that things themselves are bad. It is just that in pursuit of them they absorb all your devotion time and your God awareness. When you aren't thinking of the love and the Light, meditating, doing other practices, studying the principles, living out of your Soul's purpose all day long and instead are acting as described in the last paragraph, then you are lost.

Contrarily, constructive desire, to know your Soul's wishes, to serve in your unique way, leads to expanded activity – and the energy to manifest the constructive desire in substance and form in the outer world. God's great energy is flowing through you constantly. Creative and constructive pleasures and desires are, therefore, spiritual.

The interesting thing is that money, friends, material things and the opportunities to use your talents and training just come to you as a byproduct, through cosmic sync. The Universe doesn't want you to be poor or be without the right avenues for Soul expression!

"You have mentioned **BEING IN THE MOMENT**. This seems hard to do, could you say more?" This phrase tells us to keep our attention on whatever is going on, now. The more and more that the ego–mind gets deactivated, house trained, the easier and easier that being in the moment gets.

But some people get mixed up here. They think that if they are planning for the future, they aren't "in the moment." There *are* some moments when it *is very appropriate* to do creative–solution finding, around something that will happen in the future. That is entirely different from worrying, ruminating or letting thoughts stray. Whatever really evolved people are doing, they are doing it with full attention.

And the more the love is flowing through you, the more you are anchored in the present. It actually seems in this state that time is not passing.

"I am confused. **JUDGMENT** is wrong; okay, how do I decide what is in my best interest; don't I have to make a judgment call?" Let me talk about this subject in general before I try to answer the question. Maybe in my striving to answer your question, I can shed some of my own confusion on this nebulous subject!

Long ago on the Santa Cruz Mall, shaman's ideal location for cosmic sync to give workshop grist, he was watching us participants as we listened and watched a young woman, a street singer accompanying herself on a guitar. After she had played and left, he turned to me and said, "Janis, you are so judgmental!" What a great blessing to have someone who could see my dysfunctional behavior. Yes, I had not been listening to the young woman, because I was so busy having thoughts like, "I wonder why she has on those old, beat-up hiking boots with that long shirt? Her blouse doesn't even match her skirt. And yuck, she has beauty-shop clippies in her hair!"

What I was doing was looking with a critical attitude, a habitual mental process.

I wasn't looking from my heart! Some of the other participants told me how lovely the young woman's song had been. I had hardly heard it! Dropping my judgmentalness is something I still work on.

It is trickie. My pet peeve is a metaphysician who sees no evil. Where would India be today if Mohandas Karamchand Gandhi had not had a great case of *righteous indignation* about the way the English were ruling. Gandhi said:

> Man must fight evil always and the way to turn the other cheek is to fight back with love and truth and a fierce willingness to submit to injustice and cruelty.

There are times that I must say my truth: As I call 911 because I see a man trying to attack a woman with a knife outside a store; as I hear a mom being verbally abusive to a child in my presence – "Linda, if I were Bobby, what you just said would be emotionally devastating to me."

There are words like discrimination, discernment and preference. Sometimes, in some situations, we have to do some Soul searching to know if we are being judgmental with a sense of superiority or if what is happening is really evil. "Lord, I don't know if the way Sam treated Martha is exactly evil, but it sure doesn't resonate with me." "I really don't enjoy all the arguing of politics that George and Susan like, so I think I'll turn down their next lunch invitation."

Then there is the proper attitude when someone judges you and lets you know about it. You can take it for what it is. Maybe it is helpful feedback, and you will want to change your future behavior; maybe you won't. But the bottom line is, it doesn't matter what anyone thinks or feels about you. They are not the real judge. – Who is the judge?

Some say judgment is done in the higher realms by a member of God's all-knowing hierarchy. As an example, I pointed out a quotation earlier in a Sai Baba book that supports that view. Others say that as out-of-the-body Beings, we will lightly judge ourselves. Probably, there is some of both.

We will find out soon enough.

The reason we can't be effective judges here is because we don't know enough in third-dimension consciousness, unless we are God-realized.

In the meantime, in regard to judging yourself, try to be kind. As long as you are making slow improvements consistently, be patient with yourself and accepting. *If repeated over and over, three steps forward, then two steps backwards, is progress.* And pretty typical of human advancement.

To sum up about judgment, you are not supposed to *habitually* look at the world through a critical mental attitude. On the other hand, you may have to say your truth or act when your discrimination or righteous indignation are alerted.

"Both the Bible and you have mentioned **FORGIVENESS** as some-thing we *have* to accomplish to grow spiritually. Could you say more?" It is almost as if holding on to hate or resentment against a person, event, group, institution, or whatever – gives your Being an actual physical weight. By letting go of that weighty grudge, another stuck spot, you actually increase the vibrational frequency of your own Soul and free it up to work more effectively. Until you unload this baggage, you will never be able to evolve into the next higher dimension or dimensions. The theory is that simple. The practice takes determination and courage. It is the ego–mind that holds grudges, not the Soul!

With satisfaction, I want to report that first I forgave the alligator lady using a process mentioned in a few paragraphs. Fourteen months later, today she and I had a wonderful talk, did some collab-orative-solution finding, and finished our conversation with genuine good will.

Young children don't hold grudges. They live in the "now." Why we change our way of operating as we grow up, I don't know. I have tried to understand but can't make sense of this yet.

When we find ourselves resenting someone or something, "I for-give_____" can be said affirmatively daily until the resentment is gone. Otherwise that resentment anger will draw us to the person or thing in this life and another life, as well as the already men-tioned retardation of our Being's growth in this life. "I forgive" does-n't mean we have to have a close association with the person or thing.

I actually write "I forgive_____" on a piece of paper or three by five inch card and tabulate with pen every day I say it. I don't get discouraged if the feelings are slow to dissipate. The Bible says sev-enty times seven. If I said "I forgive" every day for that long, it would take close to a year and a half. With persistence, everything can be cleaned up. Each time, it gets easier and then even easier. If your problem is with a person, as said before, I can guarantee you, if you saw the whole cosmic picture of the Being's journey, you would naturally forgive instantly.

There are two tests which show whether or not you have really forgiven someone. The first is when you hear of his or her good fortune, you will be genuinely pleased. Contrarily, if you hear of the forgiven person's misfortune, you will be distressed.

We also need to forgive *ourselves* for difficulties we have created for *ourselves* and others. Guilt feelings are such a waste of energy. If you saw your *own* cosmic journey, you would forgive yourself for everything you have done that still distresses you. Remember you were/are in an animal body with a heavy cultural and parental stamp.

It is important that you don't use your today's more enlightened consciousness in judging yesterday's events. This is true of your own behavior or anyone else's. Again, everything makes sense at one level or another. From this angle, we are all innocent. As a student of the Light, we need to train ourselves to totally lay aside everything that is useless or undesirable.

"**SEX**. What does metaphysics have to say about sexual ethics?" They are *not dictated* by rules. Instead, staying tuned to your Being to know what is right for you at the time is advised. However, metaphysical principles do apply, the negative karma, if you took advantage of or used someone.

Let's take a look at this complicated subject. There are a number of *potential components* of a sexual relationship all relating to a specific chakra. The quality of the mating depends upon how many of these human centers are fully engaged as described:

The physical component (the sexual chakra). The actual sexual urges and mating of the two bodies. Men are often the leader at this level.

The power component (the control chakra). Who is in charge? Ideally, this is always negotiable and somewhat spontaneous.

The romantic love component (the heart chakra). When you are in love, it gives great pleasure to you to say it and show it in many ways. Love draws the two partners to become one. There is an animal magnetism between you. Sexual relating generates and continues love.

The communication and emotional components (the throat chakra and naval chakra). The respect and communication components. You are open and honest with each other, and you totally respect who and what your partner represents.

At its best, both are emotionally committed to giving as much satisfaction and pleasure as possible and are willing to communicate to each other just how to do this. Sexual relating is spontaneous, playful and fun.

The intuitive (third eye chakra) and intellectual component. You are intuitively tuned into each other and sometimes communicate telepathically.

Both of you have about the same intellectual capacity. You share common interests which excite you, and you also have individual interests or work which invites your individual study, work and pursuit.

The spiritual component (the transpersonal chakra). You and your sexual partner each have your own strong connection to God/own Being. You are both on the spiritual path. Talking together about God and the nature and principles of the kingdom bring you much joy.

You want your mate to become the best he or she can be and support his or her personal and spiritual growth efforts.

There is a triangle, man strongly relates to God, woman strongly relates to God, they strongly relate to each other.

The woman is often the leader of this spiritual component.

Before I talk more about sex, I would like to write two paragraphs on **marriage**: Men and women are opposite forces and give to each in the best relationships experiences which cannot be gained alone. They balance each other's nature. Marriage says "I want to know you to the core of your Being. I want to be your life's partner and together build something beautiful, uniquely ours. I have put all my cards on the table, and I am not withholding anything. I commit myself to this union without reservation. I will help you and cooperate with you.

Having made a total and strong commitment, the couple are supported by coincidences and events that seem magical. (Ten rainbows, an eagle and a redtailed hawk!) In engagement and marriage relationships, when people commit themselves because their Soul urges them, each in essence says, "I will be there for you through thick and thin. You can count on me. When it is important, I will be there. I will listen to you and respond to you. I will love you.

In a marriage, it is not that you won't love others of the opposite sex. It is just that true commitment takes *so much time and individualized focus*. A married person has to be ready to respond. Honest to God, one mate is more than any of us can do justice to.

Practically no communal marriages (many couples intimate with each other or a menage a trois (domestic triangle) have worked well over a relatively long period of time.

Now here is what I have been building up to: There are at least seven levels of sexual relating:

> Level VII. Components are the spiritual, intuitive/intellectual, communication, love, sexual relating, and marriage. All the major chakras have a connection between the partners and there is long–term commitment.

> Level VI. Components are the intuitive/intellectual, communication, love, commitment, sexual relating and marriage. (No spiritual component or only one partner is spiritual.)

> Level V. Components are the intuitive/intellectual, communication, love, commitment and sexual relating. (No marriage or spiritual connection.)

> Level IV. Components are the intuitive/intellectual, communication, love and sex. (No spiritual aspect, commitment or marriage.)

Level III. Components are communication, love and sex. (Missing are the spiritual, intuitive/intellectual, commitment and marriage.)

Level II. Components are love and sex. (Missing are the spiritual, intuitive/intellectual, communication, commitment and marriage.)

Level I. The component is sex. (Missing are the spiritual, intuitive/intellectual, communication, love, commitment and marriage.)

Those rare couples who create the ideal Level VII are adding to "couple consciousness" potentials in the ancestral memory/collective unconscious. For each couple who reaches this high standard and maintains it, another couple will find it a little easier. For each couple who builds their relationship in a way in which each finds creative and satisfying, their behavior makes a wider approach possible for the next couple. The old ways of the past were for a certain age. "Programmed marriage" was all right for certain times in history when rigid roles made sense. What you create together from your strong individual emotional health, spiritual connection, training, and preferences, your Level VII sexual union in its setting is a jewel for higher consciousness.

If you are in a committed relationship or married and have sex with someone other than your partner, it will destabilize the marriage, you can bet on it. Everything is energy, vibrations. Sexual energy is powerful.

When you have sex, your sex partner's energy remains in your aura field for about a month. If you are married or in a committed relationship and have sex outside it, this other–sex partner's energy will affect your relationship for that month. At the psychological level, it will affect your primary relationship forever.

Powerful energy directed away from the relationship or outside the marriage takes away from the power of the union. It is that simple. Metaphysically, it just can't hold together in quality.

So what to do if you are single and without a committed relationship? That is between you and your own Being. Metaphysically, because of its high energy, sex is bonding. It can get you into a low-level relationship that is going to waste your time, energy and money.

Also, even if you and your sex partner are just in a Level 1 relationship (sex only) or any Level for that matter, the vibrations will tend to strongly hold off other potential partners. If you are holding onto a deficient relationship because it is "better than nothing," unfortunately, it is a metaphysical principle that if you want to attract someone unattached of your caliber, you have to have an aura that is not plugged up with a "better than nothing's" vibes.

That is why Rajneesh told his followers who were searching for a love to "go as deep as you can, as fast as you can" in order to sort out relationships that wouldn't go anywhere – and get on with looking – quickly.

A single person who is a virgin has to set their own standard. It is possible that you could start with a Level I relationship, just sex, and work eventually up to Level VII.

There are no guarantees no matter what the path. That is part of being human, taking things step-by-step to see where the path leads. Obviously, the more components you know are potentially present, the better chance that relationship has of blossoming.

However, many very young metaphysicians argue that "being in the moment" means bedding down with anyone they feel like at any particular moment. That is their perfect right to make that choice.

Here is an idea I used to propose at divorce-recovery-type groups. I will share it not to write a "law," but to get you to thinking about what you want for yourself if you are single: Before having sex with a new partner, tell the person when the issue comes up that you will not become intimate until you have dated at least ten times, plus at that point you would want a commitment to explore an exclusive relationship, and extract a promise for mandatory condom use. By expressing these needs to an eager prospective lover, it always slows down, if not stops, sexual appetite. Let's face it, few people are that attracted to each other as potential lovers after even a few dates. The discussion of condom use isn't exactly romantic. However, the expressed need for time and maybe later safe sex, gives each the space to assess the potential partner at all levels. And it sets the stage for either to ask for more time.

One of the purposes of Jesus' ministry was love. He entered the earth plane at a time when the basic energy or vibrations of the planet were sex and power. He forged the pattern to the heart center. That heart pattern was held, solidified by many celibate monks meditating, mostly in the holy lands.

Since Jesus forged the pattern to the heart chakra, and the monks fortified it, celibacy as a spiritual practice in and of itself is no longer necessary. There is no longer an argument for being celibate just for celibacy's sake. But there are other arguments as presented.

If you want a Level VII relationship, you have to prepare yourself for it. We attract at the level where we are. This creates the potential of many years with some lonesome moments. I know, I had a decade of them.

If you are going to be intimate, safe sex makes sense. Rajneesh predicted to his followers in the 1970s that there would be an unnamed venereal disease that would eventually kill one-third of the world's population. He warned his followers then to start using condoms.

Again, having your own rules before sexual passion is suggested. But I won't judge your standards. It is not that any of the levels are "wrong," just potentially limiting.

Since we die if even one chakra gets shut down, regular masturbation can keep you alive when you have no one appropriate to relate to. It is a sure way to relieve sexual tension. Together with having a weekly massage (bashful, you might want to consider trading with someone of the same sex), joining groups where there is lots of hugging, going dancing often, you can keep yourself from feeling emotionally and sexually needy or having the "skin hungries." You can really enjoy your single life and the independence it allows.

Is there anything new in sexual relating? Probably not, but there is something old that is generally not well known. Called by two different names among spiritual seekers, "The Tao" (pronounced "Dow") and Tantra (pronounced "tawn–tra.")

From ancient China and India, it is a disciplined, but ecstatic way of relating sexually which seeks to activate the whole chakra system *for spiritual awakening* plus prolonged pleasure. These two old systems have in common that the male's ejaculation is restricted or regulated, through practice, which eventually gives him incredible control. This, of course, tremendously increases the woman's pleasure.

In THE TAO OF SEXOLOGY, THE BOOK OF INFINITE WISDOM, Tao Publishing, 4050 19th Street, San Francisco, California 94132, Dr. Stephen T. Chang explains in detail this disciplined, but joyful way to enhance life and develop spirituality. There are other books on this subject, ask at a metaphysical bookstore. It is a liberating process for a couple to read the book together and commit to the practices which they both find attractive.

"Do we have a **SOUL MATE**, or can we just find someone who matches us as you described in the levels?" Dear Soul, you don't have a particular love if you think in terms of a Cinderella story. Through your thousands of lifetimes, your various loves have come in to do with you the dramas to grow your Being and/or to support you. They also come to help you do a project or to work on a cause. You are drawn again to a love when you didn't leave with peace between your Souls. In the Edgar Cayce materials, divorce was rarely recommended and that is probably why. If you don't get it settled, then you have to meet again. Remember, you come here to grow your Soul. And resting comfortably just doesn't do it.

Saint Germain said, "Until something is done harmoniously, it is not done at all."

What is written in the prior paragraph was what I honesty believed. It was typed and in a floppy disk for five years. After my divorce, I had been resigned to eventually meeting someone I had heavy unfinished business with, even though it seemed a bit sad. Then, ten years after my divorce, I met my **twin flame, twin–ray soul**.

A great love also does draw as well as unfinished business. In a few precious lifetimes, we get to be with a "sweetie" with whom there is little unresolved negative karma, probably the proverbial "soul mate." If you saw the similarity of my husband's and my individual aura photographs, you would understand. This is still a mystery to me because we certainly don't look alike nor would a computer dating service have matched us.

We did not meet in this life until I was fifty-eight and he was fifty-one. For seven years before we met, single, I had been hearing a voice which said simply, "Go north." Not knowing specifically what that meant, over that time, I had just kept moving in a very general northerly direction in small increments, a dozen moves. The small northern California town, where we met, Middletown, is exactly north of Monterey. When traveling by car, they are five hours apart. All through the years, I didn't know why I was moving north.

From the moment that we met, we had this very powerful connection. It had been a decade since my then-husband had left. It was the first time my twin-ray had gone out since his divorce. David had, just an hour before, asked a single friend who happened to drop by after a two-year absence, "Where can single people go to have a good time?" Both of them came to the dance. I had seen David enter the dance and decided I would ask him to dance. I snuck up from behind before he saw me and asked him to dance. He turned, smiled at me and said, "I would love to." A metaphysical friend had introduced me to that same dance just several weeks earlier.

Shaman had forecast "a tall, very loving man" whom you would meet and "with him you will rise to your full potential." He was a bit off on the timing; he said I would meet him in about sixteen months. Nine years later I had forgotten his prophesy, when David and I merged together at last; I had long-ago stopped hoping! But three days before the dance, I had had a bit of a warning.

Three days before David and I met, I was at a metaphysical study group. Picking from a sack, not looking in, it was held by the lady who had bagged her unwanted small items to share. I pulled out a gold spoon with carved hearts on the handle. Although I didn't know what it was, several ladies in the study group, said in unison,

"Why Janis, it is an English wedding spoon!" How The Universe loves to play! I knew exactly what it meant, and I got mad. I had been at peace about not finding my sweetie in this life. "Now." I thought, "I might have to wait another ten years!" Wrong!

In the last life, my husband and I had been best friends, from our blonde, little girlhoods on. We were both women who lived during the Civil War. In another very happy life that we know about, I was his older sister.

So one's twin-ray doesn't always play the part of a lover or husband. In some lifetimes, our twin-ray has been there for us by taking other parts in our drama.

There are at least two theories on twin rays. One, that I don't buy, is that we were once upon a time one Soul that split and went out to develop in parallel ways. The other theory says that we are of the same extended Soul family and get together as husband and wife periodically to do something remarkable together.

Both my husband and I have some ideas of what this may mean for the two of us. Our thinking now is that we will probably team up to give Ego-Shrinking Playshops. It is definitely time for the human race to Lighten up! I remember shaman saying "the earth is our playpen." Proverbs 17:22: "A merry heart doeth good like a   medicine . . ."

"Would you say more about **RELATIONSHIPS** themselves?" Through the millennia, you are drawn toward those Souls or Beings who can give you your needed lessons and others who will support and nourish you. You choose to associate with those whom you have loved greatly and those you have hated passionately. You take the different roles, mother, father, sister, brother, lover, spouse, grandparent, uncle/aunt, neighbor, friend, etc. You have also taken the roles of the superior one and the inferior one, the boss and the worker, the good guy and the bad guy, the rich, the poor, and the inbetween. Unfinished business gets settled over time.

In this lifetime in the drama, there are three ways you can relate to people: with them, away from them and against them.

Ideally, if you can't relate with someone important to you, you will try very hard to restore or create a "with them" relationship.

"Can you say more about marriage and other types of close relationships? In marriages that work over long periods of time, usually the first seven years are negotiating years, where each strong person of the couple "argues" for structuring the relationship in terms of their preferences (if evolved) and addictions (if not evolved). Through trial, error, and dedication, a higher form of love is forged – with work.

It is wise to hold close to ourselves only those who are responsive to our love and return it. This is simply a linear–time expediency, we only have so much time. To be fair, as said earlier, we can't spread ourselves so thin that we aren't there to support when needed.

Unfortunately, in marriage and other close relationships, most loving is done very conditionally. That is just human nature. Human love can be very grasping, "I will stay married to you and love you as long as you are true to me." "Since I went to that show you wanted to see, I expect you to go with me to see my sister and her husband." "Since I raised you from a baby, I expect you to send me a Mother's Day card every year." As already mentioned, this conditional love demands certain types of reciprocal behavior and constantly disappoints the lover.

Divine love, unconditional love, is expanding. It just loves.

Everyone needs social support because we are social animals. Most of us put a lot of energy into keeping this support group working, which is healthy.

Besides the support, we all need the feedback and the bumping that relationships give. We get introduced and re-introduced to our ego. Thus we learn and grow.

As far as romance goes, the only way you attract the right person is to be who you really are. As already mentioned, you attract what you want by being it. And to get the most growth out of this life, it is necessary to find someone to share your life. Close relationships and marriage mean you love yourself. You grow by leaps and bounds. There is an old saying, "A joy shared is twice the joy; a sorrow shared is half the sorrow."

Happy couples have built their relationship slowly, brick by brick over years. In the process of arguing, negotiating, and truth saying, each is motivated to love, unity, and trust, even though sometimes they think they aren't going to make it.

Meditation enables you to get your life energy directly from God. You don't have to rely on a special person to fill your "gas tank." If you marry someone who also nearly always has a "full tank," your relationship will be much more harmonious. The energy of the relationship can go into enjoying each other and bringing out the best in each other.

Groups made of self–realized people function much more effectively, too.

In listening, you need to listen with attention and respect for the other person's truth. When you totally understand another person's truth, something mystical happens. You will soften, yield, stretch and allow.

Good listening helps overcome the real differences between the sexes. Carl Jung's work is helpful to understand this. When we incarnate as men, we are more likely to be engaged in these negative, pole yang behaviors. *He* says: I am using force, destroying, being strong, intimidating, aggressive, combative, initiating, ambitious, assertive, competitive, dominant, self–reliant, independent, and am willing to take a stand. Although these behaviors have created our world, they are also destroying it faster than it can be saved, thus these behaviors need tethering.

My psychic psychiatrist told me: Janis you will be doing something that will motivate the Beings in a male body this time to want to tether their yang behaviors.

Beings in female bodies this time around are more often engaged in these positive pole, yin energy behaviors. *She* says: I am loving, emotional, in tune with feelings, nurturing, yielding, warm, passive, soft, quiet, affectionate, compassionate, gentle, loyal, sensitive to others, sympathetic, tender, understanding and spiritual. Most of these behaviors include the heart energy needed to keep the human connection to God.

Perhaps you can understand why some spiritual teachers are saying that women will become the leaders in the Seventh Golden Spiritual Age. When we were males in our previous incarnations, we overdid it a bit. However, there needs to come a balance between the two energies, who would want a world run by only one side of our natures?

The prior paragraphs document the extremes, the poles. Obviously, a balanced earth male or female will have a wide repertoire of both yin and yang behaviors.

To make matters more complex, men's and women's brains are wired differently. Each sincerely sees, feels and has a different life experience, even if they are involved in the same event or are married to each other.

When a relationship gets stuck, an impartial counselor or mediator can be of great assistance and offer a new perspective.

And there are wonderful communication courses which include "listening skills" and "conflict-resolution skills."

Love relationships end because of uneven emotional, mental or spiritual growth. Today, it is very difficult to keep all of these levels, chakra connections, growing together.

As mentioned before, your Soul seeks two kinds of dynamics from your relationships. The first is emotional and physical support. The second dynamic is lessons. If a relationship is giving you neither support nor the required lessons, that person will move out of your life or become so distant that someone else can get in to play the role of the moving-out person.

Should you endure a half-mast marriage? The Bible is no help. In Deuteronomy 24:1 a man could **divorce** a woman for any reason, give her a paper stating his intent and send her out of his house. In the Old Testament, it was that easy.

In Matthew 5:32 Jesus is recorded as saying there was only one reason for a man putting away his wife, and that was adultery. In Mark 10:4 Jesus is supposed to have said that since man and wife become one flesh, if either married again, that was adultery.

I don't buy either of these as relevant to today.

A person really in tune will not allow societal pressure to rule what she or he should be doing. Go into your heart and listen to your Being to decide. The mutual obligation should stop when one very strongly no longer wants to be with the other. The problems come when expectations continue.

As mentioned before, anyone you hate, you are chained to by steel. Here is a metaphysical way to lovingly release a Being–constricting adult relationship:

Take a piece of paper or a three–by–five–inch card and write the following:

I (your name) send my higher self to the higher self of (name). I (your name) accept full responsibility for all that has gone on between (name) and myself. I give permission for angels who specialize in healing relationships to take care of this. The angels may balance it completely. (Name) thank you for being my teacher. I send you unconditional love: I wish you great happiness, health, love and prosperity. I release you to your highest and best good now.

Every morning or evening, read through it with sincerity. Put a tab mark each time. Do this for a minimum of fifteen days. When you feel a genuine release, then you know it is done. It may take a lot longer than fifteen days! But according to practical metaphysician Catherine Ponder, fifteen days is the minimum.

On the vibration level, each person of the couple has an energetic body. Together, through their relationship, they have created a third energetic body. In the breakup, this third energetic body has to be pulled apart and torn down. Herein lies the pain, real, physical pain. When there are children involved, building the after–marriage relationship has to be very lovingly and skillfully done. Only old Souls are able to do this.

"What does metaphysics offer in regards to **raising children**? In relationships with your children, first, if you are the father, in order to establish a vibrational bonding, you can be present when your child is born.

Baby has been carried in the womb of the mother. Since this is before language development, the baby depends upon mom's vibrations for security.

If the mother is happy during pregnancy, this makes for a great beginning.

Baby needs the presence of these vibrations for at least the first two years of life and preferably the first four years. Moms, in your heart of hearts, you know this is true. Mom's presence and love create the energetic bonding which later allows the grown child to give and receive love and establish normal, bonded relationships.

Edgar Cayce brought in that "homemaker is the most honorable profession." When mom stays home for some years, this is infinitely better for the child. Thrift shops make it possible for a young couple to live inexpensively. When your immediate family does not have to have two cars, when you use cardboard boxes for furniture (or family hand–me–downs), you are creating an emotional legacy for the child. And some awesome memories of how you made do.

In raising children, if you can, "leave their Light unbent, " that is quite wonderful. There is a fine line between encouraging a child's spirit and socializing the child to be operational in society. Overcontrol is counter–productive. You want loving and responsible children. This is perhaps a parent's biggest challenge.

You know you aren't "bending their Light" when babies look you straight in the eye and don't look away, when the toddler jumps into your lap and gushes love, when the pre–schooler freely tells you intimate concerns, when the child is living without strategy, doing each act in total presence.

You can try to facilitate their particular spirit/Soul path by watching what interests them and encouraging that interest. Trying to make your children a carbon copy of yourselves is terribly cruel. Contrarily, helping your children express their unique Beingness sets up a life for them to Self–actualize.

"What you said earlier about a mom staying home with her baby, doesn't that prevent something we are entitled to, **FINANCIAL PROSPERITY?**" This question takes a bit of explaining. Indeed, every person is entitled to the basics of living: simple food, water, shelter, clothing and basic medical care. You need to pray for these routinely, especially if they seem to come hard. This prayer isn't greedy. Remember who you are, you are a child of God, an actual ray from the Godhead!

In the United States, because of the standard of living and the ethics around money ("The more you have the better"), a **greed** consciousness exists. Our product advertisers fan the flames. Then we are told to hoard what we have to ensure a secure old age.

Greed can be defined as an excessive or overly intense desire for money, possessions, or more that your share of anything.

Most people are not sensitive to the already mentioned fact that greed carries very bad karma. Our culture sets us up for this; even some metaphysical churches encourage this greed business, promoting as worthy, practitioner's superficial material wants and desires.

Please don't misunderstand, God doesn't want you to be poor. And you won't be if you are true to your Soul. Marsha Sinetar wrote DO WHAT YOU LOVE, THE MONEY WILL FOLLOW, Paulist Press, 997 Macarthur Boulevard, Mahwah, New Jersey 97430. Sinetar has a perfect understanding of how good things come to you as a by-product of putting God/Soul's urgings first in your life.

It is surprising to me how many metaphysicians max out their credit cards and somehow magically expect God to come down and pay off their debt! This is backwards thinking! It doesn't work! They haven't even done the service to their own Soul and fellow humans yet, and yet they expect some positive karma, money.

Another thing that surprises me is that some metaphysicians hate to pay their routine bills. Money is just vibration like everything else.

Hoarding money stops the flow. Once I understood the principle, I have learned to love quickly paying the phone bill, the power bill, the rent and mortgage payment, and so forth.

Back when I taught Introduction to Business, there was a principle called **money velocity**. It works like this: I pay for a hair cut. The hairdresser takes that $22 and buys two music tapes. The musician uses the $22 to buy some new strings for her guitar and so forth. My $22 spent generates a lot of spending. It helps the economy. It keeps the Holy Spirit flowing.

In other words, it is best metaphysically if you don't hoard *or* over-spend.

Now, what to do when you have a Soul urge, something spiritual you just can't forget, but it is going to take money that you don't have. Let's say you want to travel to Egypt to see the pyramids. If you have meditated on it, and the energy within seems to be push-ing you that way strongly, by all means, pray and affirm that you have the money to take the trip! This isn't greed. And you will get the money. Don't be afraid to do what your Being continually urges! (Go North, go North, go North, go North . . .)

Fear stops money flow. If you go into thoughts of poverty, and get terrified, this doesn't help your situation.

I say a daily affirmation: "I have increasing financial prosperity." I let The Universe decide what that means, so with my cultural indoc-trination, I don't get greed mixed up in it.

Money is wonderful when it comes to you automatically and abun-dantly, a by-product as you seek to express your highest spiritual nature.

By the way, in one of the Edgar Cayce readings, it came through that wanting a lovely space to stay, a home, was the spiritual yearning of wanting a substitute for our true home.

"Sometimes when I think of how many **MISTAKES** I have made, I am afraid to do anything. Do you have any advice?" There are no mistakes. When we are not gaining in Being growth, then we need to make changes to get moving again. Many seeming "mistakes" taught us many lessons.

When you haven't known the principles, how could you expect to act by the principles?

Practical shaman said, "If one thing doesn't work, just try another."

Here is a rendition of the Buddhist monk tale:

> A farmer went to the monk and moaned, "My prize stallion has run away. What will I do now? He was worth so much money."
>
> The monk said, "Who knows if it is good or bad."
>
> The following week, the farmer was back to see the monk. "Oh, I am so very happy. The stallion has come back and he brought a mare with him. Now I can breed horses and make a lot of money."
>
> The monk said, "Who knows if it is good or bad."
>
> Several weeks later, the farmer was back again. "My son was riding the mare and was thrown. He broke his back. My son was my main help on the farm. Oh my, I am in such a state. What will I do?"
>
> The monk said, "Who knows if it is good or bad."
>
> A month later, the farmer was back still again. "The military conscriptionists came around and my son couldn't go because he was in a cast. I am in a state of euphoria."
>
> And the monk said, "Who knows if it is good or bad."

"Okay, so there are no mistakes. Then what can I do about my feelings of **GUILT**?" Guilt is not a natural emotion. *It is taught to us, shamed and blamed into us.* Just address it honestly, "There goes that guilt feeling again," and let it go. You don't need a priest to absolve your guilt. Dear sentient Being, truly, you are innocent. You have *always* done the best you could under all the pervading pressures and your consciousness level. – Trust me, yes, you have! And "Freedom is what you do with – after what has been done to you!"

Every Being on the Planet of the Cross has done the best that could be done under prevailing circumstances, always.   A great part of those "circumstances" has been ignorance!

When I hear someone start a sentence with " I should have," "I could have," "I would have," these are clues to guilt feelings. I call these the (said fast): "should–uh–could–uh–would–uhs."

"Well, then, are there such things as **ETHICS AND MORALITY?**" Yes. "Do what is right." That is all you can ever do, and you do it with the level of consciousness you have at the time.

Do the right thing even if the other person is not. If they continue their dysfunctional behavior, you can forgive them, bless them and move out of their vibration.

As you may recall, kindness is very important. Sai Baba emphasizes that the milk of human kindness should be taught at every level of education. Indeed, in India, he and the educators he chose have developed a whole educational program in human values. There is an English version of this Human Values Program used in the United States. I wish I knew a reference.

I would like to talk here about another problem, "**THE BOTH–AND DILEMMA.**" Most people don't recognize one.

Anyone reading a metaphysical philosophy book has to be a good person looking for the very best way to live this precious life. Practical spirituality, metaphysics, is beautiful, knowing how the invisible behind the physical works.

We have been taught that there is a right and there is a wrong. What isn't taught is that in a dilemma, argument or confrontation, both sides, at some level, have some right:

It is true that your grandmother is sick and dying. It is true that if you take time off from work to care for her, your employer will ask you to resign.

It is true that your husband's work was extra tiring this week. It is true that a three-day week-end is approaching, and the family has not been to see your folks for a long time.

It is true that your car tires need replacing. It is true that you have a great urge to go see Sai Baba in India. It is true that you have only $200 in the bank.

It is true that as good neighbors, we as a country should try to do more business with Mexico. It is true that there is some corruption in government in Mexico.

It is true that Grandma Janis got annoyed when husband David's credit card company asked him fill to out a new, lengthy application after being a user for twenty-nine years, never a delinquent payment, when all he wanted was a gold card. It is true that the request from the credit card company is only "drama" (as he reminded her, so they could both laugh).

It is true that there will be a shooting today. It is true it is only drama.

The both-and dilemma can make you crazy without you realizing what you are up against. In confrontation or arguments, if you are smart, see it, and call it by name, if something needs to be done, you can use solution-finding skills so a win/win can be worked out. Instead of beating yourself up (or each other up), the energy can go into either solving the both-and dilemma or making the decision to drop it.

"Is there really a **DARK SIDE** if we refuse to see it?" Let me answer this with a true story. In a workshop with shaman, as it was ending, he asked us all to take a stone from his personal collection. (He was going on a trip to Australia, getting rid of unneeded possessions so he would not have much to store.)

I selected a pretty, stream-rolled white and light grey rock, symmetrical in size, about four inches across. Suddenly, he came up to me and took it away. I looked at him and tears rolled out of my eyes. I did not understand. Then he said, "You only want to see the side of Light. You do not want to see ugliness, the dark side. You must learn to look unflinchingly at everything, both the ugly and the beautiful. Now go and pick an ugly rock." I went back, selected the ugliest one I could, a dirty brown irregular blob, and held it up to him. Then he smiled at me and handed me both the white/grey rock *and* the ugly stone. When I got home that evening, I put the dark rock on top of the light rock and set the pair on my altar.

Later, at another workshop, he told us to view distressing video-tapes. A participant laughed and said, "You mean like Texas Chainsaw Massacre." Laughing, he said, "Yes, in another life, you have been just like the villain. You have to realize this and forgive yourself for it." Nothing can be changed until it is faced.

Which brings up the subject of **NEUROSES**. "Can you explain?" As the human grows, various psychological events impact upon per-sonality function. When there is a catastrophic event over which a person has no control, adrenaline goes into overproduction. After it is over, if this event can be talked out with a sympathetic person, and affectionate reassurances given, the damage can be repaired. If *it is not healed*, a "black hole" or trance-like state remains in the brain process. The injured person then gets weird around certain "reminding" events. If the "black hole" is repressed and is inaccessi-ble to memory, it is especially crippling.

A young boy was strongly shamed by his mother because several times she discovered him fondling his penis. Now, as a grown man, even through he is married, he still feels guilty about having sex.

A fifteen–year old was very much in love for the first time when her father's business transferred the whole family to China. The deep emotional pain and shock hit hard. At age thirty–four, she has not had another boyfriend. If a young man shows interest, she manages from her anxiety state to indicate that she is not interested.

A little girl was severely punished by her grandfather for having played in the mud, mostly making mud pies. This same girl, now a grown woman, has a compulsive need to keep washing her hands, even though they are not dirty.

What is really sad, is that a person's neurosis can become conta-gious, a **"trans-generational neurotic virus."** That is, it gets passed on. The severely punished little girl becomes a grown women, and in her innocence, teaches her own children compul-sive-hand washing. Her children are not neurotic, just weird!

As an adult with "black holes," you use current psychological energy to avoid the pain of facing the dark side and bringing it to the Light. The older the "black hole," the harder it is to heal. The earlier the injury (preverbal), the harder it is to heal. Counselors and self-help books are available to help get you started.

When you seek out a counselor, if you don't move fast, try someone else. Just as there are many paths to God, many different types of psychotherapy can heal the same problem. Through the years I have had psychotherapy from two psychiatrists, three clinical psy-chologists, a marriage/family/child counselor, a licensed clinical social worker, and a minister. All were helpful.

Ideally, you can let everything disruptive go and heal. You will never have a totally *healthy body* until you heal your neuroses. It does take a lot of emotional energy to look at the dark side and lim-itations. Everyone of us has so many, from this life and others. It is probably unrealistic to think you can get them all; however, the major neuroses can be accessed.

We will never become enlightened *as an individual person or as a race*, unless we can heal these major neuroses. Unhealed patterns are car-ried by the Being to a future life. (An example might be fear of knives if a person were killed by one in the last life.)

My model is that as my dark side is brought out into the Light and released, the "space" in which the dark material rested *can now house Light.*

As parents, Mom and Dad, it is particularly important that you pro-tect your children from "black hole" experiences. Or if an injury has happened, that you comfort, listen to the child, again and again let-ting the child relive the memory until there is no emotional energy left in the event. (This isn't much different than cleaning a physical wound.) Can you trust a babysitter to be this committed? Every time you leave your child, you need to check the day's occurrences. If the child is old enough, you can ask, "Did we have any tears, today?" "What did you cry about?"

One way of looking for your neuroses is to watch for situations in which you overreact. Or ask a friend! Another way, is to study repetitive–emotional–pain–situations.

If you can heal yourself of neurotic behavior, this in turn helps heal the archetypical patterns. When enough people have healed themselves, of say, "alcoholism," the collective unconscious will be healed and it will be impossible for a human to exhibit that behavior.

Thus, as you heal yourself of your neuroses – or others heal you, you improve the human race. Working on yourself, "the road less traveled" of *facing and healing your dark side* is therefore a noble road. You do it for generations to come. You are a true spiritual warrior.

You have to get yourself unblocked to let the love flow through.

I have found it very exciting to know that as I became aware of, and worked on my judgmentalness, it made it a tiny bit easier for the next person to let up on theirs, no matter where they lived in the world! And that one day, no one in the world will be judgmental. Then our underground beings can reveal themselves.

Another example, as individuals face and erase their child–beating behavior, this will eventually be erased as a potential behavior of the species.

Remember, as individuals build positive behaviors, for example, learning to communicate better on the interpersonal level, these positive behaviors will be assimilated into human behavior.

Many high–level spiritual Beings have chosen to come through abusive parents so that they could grow up, heal themselves, and *thus heal the collective.* It is no accident that psychotherapies and Twelve-step programs abound. Frequently, large numbers in this generation, the majority, are old Souls.

These glorious old Souls serve higher consciousness, and give even more benefit to the ancestral memories when they generously forgive their less-than-perfect parents. They are indeed magnificent spiritual warriors. And most don't even know it!

"What is **INSANITY**?" I like the following humorous definition: Doing the same thing over and over again but expecting different results.

"Is there a **DEVIL**?" The demons we see when the lower astral plane is accessed as we open up our psychic ability, traveling the spiritual path are real – sort of. Actually, they are a wispy product of our own fears.

A former roommate saw a brown "devil" with claws in our upstairs. I wasn't afraid because that devil wasn't in my consciousness space.

Just say an affirmation every day if you are troubled by these imaginary/real entities: "Negative entities and energies don't hang around with me, because you are not wanted." Then stamp your feet, loud. They will go away.

Then there is Lucifer, of whom we have already spoken.

"If there are no mistakes, is there **SIN**?" Not if you use the model of this planet as being a place to go to school to learn, to become a better Being.

Sin might be defined as not living up to the promises you made to your Being when you chose to be reborn in a human body. Since you mostly don't remember the promises, "sin" is generally not a very useful concept.

Sai Baba, commenting on the concept of sin, advised "Do not condemn yourselves as sinners; sin is a misnomer for what are really errors, provided you repent sincerely and resolve not to follow the evil again. Pray to the Lord to give strength to overcome the habits, which had enticed you when you were ignorant."

As alluded to earlier, I am in agreement with some metaphysical churches teaching that sin is just "human limitation."

The title of this last Chapter of COSMIC MAP is "You Have Traveled in the Dark and the Light." We just finished with the dark side!

"You promised us a tool to make positive change, **AFFIRMATIONS**." Yes, an affirmation is a statement of something to be actualized in your life. This statement then prepares you to align with the universal energies that govern its workings. Since the universe has mind stuff that tends to give you back what you think into it, it is important to be positive. The universe will deny you nothing if you are very clear about what you want, and it doesn't hurt anyone.

The idea is to make affirmative statements as if the statement is true now. Discomfort with this process will stop after a particular affirmation is said long enough.

What an affirmation does is to use thought forms, thoughts as energy through "**thought molds**." With God's power at your command, it is self–defeating, even dysfunctional behavior to complain of conditions as they are, when all you have to do is affirm them as you would like them to be.

For example, let's say that I have gained five pounds and want to lose them. Here is a possible affirmation that would work over time to eliminate this weight. It is better not to have a set time for the actualization: "I weigh 118 pounds" as I visualize myself (**creative visualization**) at this perfect–for–me weight in clothes that used to fit.

Now, when I first start saying it, I just acknowledge my feelings, "This statement is making me feel uncomfortable, sad, anxious, foolish (whatever) but that is okay for now.

People new to affirmations and creative visualizations sometimes feel they are lying. Not so, you are just using word tools to build yourself a better future.

More than one sentence can be used. Let's say I am not feeling well. Here is a longer affirmation: "I have wonderful health, body and psyche. I am always guided to the right health practitioner. It is a joy to keep my this–life temple fit for my beautiful Being." Then I picture in my mind myself doing things which require splendid health, for example skiing all day and taking an outdoor vacation trip.

There have been times that I actually have had two and one-half pages of typed affirmations. I say these first thing in the morning. I have varied my practice and suggest doing what feels right to you. Other possibilities are before or after meditation or just before you fall asleep at night. And you may want to say them twice a day. In the privacy of your own home, you can say them loud and emphatically

Spend some time getting clear on what you want and don't want in your life. Then make your list. It is positively amazing the changes that come with taking the responsibility for creating a better life.

Along with affirmations and creative visualizations comes another term, **breakthrough thinking**. In breakthrough thinking, a goal or plan is created without thinking of limitations of money, personnel or time. By creating a more inspiring goal, the enthusiasm and dreampower vibrations can set in motion a practical plan to reach it. This is a great tool for a committee, too. How do you think a new park or a sky scraper gets created?

"After reading this book, although I plan to read more books, I still want a **MASTER TEACHER**. Do you have any advice for me?" You will find some of the following a review:

If you can get yourself into the presence of someone Self-realized, and hear them speaking from their Being, you will obtain some very pure information. I highly recommend it.

If you are meditating daily, in some way, a teacher will come to you. You will know if what a teacher is saying resonates with you. When it doesn't, or *doesn't anymore*, move away and find a new teacher.

A great teacher gives lovingly, leaves the followers free to choose after suggesting a course of action, is supportive but doesn't flatter or chastise, and knows that the source of his or her power is God and the Holy Spirit.

If the teacher wants to take over your life's direction, be very wary. And last, if you are asked to detach from your bank account, possessions, family, or friends, this is not a teacher who serves God. Run very fast.

It is not absolutely necessary to have teachers or a master, but if you have them, the easiest, safest and most effective path can be shown to you. For most of us, it will enable us to reach God–realization in fewer lifetimes. But we will all get there sooner or later.

As I have come in contact with my teachers, the hardest thing for me to realize was that I couldn't copy them or their lifestyle. I had to learn to evolve in my own way. But for a very long time, I kept thinking I would find one who would be my role model. I never have.

Now before I sum up the prophecies I have heard about, let's take a look at all the parts to be played in this drama of dramas, ascension on the Planet of the Cross, the outcome of which is not certain. This is a cosmic experiment. Believe me, I am not kidding when I say your help is needed!

I am sure my list of characters is not completely accurate nor all inclusive. The point is, we have an immense number of helpers, under God, who want us to succeed, our "God Squad!"

God, our Father/Mother, The Ancient of Days, has a hierarchy in our universe. As mentioned at the beginning of this chapter, all the Light brotherhood must obtain the approval and support for changes from our creator. There are twenty–four elders who always sit with God.

Metatron, under God's direction, is the incredible Light Being who makes sure the outer universe has plenty of Light. He took Hurtak in his Light body to the highest heaven. **Uriel**, another incredible Light Being, makes sure that our Soul has the inner Light for our inner–mind channels. **Michael** is an archangel, a master angel, who helps keep the Light pure and thus protects us. Other archangels are **Gabriel** and **Raphael**, who assist Michael in our dimension (and the coming dimensions); also **Jeremiel** and **Sariel** are archangels and perhaps there are more.

Melchizedek, according to Hurtak, is another incredible Light Being, co–equal with Metatron and Michael, specializing in "the rescue, regenesis and re-education of worlds going through the purification of the living Light." Memorize these three names: Metatron, Michael and Melchizedek. Sing them to yourself when you need comfort.

There are a host of Ascended Masters. Having mastered this world in a series of incarnations, most are out of body as we know the body; however, they can temporarily or for a lifetime, take a human body. There are about seven thousand actually incarnated on The Planet of the Cross. They are our best friends, actively helping to get us out of this dimension where we too often torment each other. Saint Germain, Ascended Master, currently out of body, through Godfrey Ray King said:

> The Ascended Masters are guardians of humanity and have worked through the centuries from the invisible as well as the physical to awaken, to bless, to enlighten and lift mankind out of its self-created degradation and selfishness.

And

> We have conquered death by complete and eternal domination over the atomic substance of the physical body and the world. All things obey our commands. The laws of Nature and the Universe are our willing, obedient servants.

Sai Baba, our Avatar, is a living example. All are ready to help give us a new start. It is time for the changing of the guard.

The hierarchy of Archangels and angels is working constantly on humankind's behalf. Then there are the spirit guides and nature spirits. Increasingly, a new term is appearing in the channeled literature, "**Time Lords**." Whether these Light Beings of physical creation are the same as nature or elemental spirits, is not clear, yet. Perhaps they supervise the nature or elemental spirits.

Then we have our potential friends under the earth, including the ocean, the advanced subterranean cultures. And I have not as yet mentioned the **Hakamin**. Hurtak tells us "There are thirty-six administrative directors on our planet at all times. They are the Hakamin, the wise men who can enter into the Father/Mother's presence at any time." Certainly Paul Twitchell's guide who took him to see the Godhead, Rebazar Tarzs, is one of them.

We have our millions of extraterrestrial friends who can freely circumnavigate the dimensions, the outer universe, the physical worlds, planets and stars plus their councils and federations.

None of my study has answered my question, "Who or what type was that Light Being, the seeming size of a two-story house, that met me on my way out of my body during my near-death experience; and with so much love, gave me the permission and the energy to come back?"

All the Beings and Soul minds in the aforementioned paragraphs are watching conditions on our planet Earth, changing their schedules and updating their plans to be here in concert for us.

Last but not least is us. The exact timing depends on how quickly you and I stop adding negative thought forms and clean up the collective consciousness through working on ourselves and raising the earth consciousness vibration by doing our spiritual work, including the practices.

Let me say that again, *they* are waiting for *us*!

Meher Baba, the brilliant Soul, the reincarnation of my old friend, Jesus, said it poetically:

> The individual Soul is entangled in the world of forms and does not know itself as one with the Being of God.

> This ignorance constitutes the bondage of the Soul and spiritual practices must aim at securing emancipation from this bondage.

The ascension in this Seventh Golden Spiritual Age will undoubtedly be successful. However, it is not a sure thing. That is why effort at all levels is needed.

"What exactly does **ASCENSION** mean?" It is our trip into Christ Consciousness. Ascension is a moving in consciousness from one dimension to another while in a physical body. For some, this will mean living in a fourth–dimensional reality. It may be that the fourth dimension is that time portal through which we pass, so some of us may go right into a fifth–dimensional or higher reality.

In COSMIC MAP I have attempted to lay the ground work to motivate you to want to evolve into a higher consciousness and to tell you the basics of how to get ready. I'll provide a brief review of the practices as COSMIC MAP closes. Now for the promised prophesies.

"There are the old **PROPHESIES** and many more are coming in today. You said you would give an overview. So what do you think is going to happen?"

There is a five–thousand–year–old Indian scriptural book called the Mahabharta. It prophesied an Avatar matching the description of Sai Baba. The prediction was that during the Avatar's lifetime, peace would come to earth and rulers would govern their countries with love, wisdom and fairness.

In the Bhagavad Gita, Krishna, the Avatar, talking as God promised: "When goodness grows weak, when evil increases, I make myself a body. In every age I come back to deliver the holy, to destroy the sin of the sinner, to establish righteousness." Theosophist writer Bhagwan Das said, "When the forces of evil have reached the end of their appointed time, come the history–making Avatars."

Just because most people have never heard of Sai Baba, we have to realize this has been the pattern. Few of their contemporaries recognized Lord Krishna, Lord Buddha, Lord Rama, Lord Jesus or Lord Meher as Avatars. Avatar powers and their glory have not been understood.

However, our live Avatar is more accessible and *his ministry has been long and public.* He is credited with having eight million devotees worldwide whom he has urged to accept him, not on blind faith, but through inquiry and reason. *So the prophesies about an Avatar at this time of spiritual regeneration have already actualized.* And he has said he will live for twenty–five more years.

Drunvalo predicts that by the end of this century, every last person left on the planet will ascend at least into the next dimensional level. We are going to

move into a slightly shorter wavelength and a higher energy vibration. He has also said that people who die between now and then,
may go into Christ consciousness through resurrection.

In **resurrection** the human body dies, but later is given a regener-
ated body.

About 58 A. D. Jesus' disciple, Paul, said what became incorporated
into the Bible as the Book of Romans. Here are some excerpts from
Romans 8:18–23:

> Yet what we suffer now is nothing compared to the glory he
> will give us later. For all creation is waiting patiently and
> hopefully for that future day when God will resurrect his
> children . . . We, too, wait anxiously for that day when God
> will give us our full rights as his children, including the new
> bodies he has promised us – bodies that will never be sick
> again and will never die."

Nostradomus saw an opening and a new way after the year 2000.

The Mayan calendar ends in 2012.

Hurtak once predicted that many of the most spiritual people would
leave their earth body traveling in their Light body going into a
higher dimension sometime before 2003. He teaches that the work
of friendly extraterrestrials will help in the changes. He told followers that the horrible Armageddon prophecies, a decisive spiritual
battle in the last days between the forces of good and evil, has
already taken place – in space! *The Light forces won!*

Indeed, containing lots of symbols and visions, Revelations and its
prediction of Armageddon is one of the most puzzling books of the
Bible. Apostle John's authorship is disputed.

I went scurrying for my copy of THE LIVING BIBLE and Revelations
after an event which occurred on June 16, 1994. A devout friend
called and told me this tale: "My friend from the San Francisco Bay
area who has been on the path for a long while just called me! She
was commuting to work. All of a sudden a huge Light figure
entered her car and she heard it say: 'I am the first angel here to

blow my trumpet.'"

The stunned woman started swerving and was promptly pulled over by a California Highway Patrol officer. She said to the state policeman, 'You are not going to believe this, but an angel just entered my car and told me that it was first-trumpet time.' He responded with, 'Ma'am, you are not going to believe this either, but you are the *seventh* car I have pulled over this morning who told me the same story.'"

I shared what I had heard with one of my fundamental Christian sons. His reply, "Mom! That is really interesting!   Someone I know told one of my friends the same story, only our grapevine got it from the . . . *eighth* car pulled over this morning . . .!'"

In Revelations, during the last days, seven angels blow trumpets. These are not ordinary angels, but the heads of the angel hierarchy, "seven angels which stood before God." They have earned their position by aiding the evolutionary cycles of mankind.

In I Corinthians 15:51 we learn: "But I am telling you this strange and wonderful secret: We shall not all die, but we shall all be given new bodies. It will all happen in a moment, in the twinkling of an eye, when the last trumpet is blown."

There are the predictions from Mary, Mother of Jesus, channeled through Annie Kirkwood, originally, of earth changes and terrible disasters. Annie's newsletter sometimes notes disasters that have already happened. However, Annie, in a recent newsletter said, "Now I understand that the whole reasoning for predictions and prophecy is for people to become aware, pray, raise their awareness, change themselves and through the inner changes, change the future."

Apparently we are not making changes fast enough. Between June 1994 and June 1995, earthquakes killed well over fourteen hundred people. There have been floods, tornadoes, forest fires and strange weather patterns.

In a report circulated by the Center of Attention Network newsletter, Pope John had visitations from Mary in the 1950s and 1960s which he recorded in a diary. "May 19, 1962: From the Heavens will appear the saviors. They will arrive on June 5, 1995, and begin their task of assisting the cleanup and repair of the environment and the crippled countries. There will be odd-looking beings, but they come in peace, and will, with God's guidance, [help humanity] transform Earth from a charred spinning rock to a lush oasis in space. The survivors will flourish in a world without war, disease or hatred." Of course, this date has passed, but we know that all old predictions have timing problems because of that laser and hologram intervention conducted by our Star Being friends in 1972.

Edgar Cayce's readings had the prediction of a messiah in the period around 1998. See Edgar Cayce's Story of THE ORIGIN AND DESTINY OF MAN, Lytle Robinson, Berkeley Books, 200 Madison Avenue, New York, New York 10016.

In a monthly newsletter called The Emergence, channel Benjamin Creme reports the latest speaking appearances of **Maitreya** (pronounced my-TRAY-uh,) who may be Lord Buddha come again. We take this publication in an attempt to keep updated: Tara Center, Box 6001, North Hollywood, CA 91603, SASE. According to Creme, Maitreya, astralprojecting and materializing before crowds numbering in the hundreds around the world will soon be making appearances that the world press cannot ignore.

Among other Ascended-Master characteristics, Maitreya appears in different places simultaneously and is totally psychic.

In the United States, on April 9, 1995, Maitreya appeared before approximately six hundred people in Phoenix, Arizona. Creme tells us he spoke for eighteen minutes. On June 4, 1995, he made another appearance in our country, the specific place was not reported.

"On May 28, 1995, Maitreya appeared in Sydney, Australia to three hundred Fundamentalist Christians and spoke for eighteen minutes." The people were frightened. Nevertheless, some pictures were taken.

Washta channeled us that Buddha was a Being who came from the star Arcturus. He communicated to us that "As in Christianity, Buddhism mutated into a formal concept of religion in which much of the energy was lost."

When the colony of Arcturians was destroyed by the dark brotherhood, some of the Arcturians were rescued and taken back; others
were allowed to reincarnate here in other forms. In the book, WE
THE ARCTURIANS (A TRUE STORY), channeler of Kuthumi, Norma
Milanovich, brought in that "We had begun an incredible civilization. It would take eons of time to repeat the efforts."

According to Milanovich, Kuthumi, an Ascended Master, had many
incarnations on our planet: a few are as Pythagoras, St. Francis of
Assisi and John the Baptist. He is telling us that *although things will
get worse here before they get better*, all the positive characters in this
great drama as mentioned before, are working together to transform
the energy of our beloved Earth to a Garden of Eden in the galaxy.

The Arcturians are so committed to us that they "man" space vehicles close by all the time. The short, very slender, greenish, semi-
etheric Beings defy gravity and move things with their minds. They
see more telepathically than with their large, almond-shaped eyes.
They have no ears. They don't eat as we understand taking nour-
ishment, but fill themselves occasionally with a concoction of spiritual energy vibrations. It is more like filling a gas tank. They do
have hearts and want badly to teach us how to use the heart to lead
us back to God. A chilling insight is that once they spend time on
The Planet of the Cross, they have to return to their space ship and
use a special procedure to recuperate from our dark, dense dimension.

An inconsistency, in a Shared Vision interview, a walk-in named
Shaari, from Arcturus, described these loving Beings as six to seven
feet tall – but who knows? They may vary as much as we do.

In her work, Dr. Norma Milanovich speaks of our evolution into the
fifth dimension, *with the fourth dimension being just a stepping stone*.
Stay tuned. I am not clear either how all of this is going to work.
Do read her books; they are mind benders!

In the book, YOU ARE BECOMING A GALACTIC HUMAN, channeler
Sheldon Nidle and devout writer-scribe Virginia Essene tell of a
photon belt (Light particles in the shape of a 759,864-billion-miles-
thick torus, a donut shape) which planet earth is going to flow
through. They say our scientists have known of this belt since 1961,

when it was first picked up by satellite instrumentation. This huge mass of Light will help humankind to full consciousness, the completion of the transformation of our DNA and chakra systems, and the transformation into a semi–etheric body.

Sirians have a relatively human–looking body, come in two sexes like we do – male and female, are somewhat taller than we average, and have two skin colors, one very pale and the other light greenish.

This photon belt is supposed to put our beloved Planet of the Cross into darkness with sub–zero temperatures for three days. We will be forewarned of the exact dates. Individually, our preparation will include having on hand, food, water, wool blankets and wraps. We are asked not to use fires. Electricity and batteries won't work.

Washta, through Nidle and Essene in WE ARE BECOMING A GALACTIC HUMAN, tells us that the Sirians and other committed help–earth extraterrestrials, the same Star Beings who saved the earth in 1972, may be making mass landing as early as late 1995 but before the end of 1996. Among many other helpful interventions, they intend to help re–establish the ice firmament so the earth won't have to cope with the weather. Sheldon Nidle gives a talk every few months in the greater San Francisco Bay area, assuring people about any changes of plan and is ready to give new dates when he gets them from Washta.

All star fleets of the different extraterrestrials *serving the Light* were asked here by the Galactic Command and the Ascended Masters. Each group will have a different role. Most sources are saying that the Earth itself will eventually be pulled into a different orbit closer to the Sirius complex. And most sources agree that this will make another pole shift unnecessary.

The Galactic Federation is like the main government of the entire Galaxy. It is the peacekeeper and regulator. This federation of planets work together to keep harmony throughout all civilizations.

The Galactic Command, just mentioned paragraph before last, is the military branch of the Galactic Federation. **Ashtar** is the best known representative of the Galactic Command. He is like the General Mac Arthur of the Pacific Command during World War II and just as controversial. Ashtar channels through many people today.

Ashtar is the overseer of the military forces in the area, who, he says, are seeking peace.

In the Planet of the Cross sector, part of his job is to facilitate negotiations and peace making.

Most evolved Souls say that the Planet of the Cross' *institutions and processes that are greedy, ego-centered, self-serving and/or needlessly hurt fellow humans, will have to be totally remade.* Those of us that choose to remain on The Planet of the Cross will do the remaking job, "with a little bit of help from our friends."

See the Afterword for more on the transformation of institutions and organizations from within by committed people.

Beloved child of The Universe, you can start now by refusing to cooperate with greedy institutions. Don't stand back from your own righteous indignation! And while you are at it, stop doing work that just doesn't make sense and needlessly hurts people.

I am aware that in the book of Matthew, there is the prediction of many fake Christs and false prophets who arise and do such wonders as to deceive the very elect. But also from current day Bible scholars we know that Matthew was not written in its final form by the apostle Matthew. There is uncertainty as to how the book of Matthew took shape. However, I would agree about the false prophets. There are many gurus taking a lot of people's money. They have some Light and a lot of spiritual ego.

Now, what, if anything, do I think is going to happen, and if something, when? Obviously I believe something extraordinary is going on. My sense of the Ascension is that the exact timing and the form depends on God's will and the many types of celestial intelligences committed to putting it into action. Our human race's collective ability to "lighten up" is the final piece of the puzzle.

To keep updated, you can order the newsletters I have mentioned and others of which you become aware. Mostly, *you can be as receptive as possible and keep in touch with your Being through meditation. Your own Being's resonance or lack of resonance will help alert you to truth.*

In Thessalonians 1 and 2, we are told that the day will be a surprise, "God's veiled plan;" nobody knows it.

As for me, since our mandated move to the central California coast, I have had a sharp sense of *urgency* to get Cosmic Map *published*. And when I called a devout psychic whom I hadn't had contact with in four years to ask how we should price the temple house, she asked permission to give me some free-form impressions before dealing with my question. One of the things she said was, "Beings who are not from planet earth will be contacting you in your new area. You don't have to be concerned about finding them; they will find you."

That brought to mind what Dr. Jim Hurtak said to me the time I attended his workshop. I was sitting among thirty people; Hurtak, speaking to the group about the age of the sphinx, suddenly paused, turned to the side where I sat and said to me, "Janis, you will not be stopped." He then turned to the man sitting beside me, who had been instrumental in getting me to this Hurtak workshop. This gentlemen, then a UCM minister-in-training, now a minister, got the same message, "you will not be stopped." Then, not missing a beat, Hurtak returned to his talk.

Although Drunvalo made an approximate time prediction, he says, "We are going so fast, predictions don't work anymore."

Again and again I have heard through the years that as Souls, we have all chosen, even begged to be on the Planet of the Cross at this time. Is Daniel 12:13 another Bible reference to reincarnation? Daniel was having a vision in which the end of the world was being prophesied. But he was told not to be concerned in that life. "But go on now to the end of your life and your rest; for you will rise again and have your full share of those last days." I am sure Daniel is among us.

Remembering all of the help you have from God on down through the great spiritual hierarchy and the Galactic Command and Galactic Federation, if you have let go of your fear of death and have practiced non-attachment, these possibilities you can handle: (1) Your earth body will die. Your Being will leave this dimension and earth never to return here. You will travel to higher dimensions. In the Cayce readings we find:

> When the body is no longer a hindrance to the free expression of the Soul, when the conscious mind merges with the subconscious or unconscious, the soul is as free in matter as out of it, the earth cycle is finished and the entity goes on to new adventures. It has become one with the Godhead.

And

> There is the changing from one development to another until the entity passes from the solar system through Arcturus or Septimus. [I was unable to find out anything about Septimus.]

Continuing with the possibilities of what may happen: (2) Your earth body will die. Your Being will be given a resurrected body in the new consciousness and you will help build the new society. (3) Your earth body will change as you, "in the twinkling of an eye," at the last trumpet, consciously experience evolving from a "larvae into a butterfly," from a dense, third–dimension human into a Light fourth– or higher–dimension human. In this lighter, semi–etheric body and consciousness, you will intuitively know the work which your Soul is yearning to do. You will be taught anything you need to know by loving Star Beings and very evolved humans.

(4) Like Jesus, you will simply leave this plane with your spiritual-ized physical body intact. You will have changed your garment of flesh into a garment of splendor. Sealed inside the tomb, Jesus neat-ly folded his burial cloth, set it down, and left in his spiritualized human body out through the wall! The tomb as you recall, was empty when the stone was rolled back.

And of course the last possibility is: (5) Nothing unusual will hap-pen. For now, you will not notice anything out of the ordinary.

Although many of my friends have told me which alternative they prefer for their Soul journey, I haven't given it much thought, not on the conscious level anyway, although the Pleiades draw me

because I understand that dancing and music have reached very
high levels.

I don't understand anyone seriously "choosing now;" how do you
know how much Soul energy you have or whether you have the
potential for a body that will either "turn into a butterfly" or a spiritualized body that will want to leave?

All possibilities except (5) have attractive aspects. In this last option,
I would have to ignore the earth's terminal mess. It is hard to say
which problem is the most serious. Is it the impending axis rota-
tion? As said earlier, rotations have occurred every twelve-thou-
sand, five-hundred years to thirteen-thousand years and one is due
anytime. Then there is the ozone depletion: an August 1995 report
said that at one measuring spot, there was forty percent less ozone
than there had been in 1960. And I can never be proud to be an
earthling as long as the Planet of the Cross has the inequities: poor,
starving, and politically- and socially-abused people.

"When and if they come in mass, millions of them, will everybody
see our loving extraterrestrial helpers?" This is an interesting question. Uri Geller related on a TV show his experience while riding in
an airplane. Uri is the famous man who uses **psychokinesis**, mind
power, to change elements, for example bending spoons and starting
broken watches. "I saw this UFO," he explained, "a flying cigar-
shaped vehicle right alongside our plane. I got very excited and
invited some of my fellow passengers to look out the window, too.
But no one could see it!"

Remember, I can easily believe in spoon bending with the mind, as I
saw it done by a powerful psychic woman in my own kitchen.

Then there is the story of a friend's child who saw a flying saucer.
"It came out of a hole in the sky." Apparently, there are portals
through consciousness levels through which they travel. And the
Bermuda Triangle is one of them.

We can wonder about our U. S. Government when we read Dr. Fred
Bell's THE PROMISE, Inner Light Publications, P. O. Box 753 (CS),
New Brunswick, NJ 08903. The next two paragraphs condense his
story published in 1991.

Bell was just out of high school in 1958 when he joined the Air Force and was stationed at Point Arena, California. A "techie" by nature, he was assigned to the 776 Radar Squadron. One evening, those in charge of the screens saw one–hundred eighty–seven UFOs swoop over and head toward South America at descent speeds of twenty–thousand mph, leveling to five–thousand mph. Another evening, a smaller group headed toward Mexico. He was doubly incredulous when he saw the UFO reports being shredded on the order of the base commander. Bell lasted only seven weeks in the Air Force.

Metaphysician Fred Bell is not an ordinary old Soul. During child-hood, he heard a feminine voice "in his head" that gave him loving directions. As he has grown into middle age, he has become famil-iar with the Pleiadean of the voice, who has on occasion material-ized for him in this third dimension. Several times he has been taken aboard her space ship. She is young–looking, beautiful, and has spent an amazing two–hundred years (earth–year time) in her current body, not too much different in appearance from a human except for her exquisite good looks and extra large eyes. She is helping him help us by sharing Pleiadean information.

Beings from the far–away Pleiadean star system were among our friends who saved the earth in 1972. On another silver chain hang-ing below my cross I wear a Pleiadean receptor, designed by Bell's Pleiadean lady friend and manufactured by him. He sells them at his workshops; I attended one in 1992. This receptor is supposed to be adjusting my vibrations for the coming changes. No other piece of worn jewelry gets the comments that my receptor does!

I believe that our friends, the Sirians, Arcturians, Pleiadeans and oth-ers, at this hour are working on realigning the dimensional grids and portals of the earth; they have placed their manufactured crys-tals at key spots. And I believe many are already here, going back up to their space ships when necessary. I finally accepted this when I read of Washta channeling that Sirians can completely transform their bodies to move around in many aspects of reality, even being able to increase their vibration so that the average human would think the extraterrestrial had disappeared.

What to make of all of this? First, I know I am looking through those very limited eyes I described for you, a mind with numerous channels not to mention dense third–dimensional consciousness.

Second, our many helpers operate out of the higher dimensions where events are not on a linear–time schedule. They work out of dimensions and places where things seem to flow in spiritual increments, in a harmony, in a cosmic sync, a process which we will come to understand and appreciate.

Asking for linear–time dates and hours must complicate their orchestration.

Third, I am clear that I never own anything permanently except my Soul. So, in the meantime, I can "be in the moment" for those persons and things with whom I am now associated, plus in the future are drawn to; I can really appreciate, enjoy and care, holding a state of positive expectancy.

Fourth, I truly understand why our government has not revealed UFO knowledge to the public. In fact, there is no such thing as "our government" except for our projections on the authority as we perceive it.

What we have had are individuals on career curves, each hoping their curve would move upwards. People rarely risk military court martial or the losing of a lucrative government job, including the Presidency of the United States. And each military person or government official has had only one piece of the story. What is different now, is that so many who know so much *are retired*. They are starting to tell.

Then there is this real concern: Just which nation's head is going to talk to the Star Beings? Do you think the world is going to stand aside and let the United States do all the communicating?

And what to do if the Greys and Insectoids and other negative extraterrestrials are breaking their treaties and coming back? I think they may be.

And let's be honest, have most of us world citizens *really* wanted to know?

Scientists, psychologists, UFO researchers and others are getting together and sharing. In May of 1995, one–hundred–sixty participants, including advisor to NASA, Dr. Jim Hurtak, met together under the umbrella topic of extraterrestrials. See Appendix J, "When Cosmic Cultures Meet: Exploring the Practical Ramifications of Our Reunions With Our Extraterrestrial Sisters and Brothers of the Light" for a first-hand report by channeler Mary Lynn. This is one Appendix you don't want to miss!

In her Divine Connections Newsletter (see Appendix J for where to order) Mary Lynn tells about sightings over Mexico City, "for five hours stopping traffic." The Mexican Air Force did not intervene. Ordinary Mexican citizens took videos. The TV station where Jaime Maussan, a TV journalist and director of "Sixty Minutes, Mexico City," is employed has collected over two-thousand of these moving pictures.

At the conference, Mary Lynn watched twenty-one seconds of footage, shot September 16, 1994, of a Light Being with an elongated head who had allowed herself, himself, or itself to be seen. (Was it a she, he, s/he or it?) I have seen pictures of ancient Mayans and Egyptians with these elongated heads.

We bought Maussan's compilation of those two-thousand non-professional videos. From the best fifty, he had made this just-produced commentary video. For anyone knowing how film makers can "phony up" footage, I can tell you, this was the real thing. In the background of this poorly photographed composite, we could occasionally hear roosters crowing and the excited talk of ordinary people (David can understand some Spanish).

In another newly breaking development, Steven Greer, M. D. is interviewed by Keith Thompson in the July/August 1995 Yoga Journal for an article titled, "If We Call Them, Will They Come?" The North Carolina physician is chairman of the Department of Emergency Medicine where he is on call. His second job is volunteering to be an interplanetary diplomat as head of the Center for the Study of Extraterrestrial Intelligence.

His group initiates encounters with extraterrestrial spacecraft and the Beings inside. They use group meditation and visualization (coherent-thought sequences). In March 1992 at 8:24 p.m. ". . . five craft . . . appeared with a bright circle of white light which shifted to pulsating cherry-red-orange . . . [our group of thirty-nine] signaled to the

UFO three times with a five-hundred thousand candle-power light, and to everyone's astonishment, the lead craft flashed back three times. . . When I flashed two times, then five times, the craft responded by signaling two times, then five times. During this time, our group continued sending peaceful intentions. The entire episode lasted ten to twelve minutes.

Two air force pilots witnessed the event from another location. Greer explained that "This contact convinced us that we have started down a path that will culminate in a full meeting and on-board experience with the extraterrestrials."

In a 1993 Video interview of Dr. Jim Hurtak, named Extraterrestrial Realities, available through the Academy of Future Science, Hurtak says that biological entities were taken in 1947 in New Mexico when two spacecraft crashed. Shown are drawings of these Beings.

Hurtak is calm, responsible and extremely well informed. This is the same James J. Hurtak, PhD, I have been talking about throughout Cosmic Map, the one that was taken to the highest heaven. Dr. Hurtak is a social scientist, anthropologist and futurist. Founder and President of the Academy of Future Science, he has been a consultant on extraterrestrial films and books. He has lectured before the Academy of Science, in the former Soviet Union and before the Academy of Science in China.

Dr. Hurtak has been investigating extraterrestrials for twenty years. He has explored the sightings and visitations of indigent cultures. He was the featured speaker at the first world conference in April of 1977 in Acapulco, Mexico on extraterrestrial activity. Bottom line, Dr. Hurtak says that after forty-five years, we have a sufficient data base to make intelligent decisions.

He notes further that we can choose who we work with, who we co-create with. He encourages us to choose to work with those who respect us and those who share the same Godhead. He sees us working with our brothers and sisters of the stars, our cosmic counterparts, as we learn to master space, time and energy. He says, "I believe it is time to bring forth the documentation."

This would make an excellent educational video on Star Beings, a

UFO documentary for a television station. Backing Hurtak's Extraterrestrial Realities could be Many Voices in a Cosmic Dialog, the name of the Maussan "best fifty" video compilation.

In the <u>Yoga Journal</u> article quoted here, Greer said that military and commercial aircraft pilots have reported more than three thousand, five hundred UFO sightings.

Indeed, I am getting the strong feeling that the friendly Star Beings would like us to invite them here. From Bell, Milanovich, Sharula, Drunvalo and others, we know they have many helpful technologies to share, among them a way of tapping into unlimited energy, without any negative side effects.

I am willing to forgive my government and other governments for the cover-up, now. Are you? This is the time to put forgiveness on the line. A repeat: We have to forgive every person, every event, every group, every company, every institution, everything before we can go on!

When I was just a little girl, I learned that Jesus "bids us shine." I have come to understand this as listening to what my Soul urges me to do and then following through. One day, I got the idea of sending the following letter, which I did:

> President of the United States
> 1600 Pennsylvania Avenue, N. W.
> Washington, D.C. 20500:
>
> Subject: UFOs and extraterrestrials
>
> Namaste, Mr. President, The God in me greets the God in you.
>
> I forgive the cover-up by world governments around extraterrestrials and UFOs. I know everyone involved was doing cover-up activities for some perceived good reason, and who knows, maybe the timing just wasn't right.
>
> However, I want to know the facts, *now.* I believe the people of the Planet of the Cross are grown up enough to handle the truth. I believe that many of these extraterrest-

rials want to help us on the Planet of the Cross. And God knows, we need all the help we can get on such problems as massive sun flares, depletion of the ozone layer, the on–coming axis shift, and finding a major renewable energy source.

Not to mention the photon belt which is rapidly approaching as it does every Kali Yuga, twenty–six thousand years. We may, even now as I write, be in the outer fringes of the photon belt's emanations.

This may seem naive, but I believe this to be the truth: The good Star Beings have not forced their ideas on us because they want to leave us our free will. They would like to be invited. The bad guy extraterrestrials haven't overtaken us as a nation because they are afraid to; but we need to know, on an individual basis, how to protect ourselves from them.

I would like to nominate perhaps the most knowledgeable scientific thinker on this subject to become your advisor. He will be able to add to what you already know. And what we already know. His name is James J. Hurtak, PhD. He can be reached by writing The Academy For Future Science, P. O. Box FE, Los Gatos, California 95031.

Hurtak is a remarkable human Being. He is a most devout man committed to God and the human race. Researching extraterrestrials for twenty years has been an important part of his life's work. And he has already worked with NASA!

From his research he had identified approximately seventy of the good guy races of ETs and approximately fifty–four races of the less than desirable ETs. He says we now have tremendous opportunities for planetary growth. With the right leadership, this information could be shared with all citizens in all nations, giving the opportunity to bring the world together.

Indeed, the "bad guys," often with grotesque forms, have a history of among other things: (1) Capturing with a hypnotic–type of mind control, men, women, and children. (2) Through the use of surgery, putting "chips" in a person's body that send signals over time to destroy a person's health. (3) Taking by surgery, sexual cells, mixing them with their own, with the purpose of creating a race of sub–humans. They have implanted these embryos in unwilling, but unable to protest, women, forcing them to give birth to their horrible hybrids.

The "good guys" know how to help with our problems as stated. They respect our free will, our knowledge, our human rights, and our spirituality. They also respect the Galactic Command.

The very highest of these extraterrestrials, whom Hurtak calls "**ultraterrestrials**," the angelic ETs, are the Ascended Masters like Jesus, Mary and Saint Germain. These beings travel in their own Light "envelopes," called a **Merkabah**, energy envelopes with superluminal Light. This advanced intelligence doesn't require a specific, solid material form. The advanced ETs bring along with their practical solutions to our problems, prophesy, revelation, spiritual sanctification and a sense of uplift.

James J. Hurtak, PhD says we now have tremendous opportunities for planetary growth. By sharing information about extraterrestrials with the world's nations and citizens, with the right leadership, this could bring the people of the Planet of the Cross together and be one of the factors to create heaven on earth, as we evolve from homo sapien to homo nova.

God bless you, Mr. President
Grandma Janis

If intuitively, you feel you need to write a similar letter, I would invite you to follow that urge.

Beloved ray of God, here is a final synopsis of the Soul practices presented in Cosmic Map for this time of spiritual regeneration.

No matter what happens, these will give you more Soul energy plus helping the Planet of the Cross:

Grandma Janis' Compilation from COSMIC MAP:
How to Help in the Positive Transformation of the Human Race

Laugh; downsize your ego; let God's love flow through you; find spiritual community; support, reinforce, inform and love each other; breathe deeply, often; meditate; relax, relax; develop your intuition; get to know your eternal Radiant One, your "mommy/daddy," Yahveh, through becoming acquainted with your Being; chant and sing devotional songs; worship; be kind; be appreciative; pray; have positive thoughts, attitudes and behaviors. Practice the positive-karma–generating behaviors. Discipline your thoughts so as not to create negativity (ugly, dark energetic blobs that some one has to clean up – or the insectoids "eat!") Ask for guidance daily, "Yahveh, what would you have me do?" Process your dreams; find and heal your neuroses so God's love finds no stuck spots (remember, this love hitting too many stuck spots can make you sick and cause physical body death by its intense, pure vibrations); quickly process and let go of your negative emotions; be of service to those around you; become acquainted with some Ascended Masters, your guardian angel, spirit guides and – prayerfully thank them for their constant help; take care of your body/mind; forgive every single person, group, institution (including government) and God; build spiritual realizations; read the advanced books; quickly process your negative emotions; downsize attachments into preferences; use discrimination, but don't be habitually judgmental; allow occasional righteous indignation and its cousin, predicament anger; say your truth softly and diplomatically; use positive affirmations, creative visualizations, reverse-thought forms, and breakthrough thinking; help in the positive transformation of the organizations you work in, play in and worship in [see Afterword]; and allow yourself the permitted pleasures.

"In my Father's house are many mansions; if it were not so, I would have told you," John 14:2. I don't know how many material universes there are. However, to help you keep your sense of proportion, may I remind you that *our* material universe has approximately one hundred billion galaxies. And, in our Milky Way galaxy, there are about one hundred million inhabited planets and stars.

Now, I am about to end this basic survey of metaphysics. A long journey, COSMIC MAP - METAPHYSICS DEMYSTIFIED has introduced you to more than you knew before. I am an **all-pather**, a new word I just invented. What it means is I found as many parts of the crystal, the different color rays of many strong teachers, as I could. I tried to create a Maypole for you by weaving the colors of the different "crystal pieces" together.

As suggested, just keep what has resonated, drop what doesn't, and pursue for more depth what interests you. Take up or continue the spiritual practices that you are especially drawn to. No one can do everything. We are all in this together, every one of us. We'll compensate for each other exactly right as long as we listen to our own Soul. Since I may have bogged you down in the details, please remember what is important. About Atma, Soul, Sai Baba says as you go into meditation:

> Your duty is to abandon. Abandon all your plans, even the best ones. Abandon all the theory you cherish, the doctrines you hold dear, the systems of knowledge that have cluttered your brain, the preferences you have accumulated, the pursuit of fame, fortune, scholarship, superiority. These are all material objectives. Enter into the objective world after becoming aware of the Atma. Then you will realize that all is the play of the Atma."

For spiritual growth, beloved spiritual Being, you made a wonderful choice in finding your way to the Planet of the Cross where Soul growth is relatively fast and the opportunities for this growth are infinite. Your choice to come here, in spite of all the pain, is an excellent one.

Surrender to the Light of your Soul. Then come back to this "reality"and do your work. And play your play. It won't be long now. Godspeed.

When difficult situations arise, you can keep focused on your Soul to keep the outer condition in perspective, leaving you alert to act as necessary. Keep talking with your favorite Ascended Master, your angels, Sai Baba, spirit guides, Metatron, Michael, Melchizedek, whomever you know on the other side that you easily communicate with.

With all the help you are getting, you can have total confidence that your Soul will know what to do – it always does!

AFTERWORD

And it came to pass that as Cosmic Map – Metaphysics Demystified was being typeset, a series of four events happened that I must share with you: (1) Sai Baba, over a three-week period, frequently visited both David's and my dreams. Since then, we both feel a pulling toward India. (2) I was invited to – and attended – a reunion of the staff at the United States Army graduate school where I had been a GS-12 civilian trainer. (3) In our new central California Coast location, through Divine Connection's Mary Lynn, I became acquainted with an incredible woman, Jean Martin, who for fifty years had learned and practiced the "I Am" through the study of Saint Germain as taught to Godfrey Ray King (See the Advanced Book list.) (4) I received a book I had ordered by Meher Baba, which has a beautiful, deep, compelling quotation about "Love."

Now the details:

(1) Never tugged toward India before, we are leaving the week after Thanksgiving and the publication of Cosmic Map, to spend five weeks at Sai Baba's ashram in Puttaparthi, India. We will return January 3, 1996, the official publication date, at which time I will commence a publicity tour and be available for talk shows. Interviewers, you can write to me c/o my publisher, Meadow Park Press, P. O. Box 14410, San Luis Obispo, CA 93406.

(2) I was invited to a reunion the last weekend of September 1995, of the staff of the graduate school where I had taught for three and one-half years, 1981 – 1983, the United States Army Organizational Effectiveness Center and School, Fort Ord, California.

This was a graduate school at which we trained army officers to become management consultants. In a curriculum way ahead of the times, especially in an authoritarian-structured army, for seven years this graduate School trained officers and outstanding Non-Commissioned Officers to help organizations, using a consultant role, to create positive transformation from the inside.

My most challenging job, it was a privilege to develop instructional materials, train, consult, and supervise officers on their first management consulting practicum. Indeed I traveled all over the United States visiting Army installations to fulfill my duties. Consulting for a two-star general was not unusual.

At this September, 1995, reunion on the Monterey Peninsula, one-hundred strong, (including friends and spouses,) we reaffirmed our love for positive organizational transformation from within.

Remaining neutral, the trained consultant helps your organization identify the problems, research the problems, make plans for change, and then facilitates reaccessing four months after the changes.

Here is one mission of the human race: "All organizations and institutions engaged in greed, self-servingness, and processes and procedures that needlessly hurt Beings in a body have to be totally remade."

We can have orderly change under positive leadership. Or we can have chaos, anarchy and disorder. It is our choice. Turning our Planet of the Cross into a heaven on earth must be done, one way or another, now. Remember, the first angel has blown the trumpet.

Lynn Herrick, who had been the School's librarian, working twelve years after the School closed, was able, through the old grapevine, to get the names of three-hundred staff persons. The School had been closed by a General unknown to me who considered the curriculum too maudlin.

We were reminded that the School trained four thousand organizational transformation consultants!

Karen Culpepper, an administrative assistant at Meadow Park Press, has agreed to keep a list of consultants who will come and help you, constructively transform your organization. The consultant's first job is to help you identify areas of greed, self-servingness, and processes and procedures that needlessly hurt Beings in a body.

Then facilitate your management's deciding upon plans to make ordered change. Then to come back four months later and facilitate a feedback and follow-up session to help your management and organization's members know how they are doing.

The consultant remains neutral and does not have to know the details of your organization. The OT process releases the energy of the organization's members for positive change. All information that the consultants gather is done anonymously, so no individual becomes the fall guy. And the organization's "secrets" are kept confidential. *No one* may go to the press.

If you would like to have a list of these traveling consultants, so that you can pick someone you know or someone physically close to you, send a self-addressed, stamped envelope to Karen Culpepper, Administrative Assistant, Meadow Park Press, P. O. Box 14410, San Luis Obispo, CA 93406. Ask for the "The Organizational Transformation Consultant List." You can communicate with them directly about the details of their services and what they charge. Remember, these highly trained and experienced consultants can't be greedy in their consultant fees. However, they are giving you the irreplaceable hours of their lives, so you can't expect a free service, either.

And if you are one of those four thousand trained, and you want to be on this list, send Karen a letter of explanation with your current mailing address, Fax No., and phone number.

If, as a member of an organization, you cannot talk your organization's managers into hiring a consultant, you can still make change, although it will be a thousand times harder. Here are two books that Meadow Park Press publishes that can help you. They are both written by J. K. Day, PhD: (1) ORGANIZATIONAL TRANSFORMA-TION, HUMAN RELATIONS AT WORK and (2) CO-CREATING THE FUTURE, COLLABORATIVE-SOLUTION FINDING. You can spiritual-ize an organization from the bottom up, but there must be a large group of you from different segments of the organization, and you will have to individually master these materials before you begin. If you have *no other choice than to work from the bottom up*, after all in your group have mastered these two books, have the leader of your self-appointed group write to J. K. Day, c/o Meadow Park Press, telling the details of your efforts, how many people are involved, and what top management thinks of your plans. You will receive tailor-made suggestions.

For those involved in organizational transformation, watch out for the ego. Meetings could have a sign posted at the entry door, "Leave your Ego Outside." You are supposed to be playing and having fun while you create heaven on earth, not be deadly serious. If you fail to transform your organization, or if you die trying, so what? Maybe we can all have a party, with music and dancing, at the Pleiades star system. David Viscott, M.D., psychiatrist, writes:

> If you do not find play in your work, you may appear grown-up and serious to others, *but you have just grown old.* [Italics mine.]

Beloved of God, I hope you realize what I have just said. Let me reiterate: With a little bit of help, we can create heaven on earth by both working on ourself, always, and spearheading change, co-creating the future, in the organizations we work in, play in and worship in. We have the free will to do this. Let us, as children of the living God, make our parent proud of us! **Let's do it, homo novas!**

(3) Jean Martin is the lady who often mentally communicates or "talks with" Saint Germain, Mother Mary, Jesus, and other Ascended Masters. Indeed, at her high level, she does talk to them. And, she says, we can talk to them too

Jean gave me a new nickname, "Cosmic Whirlwind."

On the day Jean Martin and I met, we had gone to lunch. She was dropping me off and we sat and talked for some time in her car. I asked her, "Were you there with Jesus?" "Yes," she answered, and she described her ancient role as a woman, a powerful and wealthy supporter of Jesus Christ.

Then I said to her quietly, "I am Peter."

She later shared with me her experience at that moment, a moment she said ranked as one of a powerful dozen in her life, potently paranormal:

> Your voice, as you said, 'I am Peter,' changed; it was different. At that instant, I saw this transparent overlay cover your face, sort of like a holographic image. I saw an older man with greying hair, and deep, worried eyes. The

overlay seemed to sink into or become part of your face, which took on the same worried look. In this mode of Peter, you talked about how you failed, still blaming yourself.

My very new friend went home and "talked with" Saint Germain about me. She sent me by Fax this message from Saint Germain, talking to her:

> Your recognition of "Peter" was magnificent. We knew you would "sense" an old connection, but had to wait to know if you would "see" in this new friend, the friend of old. You had a great respect and love for the Peter of old, often counseling him and comforting him. In that embodiment, you had the wider (than he) perspective of the world and its then evolving nature, and you often tried to share that with Peter, who was still very much in the grasp also, of his human nature. Thus, we see his dilemma . . . powerfully "religious" within the framework of the old Judaic thought . . . even while his higher nature was responding to the call of Jesus to think in a new way . . . his human fear at work in his doubt of the legitimacy of the teachings of Jesus and finally in his denying . . . not once, but three times in a matter of hours, that he even knew this person he recognized to be an incredible Soul incarnated on earth.

> And then it fell to Peter to be the leader of the "New Age" thought of his day in Jerusalem. What a "hot-bed" of ideas that was. (And still is to this day.) Dear fellow, he hardly knew which way to turn, so much was expected of him . . . He expected so much of himself. To the last breath Peter strove to be true to the teaching of Jesus, while being pulled every which way by the prevailing ideas of his day and by the varying interpretations of the teachings of Jesus.

> In subsequent embodiments, he has tried to keep this new teaching from becoming politicized . . . from becoming a teaching that would be used to control mankind rather than the gift of Life it was meant to be to uplift and evolve God's people.

> Yes, Peter chose a difficult role for himself . . . and believed

. . . to this day . . . believes he failed his friend in that long ago day. But, in every embodiment since, he has given every drop of his life's energy to make amends and forever more be a force that the Ascended Masters could and can count on. And when out of embodiment, he works closely with His Dear Friend and others of those who came forth to serve at this time . . . I, [Saint Germain], being one of them. (Saint Germain embodied at that time as Joseph, the husband of Mary, the Mother of Jesus.)

Thus, you have now met, in this time, this friend of old, and you see the work she is doing and the dedication with which she "tackles" what she has set herself to do. We say, "God Bless and assist her in everything she sets her mind to do in the service of her Great Friend and of God and His Creation. Hers is a very great Soul."

I wept deep tears upon reading this. David, also, was very, very deeply moved by it. We were even more moved when Jean said I could print it as part of COSMIC MAP.

L O V E *

Love is essentially self–communicative; those who
do not have it, catch it from those who have it.
Those who receive love from others cannot be its
recipients without giving a response that, in itself, is
the nature of love. True love is unconquerable
and irresistible. It goes on gathering power and
spreading itself until eventually it transforms
everyone it touches. Humanity will attain a new
mode of being and life through the free and
unhampered interplay of pure love, from heart
to heart.

– MEHER BABA
Jesus' Incarnation, 1894 - 1969

*From Discourses, Meher Baba, Sheriar Press, 1994, Book Division,
3005 Highway 17, Myrtle Beach SC 29577.

Appendix A

Dedicated to those I love a lot . . .

to my Pop, born in 1909, scientist, mathematician, and agnostic. Pop, Cosmic Map is my Soul's song, and I sing it to you. It took eighteen years on the spiritual path, seven of it stop-and-start writing, before I could offer you this basic primer. As you say, a philosophy is needed that sees no disparity between religion and science. Thank you for your sustained interest in being the work's severe critic, your sharp questions and your willingness to edit.

to my Mom, born in 1909, high-school-class valedictorian, graduate food scientist. Mom, thank you for explaining the world in terms of beauty, truth and good, and thank you for the touching gift of your own Bible when I was a young woman.

to my devout husband, "master of the material world," carpenter, electrician, plumber, rigger, etc. Dearest Being, my twin-ray soul, you are the most loving, deep, handsome, capable, sexy, egoless, playful and fun man I have ever known. Your presence has created the energetic space to finish Cosmic Map. Thank you for your great wisdom, love, support, understanding and neck massages!

to my devout metaphysical son and his same-faith wife, spiritual music makers and Hebrew-chant teachers. Sweet twosome, thank you for your Beingness, support, love, and for introducing me to your teacher of nineteen years, Jim J. Hurtak, PhD.

to my devout identical twin sons, one an engineer and one a soil scientist, fundamental Christians, and their beautiful same-faith wives. Neat young folks, if you could stretch and read this, you might be surprised about what mama Janis believes about the Divine. As we have discussed, our different views of God, the Radiant One, have many commonalities. Thank you for your love, respect, and for sharing with me your scholarly knowledge and understandings of the Holy Bible.

And Dedicated to more of those I love a lot . . .

to my six grandchildren (and those yet to come) who can't read this yet. Little darlings, I would love to know what my grandmother believed, or for that matter what any relative believes, about the Divine. I wonder if you will read COSMIC MAP later? Your Grandma Janis so appreciates your wide-eyed, unconditional love.

to my two school–age stepchildren. You were my loving parents in a past life. To be sharing family life with you again is a treasured experience. It is my privilege to be your teacher this life. Thank you for your interest and astute metaphysical questions.

to my budding metaphysical friends. Clayton (my exquisitely beautiful wife in a past life when I was a man), Norm, Jason, Marcie and Susan. Thank you all for reading rough draft number one and encouraging me.

to my evolved metaphysical friends. Light lady Anne (who keeps me updated), Rev. Lavona, Ralph, and LaVerne. Thank you for reading rough draft number four and lovingly critiquing the work.

to Taira and Joanne, editors. Advanced metaphysical philosophers, thank you for your high–level skills and knowledge, used with such grace and kindness.

to Marcie. You typeset COSMIC MAP and did the cover and graphics, my dear friend, your work speaks for itself.

to Dan and Barbara. "Book promotion idea" people. You do your jobs with an immense amount of love and wisdom. My Soul is indebted to you, forever.

to Lois, Margaret and Mavis. Last minute editing angels.

MAY YOU ALL BE CONTINUOUSLY BLESSED BY DIVINE LOVE IN MANIFESTATIONS, SEEN AND UNSEEN.

APPENDIX B

This is an edited-for-Cosmic Map article that appeared in the local newspaper, Lake County Record Bee, Friday, April 8, 1994.

UCM, A LAYING-ON-OF HANDS, HEALING MINISTRY

by Grandma Janis

Namaste. That means, "The God in me greets the God in you!" Namaste is an Indian word, from the country of India, pronounced rapidly, "naw–maw–stay." It is usually said with palms of both hands pressed together vertically in front of the chest and at the same time bowing slightly forward.)

I am one of over seven hundred Universal Church of the Master ministers in the world, not including the several hundred registered spiritual healers. Non–denominational, this church was started in 1908 and is headquartered in Santa Clara, California. Only a handful of us have an actual physical church. Most serve, as I do, in a small way, out of our home.

To earn my living, I give staying–well classes. These include yoga, meditation, other relaxation techniques, and vegetarian nutrition. I also do couple relationship mediation, the only kind of marriage counseling I do.

The Universal Church of the Master, by its name, recognizes and emphasizes not only the personal mastery that Jesus exhibited over his life and his physical environment, but also the remarkable spiritual gifts that he demonstrated during the three years of his public ministry. It is the position of UCM that this same mastery and that these same remarkable spiritual gifts, with self–discipline and suitable training, can be and have been demonstrated by far lesser persons than Jesus Christ, the great Avatar. For Jesus himself said, "He that believeth on me, the works that I do shall he do also; and greater works than these shall he do." (John 14:12)

The four gospels document many examples of the paranormal or mystical, adept and mediumistic powers that Jesus exhibited. Beyond clairvoyance and telepathy, scriptures mention numerous instances of psychic and supernormal healing, psychic communication between worlds, physical materializations and other occasions where Jesus employed his paranormal powers. In the primitive Christian church, teachers and preachers were filled with the power of spirit, doing many of the things that Jesus had done: healing the sick, prophesying, seeing visions, and communicating with spiritual realms. In the course of time, as the Western Church became more focused upon worldly power, personal manifestations of spiritual power became more and more discouraged.

UCM lets us use God's energy for life. I encourage those who are attracted to the idea of "finding and traveling their own path in the Light without dogma" to use their own healing and psychic powers, which we all have. (We are even allowed a belief in reincarnation.)

On Wednesday mornings at 6:55 a.m., a few of us gather in my home for a serious meditation, 50 minutes. I believe that meditation is listening to God through the divinity of our own Soul. Then, from 8:15 a.m. to 9:30 a.m., we have an Angel Prayer Healing Group. Prayer, of course, is talking to God.

Both UCM ministers and spiritual healers work with a person's physical body, their mind, their psychology, and their aural or Light body. All living organisms have this vibrancy, an aura, around them. Current scientific instruments can photograph this Light body.

The aura can be balanced and healed, which in turn heals the physical body. Healers are effective for two reasons: (1) They have very loving, open hearts and compassionate Souls. (2) They have clarity that they don't do the healing; God does. They just allow themselves to be a channel to let the healing energy come through.

People often respond to spiritual healing after their medical doctor has given up on conditions like chronic fatigue syndrome and arthritis.

It is my belief that there is another Avatar of Jesus' stature alive in the world today who has a very well-documented fifty-two-year ministry. He is a different Soul, not Jesus returned. I would like to write about this Avatar, Sathya Baba of India, in a future column. Baba supports all faiths. As a UCM minister, I can choose to believe in Baba because my church encourages me to use my intellect and intuition. I do not believe our Radiant One, Divine Love, God, would remain silent since Biblical times.

God is real. God is now. And at the birth of the Seventh Golden Spiritual age, his love is more accessible than ever for healing, help and direction. Heaven is interactive! If you feel the quickening and have felt separated from God, it is now the time to connect or reconnect. Baba says that if you take one step toward God, God will take one hundred steps toward you.

If you are able to sit perfectly still for fifty minutes, you are invited to attend our meditation. Anyone drawn can attend the Angel Prayer Healing Group. There is no charge. No plate is passed.

Scientific research is showing that prayer really works. Of course, we knew the power of prayer all along.

Come to heal or be healed. I and the others will support your spiritual path. Also if you would like us to say prayers for you or your loved ones, please telephone me.

A PPENDIX C

Author's Biographical Information

My name at birth was Janis Kathleen Eaton. I was born March 7, 1935 at 12:32 p.m in East Chicago, Indiana. This was the year that Hitler reintroduced conscription and scrapped the Versaille Treaty limiting arms and Japan walked out of the United Nations.

My bachelor's degree is in Office Administration, California State University, Fresno, magna cum laude, (1968). I hold an MBA with distinction from CSUF (1969) and a PhD from Columbia Pacific University, a university–without–walls headquartered in Mill Valley, California, in human relations in management (1982).

My writing history includes published articles, thousands of pages of instructional materials and a textbook published in 1980, an experiential text for human relations, business psychology and organizational behavior classes. Titled A WORKING APPROACH TO HUMAN RELATIONS IN ORGANIZATIONS, 1980, it was originally published by Brooks/Cole Publishing Company a Division of Wadsworth. I created a matching book on experiential education for professors using that book. These can be ordered from Meadow Park Press, P. O. Box 14410, San Luis Obispo, CA 93406–4410. (See the order form at the back of Cosmic Map for descriptions of forthcoming books.)

For nineteen years I taught at the college level, including three and one–half years as a GS–12 civilian, instructing army officers in human relations, management consulting, stress management and time management at a graduate school at Fort Ord, California. The army training experience was my most challenging, but a close second was seven years of teaching Introduction to Business to a community college class of two–hundred students. (I so appreciate this wonderful country and its incredible economic system!) Including the staying–well classes I have been teaching privately since 1984, this is my twenty–seventh year of standing up front.

In 1988, I was ordained in the Universal Church of the Master, a spiritualist Church.

For exercise, I love walking and all kinds of dancing. For joy, I play the recorder (a flute-like instrument). Toning and chanting with my crystal bowl is delightfully fun and helps align the chakras of myself and anyone listening.

APPENDIX D

I composed this to put in a frame in our home just before giving a party for a group of metaphysical seekers.

WE ARE THE CHILDREN OF THE LIGHT

* We feel a powerful draw toward the Divine.

* We think that our own Soul or Being is a ray of the Divine, creative light, God. (I am the vine, ye are the branches, John 15:5)

* We often meditate and/or sing and/or hum and/or chant spiritual songs. Sometimes, we write them! Celebrate!

* We have had paranormal experiences – times when we saw or felt or heard something beyond the normal reality.

* We entertain the concept of reincarnation – our Soul being born again and again, to become the best we can be.

* We know the Holy Bible does not say that reincarnation doesn't happen. And we know the Holy Bible cites references that show reincarnation does happen: Matthew 11:14 and 17:52 – 53; Malachi 4:5; Matthew 17:10 – 13; Luke 1:17; Daniel 12:13, plus all references to Jesus coming again.

* We have opinions on the rest of religious theory, but we don't press it on others, knowing that whatever "Is" is, no matter how we conceptualize it.

* We are sure that the Seventh Golden Spiritual Age has begun.

* In this Golden Spiritual Age, we want to express our unique talents and training in ways which serve and enrich our fellow humans.

* We know that no Being is superior to another Being, any more than a four-year old child is superior to a two-year old. We have all come to fill a unique, special place, like an individual piece of the puzzle.

* We love a lot.

Grandma Janis,
January 1993

Appendix E

This is the memorial service for a young man conducted June 3, 1994 at Upper Lake Park. He was found dead in his pick-up truck May 29. His death was reported as drug-related in the Lake County Record Bee and in the Santa Rosa Press Democrat. It is suspected that the recreational drugs he took had impurities, which caused him to have fatal lung hemorrhages. Here is the talk Rev. Janis gave at the Memorial Service in the form of a letter. Here we will not call him by his real name, but instead "Dear Soul."

Dear Soul,

Today we gather to remember you and to try to come to terms with your untimely death – a young man stolen from life in what should have been a prime time.

Your parents are still in a state of shock, for you see, Dear Soul, the loss of a child is the hardest human loss one is required to bear. And your eight–year–old daughter and brother grieve too, as well as the other members of your large family.

When Polly Klaus was kidnapped, her community gathered around the family. Later, legislation was commenced that would keep repeated offenders in prison. Polly didn't die in vain.

Dear Soul, we are going to see to it that you didn't die in vain either. Other young people buying drugs are having chest pains. Your death will get their attention. Maybe they will stop. Maybe some-one who hears or reads this will have the courage to turn in a drug maker or seller. Maybe like a hero fighting in a war, your death and the attention drawn to it will work in the war against drugs. Maybe this was the reason for your life?

But before I say more about that, let me share briefly how I think the universe works. I believe God is a giant Light Being. I believe that as Souls, we are "chips off the old block." Our Soul is a ray of God; as such, we really are the children of God. Then, I believe that as Souls we enter the human body and live a life in that body.

As a metaphysical minister, I believe in reincarnation. I believe that most of us live thousands of lifetimes as we perfect our Soul on this Earth School. Each life is an extension of our Soul's "childhood."

So you, Dear Soul, are an eternal spiritual Being who just had another temporary human experience.

Why am I talking about this today? Well, to introduce the concept of old Souls and new Souls. Old Souls have been around the most times. They are wise, kind, courageous, sincere, and deeply interested in the welfare of their fellow humans.

On the other hand, like little babies, new Souls are self-centered, greedy, and with little conscience. Drug dealers are greedy new Souls.

Drug takers seeking bliss states unknowingly put their beautiful bodies, their own personal temples of the Holy Spirit, into the hands of greedy new Souls.

There is nothing wrong with bliss states. However, it is unfortunate that most young people don't know that there is a healthy way to get into a bliss state through meditation. Experienced meditators can quickly access the alpha state which sort of disconnects the mind, the anxiety producer, and lets a person have direct access to God. Behind the mind there is joy.

It is up to old Souls to police the behavior of new Souls, like big sisters watching out over little sisters.

I hope all concerned people in the community will gather around your family in this time of sorrow. These concerned people have to be old Souls or they automatically wouldn't be concerned! And if anyone who gets this message knows greedy new Souls who make and market drugs, tell the proper authorities what you know.

And let's remember how to get into that bliss state quite naturally without drugs. There are many books on how to meditate. I will have a book out soon, COSMIC MAP. It will include meditation instruction. You can meditate by yourself or get some friends together.

Now, Dear Soul, I would like to try to offer a little comfort to your family and friends.

As soon as the body dies, the eternal part of us, our Soul, leaves. That means your son probably did not suffer long. And the journey of the Soul as it leaves is freeing and beautiful. The departing Soul is met by other Light Beings and angels who assist with the trip. It is my belief that your loved one is having a wondrous journey, as he has done many times. He has business to do, such as constructing a "did well" and "didn't do well" list. He is totally forgiven by God, as all people are, for being less than perfect. Even new Souls are forgiven. After he recalibrates himself, he will choose the time to be reborn again, commonly in about eight years.

So, your son is not dead at all. Only his temporary human body is gone. The Soul has its own eyes, ears and mind.

God bless you that suffer at this loss. Try to remember through your pain that although he has gone home for awhile, he will be back.

Added notes:

On June 22, 1994 the Associated Press reported on a survey of 5,655 students in public junior high and high schools. After years of declining usage in the late 1980s, drugs such as alcohol, amphetamines, marijuana, and LSD are on the rebound. LSD use more than doubled among eleventh graders since 1985-86. Twenty-nine percent of high school juniors and 21 percent of freshmen were classified as "excessive" alcohol users. That group included those who had consumed five or more drinks in a row at least twice in the previous two weeks, had gotten very drunk or sick at least three times in their lives, or drank to get drunk.

Similarly, 28 percent of eleventh-graders and 23 percent of ninth-graders were described as "high-risk drug users" who used marijuana or other drugs frequently, mixed their drugs, or tried cocaine.

Among eleventh-graders, 40 percent said they had driven a car after drinking or been in a car with friends who were drinking and driving.

Nearly 30 percent of eleventh-graders, and 20 percent of ninth-graders and 6 percent of seventh-graders said they had been high on alcohol or other drugs while at school.

Marijuana, inhalants, and LSD showed significant increases in the past two years. Forty percent of eleventh graders and 30 percent of ninth graders said they had tried marijuana, up from 29 percent and 19 percent, respectively, in 1991-92.

Sniffing inhalants, such as nitrous oxide or aerosols, nearly doubled to 21 percent of ninth-graders. LSD use increased from 12 percent of eleventh graders and 8 percent of ninth graders, to 18 percent and 12 percent, respectively.

The AP article mentioned that drug education courses have declined in number.

It is apparent that human Beings need bliss states, which can be gained drug-free by meditation.

Obviously, our educational system is failing to teach meditation and is not putting a priority on continued drug education. These will change in the coming years as all institutions are brought into line with the Light and the love by the old Souls that have chosen to be the Light workers therein.

The Light workers are now in place everywhere that is needed. Are you one of those ready in drug prevention? Now is the time to create heaven on earth! As Yogananda said, "Love, serve, remember [God]."

APPENDIX F

HARVEST

DEVAPREM DEMYSTIFIED ENLIGHTENMENT

This article was written by Grandma Janis in 1992 and approved by Devaprem for submission to a Sacramento New Age publication. He wanted to encourage seekers to come to meditate with the group.

Into the large, empty room they come, sock–footed people with assorted pillows and seats. Many have arrived an hour early to get close to the front. All are seated, most meditating, before Devaprem arrives at the appointed hour. After he enters, a volunteer locks the door. There are usually seventy to one hundred people seated on the floor. Some have previously reached enlightenment; others have heard of "What's Happening" and are here to "get it." The news of "What's Happening" has been passed by word of mouth. At least a dozen have flown in from Europe.

In the Mill Valley area, over a year and one–half ago, Devaprem started doing group meditations and Satsangs. Satsang is a Sanskrit word meaning an intimate group meeting with the Master, the Enlightened one. It allows time for meditation plus additional time for questions answered by the Divine Master.

When Devaprem started doing Satsangs five times a week plus hour–long meditations several times a week, there were only three people in his audience. Two of them became enlightened. They passed the word and now the numbers are growing exponentially. Well over one hundred people have become enlightened.

A chemical engineer from Germany with English as his second language, Devaprem is just thirty–three years old, about the same age that Jesus was when he did his powerful teaching.

As a young spiritual seeker, during a ten–year period, Devaprem meditated in a Buddhist monastery, sat with Rajneesh, and got his own enlightenment in India with a Divine master named Ponjaji just a few months before he came to Mill Valley.

Devaprem modestly takes no credit for anyone's enlightenment. He tells us that it is like "The other masters tilled the field, planted the seeds and watered the crops. Then many had to leave before hardly anyone became enlightened. It is just this time, now is ripe. I just happen to be one of those people who gets to bring in the harvest."

In the meditations, to his right, always sits another former Rajneesh devotee, Hari Devi. Already enlightened herself, she is Devaprem's cook, housekeeper and administrative assistant. In my opinion, this lovely vibrating Soul has as much to do with the flavor of the sat-sangs as Devaprem himself. Extremely modest, she seems at ease in her subordinate role.

For the meditation itself, Devaprem uses a combination/flow of timed music and timed silence, music and silence, music and silence. He consciously selects the ethereal–sounding music from a wide variety of artists to insure the best possible visit with the Being (Soul). I respond well to this diversion – somehow, my mind gets fooled and it lets loose. And Devaprem's explanations in the Satsangs are delightful.

Very tall, thin, spontaneous, frisky and full of smiles, he eats, he says, "food" – and then I listen to my body to see if it likes what I ate. I am getting more careful in a natural way. I don't deprive myself. This in–touchness is a natural process. My Being is feeding my intu-ition all the time. My Being manifests my body."

Devaprem lives a simple life in a mostly unfurnished apartment. Financially independent because of a wealthy family, he takes no money for his services. The $3 we pay to get into a meditation or Satsang goes toward paying for the rental of the hall and buying the ever–present flowers.

He uses a simple model: "There is just the body, the mind, and the Being (Soul). He says laughing, "Of course my model is not com-plete, but it works!" The ego is part of the mind.

His forthrightness is so refreshing. Here are the kinds of things he says in the Satsangs I have attended:

"The reason we hold on to negative emotions is that without them, there is nothing there. And that emptiness makes us feel uncomfortable. We would rather have a familiar – if uncomfortable feeling – than to deal with that nothingness. So we invent a negative thought or create an event around which to have negative feelings."

"In meditation, you can't have a visit with the Being unless your body is totally relaxed. You have to learn to trust that the Being is eternal and that the Being is the real you and is not going to die. When you have mastered the fear of death, you can really let go in meditation. The body has to be guided into manifesting enlightenment. Complete relaxation is absolutely necessary. You have to be able to forget you have a body."

"When you don't have the fear of death, you still want to live."

"The Being is love and compassion, your natural state. You will use your heart to manifest these behaviors in the world."

"The more imposed rules you abide by, the less you will experience. Spirituality is responding to the inside, to your Being. What society is telling you isn't necessarily right for you."

"The Being is a space inside that is always the same. Before enlightenment, your body feels good and bad, up and down. After enlightenment, you don't identify with the emotions any more; and the ups and downs come less and less."

I asked him, "Why are so many people getting enlightened with you?"

He said, "A strong Satsang comes when many good people have come to meditate. The mood and energy of each person adds to the flavor. Always, the right people and right number of people come to the meditation. It nearly always works. I don't do anything except watch the energy. The flavor is also enhanced by the capacity of the people to take in energy and their level of openness."

"Having men and women setting on opposite sides would seem funny in this day and age when enlightenment is for the market place. It is not just for males in a temple or ashram. Women are becoming enlightened just as often as men. And their age is inconsequential. Unfortunately, the old conditioning of how to get enlightened is still hanging around."

"When I meditated in the Buddhist monastery, there were twenty men sitting around staring at the wall. It was very dry and boring. Today we can make it totally appealing and have it work better than it ever has!"

"In the old days, a man would sit in a stone hut for years with the windows boarded up except that one window was left for the passing of food. That man either went crazy or he became enlightened. Either way, he would come out, and take up the begging bowl. Now I ask you, what good was that?"

What isn't inconsequential statistically is that most of the people – but not all – of those coming to Mill Valley have meditated for between five to ten years. Most had been with Rajneesh – old friends passing on the information through friends. But this is not an organization related to the deceased Rajneesh. Semi–organized volunteer workers did create a name called The California Center for Creative Living. Ironically, there is no Center and anyone working for Devaprem – for example a person taking the $3 from people at the door, another person selling for $5 tapes made during each Satsang, or still another person ringing the bell indicating the start of meditation – all work in a volunteer capacity.

Devaprem describes enlightenment as "the letting go of the mind, the ego part of the mind. After enlightenment, your mind will register but will not hold the vibrations of the negative emotions, for example fear and anger, or of a puffed–up ego. Your misery comes from your ego. However, the mind retains its functions of memory and the ability to analyze when necessary – like in creative–solution finding. And the heart is released to let out more love. After your enlightenment, your environment will benefit."

Enlightenment is simply, utterly becoming yourself, the way you are meant to be, the way you have the most fun in life, having more richness and more choices. After enlightenment, you go back and do most of the things you were doing before, work in your job, drive your car. It doesn't blow all your mind away, just the non-essential portion."

"Enlightened people feel at one with Existence," says Devaprem using the same word for God as did Rajneesh. "Choose your own spiritual words, everyone has a different spiritual history and vocabulary."

"After enlightenment, the need for sex is very individual. Some people are turned on more by sex after enlightenment. For others, they lose interest in sex. We all need the variety of experience." He says, "I know what it is to live without sex and at the other extreme to be obsessed with it. I also know how it feels to have no money and at the extreme to be rich."

"The drive in the universe is always toward higher consciousness. The more consciousness you have, the more you will experience life."

"After enlightenment, instead of having three or four thoughts at the same time, you will only have one – maybe sometimes none. You are always in the moment without effort. The past and future are no longer grinding concerns."

"Unenlightened people have fears which come out of past conditioning. The enlightened person knows that the father that beat him is not going to come."

Ego-mind can be put into a subordinate role at age twenty-two, forty-four or sixty-six. Then you will be your real Self. You have known enlightenment when you were small. Now you just have to remember it."

"After enlightenment, you will just relax and make your life easier, simpler. You will know when something comes up whether to drop it. Your mind doesn't go over and over something that happened an hour ago. Ego–mind perverts. It questions, judges and meanly or selfishly analyzes."

In answering questions about how to become enlightened, Devaprem made these comments: "Just put yourself in the flow and it will happen for you. And don't be discouraged. Sometimes you'll come to Satsang, and your mind will be more active than at home. That is okay. You will sit in another Satsang and you will go very deep in meditation. Don't get hooked on any former experiences. Come and be here in the moment, freshly new. And don't compare your experiences with others' experiences in order to judge their experience or yours."

"The enlightened moment comes TO YOU. You cannot possibly pro-duce it, although meditating for sixteen days in a row will set the stage for it, increase your chances. And you must relax. Drop all techniques now; they have brought you this far."

"Even if you don't get enlightened, go as far as you can. Meditation increases your ability to have more insights and to see more. You will grow and learn more. And you will be healthier."

"Enlightened is the way the human race is supposed to be."

"The ego part of your mind doesn't want to let go because it is afraid. So just say to it, 'I have had enough, ego–mind, I want to go into my Being.' The doer, the ego–mind, pushes the Being away. We have to keep trying to figure out which is the ego and which is the Being. It is a paradox, but we really don't know what the ego is until we have lost it. There is a natural drive toward simplicity in the universe, except for the human ego. Meditation brings together good and bad. Finally, they collapse together into enlightenment."

"You may be disappointed in enlightenment if you think it is a super moment, a gigantic orgasm, or that all your life's concerns are going to go away. But after enlightenment, life is really simple."

After fourteen years on the path, I, Janis, age fifty–seven, was stuck and had given up getting enlightened in this lifetime. I am really grateful to have been introduced to Devaprem and his huge gift of enlightenment which came to me on the sixteenth day in a row that I meditated. Although some of the beginning meditations in my series had been in the Devaprem group, on my sixteenth day, I was in Texas meditating by myself late at night in my atheist- brother's home. My body and thoughts were gone, but again I felt my head "float into a bubble." Previously a friend had suggested the bubble was my ego-mind and that the next time it happened, I should tell it to "fuck off." Taking the friend literally, when it did happen again, I literally shouted into the empty room, "Ego-mind, fuck off." My head filled with white Light. And for the next four months I was the sleepiest person alive. Others had this sleepy experience, also, but not the majority.

We can move or adjust ourselves slightly during the music. We can take a cough drop if we have the urge to cough. However, twice he commented to me sweetly in front of all one hundred twenty persons when I, because of cramps in my muscles, made noise in altering my position. And following those times on another occasion, he spoke out loudly and angrily, momentarily losing his patience with me, as I, sitting at the very back of the room, unwrapped a cough drop – I had thought silently – and he heard the paper being torn off. "Take the paper off ahead, Janis!" He is assertive in getting his needs met and protecting the silence for everyone.

The word "Devaprem" is sanskrit and means "Divine love." It is not his given name; he has an ordinary German-sounding name he mentioned once and I forgot it. But his administration of the meditations is not ordinary. The energy is so very powerful and the vibrations so loving. The first time I entered that room, arriving just before the meditation was to start with other meditators already meditating, it felt as if someone poured a warm liquid into my heart, which then became so heavy I immediately had to sit down!

And one doesn't have to go to India to sit in this extraordinary vibration.

Post–scripts. This article was never submitted or published. Devaprem, without explanation, hurriedly left the United States for Europe.

Rumors said that the U. S. government was hovering over Devaprem and that he decided not to allow himself to be detained like his master, Rajneesh had been. It had also been rumored that Rajneesh was given a slow–acting poison during his two years in a U. S. jail, and that this great teacher, this greatly misunderstood teacher, Rajneesh, died a slow, agonizing death after being returned to India. It is said that his followers took Rajneesh's body to a German laboratory where the presence of this poison implicated our government.

Some of these people get indignant if you ask about those Rolls Royces. They say the holy man didn't own them: He just let followers bring the cars to Oregon because he knew they loved to see him ride by in their car.

Three years later, my life experience is exactly the way Devaprem described it. Except that I would say I am just third–dimension Self–realized.

APPENDIX G

Bible Scripture References for Mystical Phenomena

CLAIRAUDIENCE: Acts 9:4, Job 4:15–16, Ezekiel 12:1–8.

CLAIRVOYANCE: 2 Kings 6:16–20, Acts 7:55–56, Matthew 17:8.

FIRE IMMUNITY: Daniel 3:21–27.

HEALING BY MAGNETIZED OBJECTS: II Kings 4:29, Acts 19:11–12.

HEALING: Matthew 8:13–15, Matthew 12:10–13, Luke 4:40, Acts 3:4–8, Acts 9:33–34 and 39–41.

HEALING OF OBSESSION: 1 Samuel 16:14–23, Numbers 21:8, 9; I Kings 17:7–14, II Kings 4:18–29, 37:2, Kings 4:1–14, Matthew 8:16, Luke 4:35, Luke 9:11 and 14:2, John 4:47–54, Acts 16:16–18.

IMMUNITY TO POISON: Acts 28:3–6.

INDEPENDENT VOICES: Ezekiel 1:28, Deut. 9:12–13, I Samuel 3:2–9, Matthew 17:5, John 12:28–30, Acts 7:30–34, Acts 8:26, 29, Acts 9:14–18, Acts 12:7–10.

INDEPENDENT WRITING: Exodus 24:12, Exodus 34:1 also 31:18 and 32:16, Deut. 5:22 and 9:9, Daniel 5:5, also II Chronicles 21:12.

INSPIRATION OF SPIRIT: Ezekiel 2:2, Job 26:4, Mark 13:11, John 14:26, Luke 12:12 and 1:15, Acts 4:31 and 6:10, Acts 2:2–4, I Corinthians 11:8, and 2:10–16.

MATERIALIZATION: Genesis 3:8, 18:1 and 32:24, Exodus 24:10–11, Daniel 5:5 and 10:10, Ezekiel 2:9, Matthew 28:2, Luke 24:15–31, John 20:17–30, Acts 5:19–20.

DEMATERIALIZATION: Acts 1:9.

MINISTERING SPIRITS: Hebrews 1:13, 14 and 2:5.

PROPHECY: Acts 2:17, 18, also 19:6 and 27:10, 11, 21–166, 31, 34:1, I Corinthians 12:1–11 and all of chapter 14, I Thessalonians 5:20.

REINCARNATION: There is no statement in the Bible that reincarnation does not exist. References that say it does are Matthew 11:14 and 27:52–53, Malachi 4:5, St. Matthew 17:10–13, Luke 1:17, Daniel 12:13, plus all references to Jesus coming again.

SPIRIT LEVITATION: Ezekiel 3:14 and 8:3, 1 Kings 18:12, Acts 8:39.

TELEPATHY: Luke 5:22.

TRANCE: Genesis 15:12, Daniel 8:18 and 10:9, Acts 10:10–16, Acts 11:5–17 and 22:17.

TRANSFIGURATION (transformation): Acts 6:15, Matthew 17:2–3.

TRUMPET SOUND: Exodus 19:13, 16, 19, Exodus 20:18, 31:18 and 34:1, Deut. 5:22 and 9:19, Revelations 1:10.

SPIRIT POWER: Acts 16:25–26.

Compiled by Byron J. Fitzgerald, second president, Universal Church of the Master, from 1931 to 1967, and author of *A New Text of Spiritual Philosophy and Religion*, 1934. (Except for the reference to reincarnation.)

APPENDIX H

Bible Scripture References for Troubled Times

REST FOR THE WEARY, Matthew 11:29–30, John 14:27.

DISCOURAGED, Psalms 23, 42, 43.

EVERYTHING SEEMS TO BE GOING FROM BAD TO WORSE, IITimothy 3, Hebrews 13.

SORROW OVER TAKES YOU, Psalms 46, Matthew 28.

THINGS LOOK "BLUE," PSALMS 34, 71, ISAIAH 40.

YOU CAN'T GO TO SLEEP, Psalms 4, 56, 130.

WORRIES OPPRESS YOU, Psalms 46, Matthew 6.

FACING A CRISIS, Job 28:12–28, Proverbs 8, Isaiah 55.

ARE IMPATIENT, Psalms 40, 90, Hebrews 12.

ARE BEREAVED, I Cor. 15:1, Thes. 4:13–5:28, Revelations 21, 22.

ARE BORED, II Kings 5, Job 38, Psalms 103, 104, Ephesians 3.

THINK GOD SEEMS FAR AWAY, Psalms 25, 125, 138, Luke 10.

ARE LONELY OR FEARFUL, Psalms 27, 91, Luke 8:1, Peter 4.

Compiled by an anonymous U. S. Army chaplin.

APPENDIX I

List of Concepts in Order Presented

COSMIC MAP, METAPHYSICS DEMYSTIFIED

Chapter 1 – THE IMMENSENESS OF YOUR JOURNEY IS AWESOME

Relative truth, "tentative shelf," [Foreword], real knowing, paranormal experiences, telepathy, seeing experience, metaphysics, New Age, Age of Aquarius, God, collective consciousness, collective unconscious, Existence, The Universe, Ascended Masters, Divine, The Holy Spirit, grace, quantum physics, thought forms, pre–matter, reverse–thought forms, intent, Soul, our Being, our Self, persona, higher self, higher selves, spiritual ego, Ehyeh Asher Ehyeh: I Am That I Am, spirit, silver cord, new Souls, old Souls, lost Souls, higher realms and other dimensions, Christ consciousness, Edgar Cayce, trance, Nostradomus, karma, karma bank, free will, reincarnation, Soul families, Spiritualism, occult practices, seance, medium, goddess worship, satanic spells, hexes, curses, voo–doo, sorcery, chakras, astral or Light body, ghost, kundalini, Avatar, God–realized, Sai Baba, Jesus Christ, Meher Baba, immaculate conception, omniscient, omnipresent, and omnipotent.

Chapter 2 – CLOSE TO HOME

Physical body, realizations, physical eyes, physical heart, love, God's love, physical human brain, Grandma Janis' Human–Mind–Channels Model, Supreme–Being mind, Big Mind, archetypes, morphogenic fields, ancestral memory, one–hundredth–monkey theory, ego–mind, lower mind, Akashic Records, solution–finding mind, beta; "coming-going;" theta; dreams, delta, sleep; astral plane mind, hell, atheist, agnostic, heaven, saint, the subconscious mind, hypnotism, modern shaman, the humor–mind, subjective world, objective world, mind, time, Soul time, matter, drug–induced altered states, emotions, fear, anger, predicament anger, chanting, bhajans, mantra, om, music, enlightenment, self–realization, shaman, saint, satori, meditation, entrainment, purpose, mission, Zen, samadhi, biofeedback training, third eye, fall of man, intuition, psychicness, cosmic sync, synchronicity, clairvoyant tools, astrology, crystal readings, psychometry, numerology, palmistry, phone readings, tarot cards, other cards and games, I Ching, runes, clairvoyant, telepathy, clairaudient, clairsentient, x-ray clairvoyant, precognition, channeling, health, healing, Grandma Janis' Health Tips, skin brushing, yoga, aerobic exercise, vegetarianism, death, conscious death.

Chapter 3 – YOU TRAVEL IN THE DARK AND THE LIGHT

Earth, Metatron, Washta, walk-in, Lemuria, Atlantis, fall of man, starseed, Kali Yuga, Light Brotherhood, dark brotherhood, duality, polarity consciousness, dramas to grow the Soul, dark night of the Soul, spiritual path, war, peace, Holy Bible, religious institutions, cult, angels, angel choirs, music of the spheres, spirit guides, spirit band, elemental spirits, nature spirits, fairies, prayer, Angel Healing Group, prayer chain, truth, listening, non-attachment, giving and receiving, service, pleasures, desires, being in the moment, judgment, forgiveness, sex, marriage, Soul mate, twin flame, twin-ray Soul, relationships, divorce, raising children, financial prosperity, greed, money velocity, mistakes, guilt, ethics and morality, both-and dilemma, dark side, neuroses, transgenerational neurotic virus, insanity, devil, sin, affirmations, thought molds, creative visualizations, breakthrough thinking, master teacher, Uriel, Michael, Gabriel, Raphael, Jeremiel, Sariel, Melchizedek, Time Lords, Hakamin, Ascended Masters, ascension, prophesies, resurrection, Star Beings, Maitreya, Ashtar, psychokinesis, Afterword: India, organization transformation consultants, Peter, Meher Baba on "Love."

Appendix J

When Cosmic Cultures Meet

Exploring the Practical Ramifications of Our Reunions with Our Extraterrestrial Sisters & Brothers of the Light, Star Beings

The following article was written by Mary Lynn, founder and editor of Divine Connections, a newsletter dedicated to getting into print those who channel evolved Beings. This rapturous publication is filled with the love coming down to us. You can order it from Divine Connections, P. O. Box 1021, Middletown, CA 95461-1021, $22 for four issues.

Mary Lynn attended the international conference, "When Cosmic Cultures Meet," in Washington D. C., May 27 - 29, 1995. Sponsored by the Human Potential Foundation and led by Founder, Scott Jones, PhD, this gathering brought together one-hundred sixty participants and twenty-four presenters to further activate a public dialog. Published in International UFO Library Magazine, portions of her article are printed with her permission:

Richard J. Boylan, PhD, a clinical, research and consulting psychologist and author of CLOSE EXTRATERRESTRIAL ENCOUNTERS, stated that we will need to establish support groups soon . . . that a lot of people are going to need help expanding their perspective to include other cosmic cultures. These support groups are likely to be led by you, the readers of this magazine, by conference participants and by all the people who have believed . . . with or without seeing.

Boylan believes that the U. S. government will acknowledge the presence of the Star Beings before the end of 1995, that a public meeting with them will take place in 1996 and that our star brothers and sisters will establish a community on earth by 1997.

Michael Hesemann, German author (A COSMIC CONNECTION and other UFO books), publisher of Magazine 2000, and TV producer, noted that contact will affect every aspect of thought . . . that our socio–economic set-up will change . . . and that contact will definite-

ly challenge our psychological stability . . . our concept of our ability
to control the future.

He believes that a good strategy for preparing for contact is to grad-
ually leak more information into the common consciousness every
day. Since much fear is caused by ignorance, increasing the public
dialog will help us meet the challenge of contact.

Hesemann pointed out that fear is only one possible response to
contact . . . curiosity, amazement, amnesia and joy are also choices.
He would like to see more military people permitted to speak openly
about what they know and have experienced. Openness leads to
acceptance.

The Fear Panel at the Cosmic Conference . . . which included Dave
Hunt, author; James J. Funaro, Professor of Anthropology and
founder of CONTACT;Paula Underwood, Native American author-
educator; and William J. Baldwin, PhD, psychologist, pastor and
author . . . discussed fear of the unknown . . . fear of more advanced
technologies . . . fear of greater psychic abilities . . . fear of giving
away our authority/sovereignty . . . fear of excess emotion making
us too vulnerable . . . fear of multi-national corporations attempting
power deals . . . fear of non-similarity and fear of strangers.

The panel pointed out that fear of the unknown is not universal and
not necessary . . . and that to eliminate fear we need to reconcile
spirituality with the nature, origin and purpose of Star Beings . . . to
determine the truth.

Jim J. Hurtak, PhD, Founder, Academy for Future Science and author
or THE KEYS OF ENOCH, sees love preserving the integrity of contact with cosmic cultures. Hurtak reminds us that we can choose
who we work with, who we co-create with. He encourages us to
choose to work with those who respect us and with those who share
the same Godhead. He sees us working with our brothers and sisters of the stars . . . our cosmic counterparts . . . as we learn to master space, time and energy.

Hurtak is doing research with indigenous cultures all over the earth

. . . people who have long been aware of and in contact with other cosmic cultures. He is learning the characteristics of many forms and races of space beings . . . some feared, some very advanced, some simply curious and some reminiscent of figures in ancient, advanced earth civilizations. In other words, they have been here many times before with us. Now they are coming to be with us again . . . part of the eternal return . . . which includes our return to other realms where we have been before. [Eve Bruce interviews Dr. Hurtak on video, *Extraterrestrial Realities*, which can be ordered from the Academy of Future Science, P. O. Box FE, Los Gatos, CA 95031. SASE. This responsible and mature coverage would make an excellent TV program.]

Zecharia Sitchin, historian and author of THE EARTH CHRONICLES AND GENESIS REVISITED, believes that we are the offspring of Star Beings. He believes that we are going to meet ourselves at a much earlier and more advanced stage, like in Lemuria and early Atlantis before "the fall."

Leo Sprinkle, PhD, counseling psychologist and UFO researcher and experiencer, also believes that this is a time of remembrance . . . that many of us have extraterrestrial heritage, especially the experiencers . . . and that this is definitely a family reunion.

John E. Mack, M. D., Harvard professor, author of ABDUCTION: HUMAN ENCOUNTERS WITH ALIENS and part of the Program for Extraordinary Experience Research, believes that most contact, including abduction, is a spiritual outreach . . . that all contact is growth promoting and opens consciousness. Mack noted that all abductees are told a story about us and the earth. He said that the star Beings always express puzzlement about us destroying life forms here. Jim Hurtak also spoke of the cry of Mother Earth . . . that she is suffering.

Charles T. Tart, PhD, professor, Institute of Transpersonal Psychology, Professor Emeritus, UC Davis, and author of LIVING THE MINDFUL LIFE, ALTERED STATES OF CONSCIOUSNESS, reminded conference participants that emotions are a kind of intelligence . . . a way to know . . . and that a balance of emotional and intellectual intelligence is useful. Tart suggested that if we choose to receive the Star Beings with an enlightened quality of being, then we will feel a familiarity and an appreciation as we feel the relatedness of all life. He sees us staying completely present in every moment, becoming observers, and receiving them as equals rather than special. If we place ourselves in a highlighted, yet detached state of being, we will be able to receive the Star Beings effectively, intelligently and compassionately.

Recommended books
All Classics

BASIC BOOKS

Below are basic books for the mystical seeker who is fairly new on the path. Once you have committed yourself to the search, the books and teachers you need to keep growing spiritually will come to you. Following this list are some advanced books.

ASHTANGA YOGA PRIMER, Baba Hari Dass, Sri Rama Publishing, Hanuman Fellowship, Santa Cruz, CA, 1981. Profits go to orphanages.

Beginning, intermediate and advanced postures as clearly portrayed as I have ever seen. A beautiful book to learn the various breathing exercises, hand mudras, plus practices to keep the body clean.

AUTOBIOGRAPHY OF A YOGI, Paramahansa Yogananda, Self-Realization Fellowship, 1946.

A humble man from India with a passion for the Divine tells his life story. A best seller and a masterpiece.

DR. DEAN ORNISH'S PROGRAM FOR REVERSING HEART DISEASE, Random House, New York, 1990.

Tells how to use meditation, yoga, vegetarian eating, improved inter-personal communication, group support, and exercise to actually reverse plaque in the veins and arteries therefore avoiding coronary bypass surgery. Contains elaborate, gourmet vegetarian recipes. The spiritual lifestyle is so healthful!

EDGAR CAYCE'S STORY OF JESUS, Jeffrey Furst, Berkeley Books, 1968.

The most-documented clairvoyant's work, combed for messages about Jesus' Soul history. Stunning. *All* books about Cayce's work are recommended.

LIVING WITH ANGELS, Dorrie D'Angelo, Angel Press Publishers, 1980.

Simple, lovely, almost childlike advice for using the abundance of angels to cope with the dramas and raise consciousness.

JOY'S WAY, A MAP FOR THE TRANSFORMATION JOURNEY, Brugh Joy, M. D., Jeremy Tarcher, 1979.

A courageous, sincere physician takes the inner journey away from traditional medicine and brings back for us what he has learned.

HANDBOOK TO HIGHER CONSCIOUSNESS, Ken Keyes, DeVorss & Company, 1975.

Here is how to evolve with a looser hold on the things and people you hold dear. He makes non–attachment seem logical.

HOME COMING, RECLAIMING AND CHAMPIONING YOUR INNER CHILD, John Bradshaw, Bantam Books, 1990.

How to heal your own neuroses and gain love for yourself. Bradshaw generously shares his own healings.

PERFECT HEALTH, Deepak Chopra, M. D., Harmony Books, 1989.

Chopra tells us everything we need to lead a complete ayurvedic lifestyle, starting at dawn with a combined hour's worth of meditation, exercise, massage, internal and external cleansing, and the proper breakfast for our body type. He is electric.

SAI BABA THE HOLY MAN AND THE PSYCHIATRIST, Samuel H. Sandweiss, M. D., Birth Day Publishing Company, 1975.

A doubting psychiatrist meets the Divine "Baba" repeatedly, struggles to understand the miracles and his own feelings – and becomes a believer. Here is a good place to start your learning about our awesome Avatar! *All* books about Sai Baba are recommended.

A CATHOLIC PRIEST MEETS SAI BABA, Don Mario Mazzoleni, Leela Press, Inc., Rt. 1, Box 3396, Faber, Virginia 22938, 1984.

An Italian Catholic priest is irresistibly drawn, has to face up to his learned dogma and when excommunicated says painfully, ". . . I must state that every human judgement is empty."

THE BOOK OF SECRETS I, Bhagwan Shree Rajneesh, Harper Colophon Books, New York, 1974.

Osho, formerly Rajneesh, gave an amazing number of discourses. His disciples have put together over a hundred discourse books. This is but one of them.

Our culture understood and treated Rajneesh at the level Jesus' culture understood and treated Jesus.

THE DREAM BOOK; SYMBOLS FOR SELF-UNDERSTANDING, Betty Bethards, Inner Light Foundation, 1983, P. O. Box 761, Novato, CA 94948.

Bethards talks about the meaning of dreams, how to work with them, and gives a rather comprehensive list of dream symbols with interpretations.

THE GYPSY DREAMBOOK, Sergius Golowin, Samuel Weiser, Inc., York Beach, Maine, 1983.

From other cultures a collection of dream symbols/interpretations. *Outstanding* and "right on."

QUIET TALKS WITH THE MASTER, Eva Bell Werber, DeVorss and Company, 1934.

God talks to you in the first person in these inspirations and lessons. Start the day refreshed with one of these.

HEAL YOUR BODY, Louise L. Hay, Coleman Publishing, 1984.

Contains metaphysical reasons why we may have certain illnesses. A brave spiritual warrior *has* to entertain her ideas. All books by Hay are recommended.

ADVANCED BOOKS

COMING BACK TO LIFE; THE AFTER-EFFECTS OF THE NEAR-DEATH EXPERIENCE, P. M. H. Atwater, Ballantine Books, New York, 1989.

Atwater was already a metaphysically knowledgeable, practicing psychic and hypnotherapist when she accidentally died – three times! Using these out-of-the-body times to will experiences, she saw her own thought forms, black blobs. In that dimension of consciousness, she created a house, then inspected it; then she imagined and created a live tree. She concluded: "Thoughts are pre-matter itself, they have substance and mass, and thus can be shaped into form at will. It can be done and I did it." Then she "disappeared" what she created!

She generously shares her extensive knowledge, her life, her Soul, and her hypotheses about creation, along with the title promise. A must read for anyone who has had a near-death experience. I did not discover this gem until fifteen years after my NDE or for anyone wanting to have a full understanding. It would have been such a comfort to know that what I was going through was common.

One's metaphysical education is not complete without a cover-to-cover reading. There is a forty-page resource section at the back of the book. Bombastic!

KNOWLEDGE OF THE HIGHER WORLDS AND ITS ATTAINMENT, Rudolph Steiner, Anthroprosophic Press, Inc., Bell's Pond, Hudson, New York, 1947.

Steiner lived from 1861 to 1925, wrote the preface to this work in Berlin in 1914. It was translated later into English and doesn't read easily. He tells practical ways to develop high-level spiritual knowledge and growth. An interdisciplinary worker, Steiner helped found the Waldorf School, touched economics, agriculture, drama and other fields. I was lucky to study under Steiner's reincarnation in this life, my beautiful shaman teacher.

NOTHING IN THIS BOOK IS TRUE, BUT IT'S EXACTLY HOW THINGS ARE, Bob Frissell, Frog/North Atlantic Books, P. O. Box 12327, Berkeley, CA 94712, 1994.

Frissell takes his learning from Drunvalo Melchizedek's Flower of Life Workshops and his own background in facilitating rebirthing to clearly make us comfortable with extraterrestrials and our own physical and spiritual quantum leap into the next level of consciousness. Beautifully and simply written.

THE BOOK OF KNOWLEDGE: THE KEYS OF ENOCH, J. J. Hurtak, PhD, The Academy for Future Science, P. O. Box FE, Los Gatos, CA 15031, 1973.

Hurtak wrote this advanced knowledge after being taken to the highest heaven by Metatron to experience God, and to have information encoded into his consciousness. Given on seven levels to be read and visualized in preparation for the actualization of the Brotherhood of Light, you will understand from this book what you need to understand. You won't understand it all but will gain more as you progress on the path. Each time you read it, it resonates deeper. A masterpiece without equal.

THE FAR COUNTRY, (and all books by Paul Twitchell), Eckankar, P. O. Box 27300, Minneapolis, MN 55427, 1971.

Astral travel with out-of-body Paul Twitchell and his satguru teacher to some of the spectacular worlds in our Father's house of many mansions. Twitchell's books are wondrous.

If you should have the opportunity to have a satguru teacher, *follow the opportunity.*

THE MAGIC PRESENCE, (and all books by Godfre Ray King), Saint Germain Press, Inc., 1935, 1120 Stonehenge Drive, Schaumburg, Illinois 60194.

Ascended Master Saint Germain appears repeatedly to King (pen name) plus takes him to other dimensions to teach and enlighten. From time to time Saint Germain temporarily embodies himself in a human body and teachers King on earth. A beautiful, pure and high book. Read all books in this series.

WE, THE ARCTURIANS (A TRUE EXPERIENCE), Norma Milanovich (and all books with Milanovich as one of the authors, this one with Betty Rice and Cynthia Ploski), Athena Publishing, Mossman Center, Suite 206, 7410 Montgomery Blvd, NE, Albuquerque, NM 87109-1574, 1990.

The information in this book was channeled by Milanovich from Beings who say they are fifth dimensional Beings from the star Arcturus. We meet Kuthumi, World Teacher, and others prominent in helping humanity evolve. According to their self descriptions, they don't look anything like us. Their culture is not anything like ours either, because it sounds like heaven. They pretty much know what path we are on, the changes we need to make, and the eventual outcome. They, thank God, are coming to help.

YOU ARE BECOMING A GALACTIC HUMAN, Virginia Essene and Sheldon Nidle, Spiritual Education Endeavors, 1994, 1556 Halford Avenue, #288, Santa Clara, CA 95051.

Nidle channels Washta and the Sirian starcluster council. Essene asks questions and is the scribe. What emerges is electrifying if for no other reason than the time prophesy: The photon belt that will help turn us into semi-etheric human beings will arrive as early as December 1995 but before the end of 1996. Also contained is much earth history.

Index

See also Appendix I

Advanced Book List 318
aerobic exercise 167–168
affirmations 252
Age of Aquarius 11, 34, 63
agnostic 101
Akashic Records 92–93
Akashic Record's mind channel 85
Aldebarans 186
all-pather 275
alpha 85, 98, 135
ancestral memory 88, 89
Ancient of Days 15
Rich Anderson 160
angel choirs 201, 202
Angel Healing Group 207–217
angel(s) viii, 20, 199–201
anger 116–117
Annie Kirkwood 149
archetypes 88
Aquarian Age 11, 34, 63
Arcturus 182, 184, 261, 267
Armageddon 258–259
Aires 144
Ascended Master(s) viii, 18, 19, 20, 255
ascension ix, 256–257
Ashtar 262
Assoc. of Research & Enlightenment 10
astral/Light body 51–53
astral plane/lower astral plane 91–101, 102
astrology 143
atheist 90, 101
Atlantis 182, 183
P.M.H. Atwater 29, 33, 318
aura 52
aura camera 52
Avatar 18–20, 38, 55–57, 63, 68, 73, 74, 88, 257
Meher Baba 70–71, 110, 256, 276, 282
Baba Hari Dass 167, 315
Baha'i 10
Basic Book List 315
Being 12, 13, 19, 22–30, 32, 42, 46, 47, 56
"being in the moment" 225–226

Dr. Fred Bell 266–267
Herbert Benson M.D. 133
Itzhak Bentov 119, 126
beta 85, 98, 137
Bermuda Triangle
Bhagavad Gita 26, 195, 257
bhajans 120
Bible vi, 194–197
biofeedback training 136–137
body (our physical body) 79, 150–172
both-and dilemma 246–247
brain (physical human brain) 85
Bennent Braun, M.D. 103
breakthrough thinking 253
Buddha and Buddhism 69, 198, 260
Cancer 144
Capricorn 145
Eckankar 10, 15, 16
Edgar Cayce 10, 25, 26, 29, 36, 37, 39, 65, 68, 69, 100, 101, 107, 139, 180, 182, 183, 242, 260, 315
chakras 51–52, 79
channeling 148–149, 267, 310
chanting 119–122
chi 19
children 242–243
Deepak Chopra, M. D. 17, 107, 108, 127, 133, 157
Christ consciousness 34, 58, 89, 93
clairaudience 148
clairsentient 148
clairvoyance 147
clairvoyant tools 146–149
collective consciousness 13, 90
collective unconscious 13, 88,
cold remedy 151
colon cleaning 160–165
colonics 160
Confucianism 198
Cosmic Cookies 152
cosmic hum (OM) 121
cosmic "sync," cosmic synchronicity 141
Cosmic Mind 21
consultant list 278

creative visualization 252
crystal reading 145
cult 198
curses 49
Dalai Lama 154, 193
dark brotherhood 187
dark night of the soul 192
dark side 247-248
Baba Hari Dass 167
death 172-175
delta mind state (sleep) 85, 98, 138
desires 28, 225
devil 251
Devaprem 123, 128, 129, 132, 297-303
John Diamond, M.D. 164
Divine 19
divorce 240-242
dreams 2, 85, 94-98
dramas to grow the Soul 189-192
drugs, recreational 33, 109-111, 293-296
Drunvalo (see Drunvalo Melchizedek)
earth history 179-188
Eckankar 10, 15, 41, 101, 135
ego-mind 85, 90-92
elemental spirits 203
emotions 111-116
enlightenment, (Self-realization) 37, 90, 92, 93,
95, 106, 110, 115, 119, 122-125, 132, 191, 297-302, 308
entrainment 126-132
Virginia Essene 71, 180, 261-262, 320
ethics and morality 246
exercise 167-168
Existence 167-168
extraterrestrials i, vii, 117-118, 179, 182, 184-189,
203, 258, 262, 268-273, 275, 311-313, 319
eyes (human physical eyes) 80, 157-158
fairies 203
fall of man 138, 183, 184
fear 115
five languages of the Soul 119
Bob Frissell, Flower of Life Workshops 181, 188
forgiveness 74, 228, 299
free will 14, 42-43
Gabriel 254
Galactic Command 182, 262-263
Galactic Federation 181, 262
Mohandas Karamchand Gandhi 226
Gayatri 121
goddess worship 49

Uri Geller 266
Gemini 144
giving and receiving 222-223
ghosts 53
God 11-18, 20, 22, 23, 28, 29, 74, (too many to list)
God-realized 34, 55-56, 63, 93, 195 (see Avatar)
Golden Spiritual Age 11, 34, 63
grace 20
greed 40, 46, 91, 154, 155, 196, 205, 243, 263, 278
Steven Greer, M.D. 269
Grandma Janis' Human-Mind-Channels
    Model 85-107
Grandma Janis' Health Tips 151-172
guilt 245-246
Louise Hay 165
Hakamin 255-256
Hindu 13, 62, 198
healing 150-172
health 150-172
heart (in physical body) 81, 154
heaven 43
hell 100
higher realms, and other dimensions 33
higher self, higher selves 25, 26
Lawrence Hinckley 27
Holy Bible vi, 194-197
Holy Spirit 19, 20, 21
Ernest Holmes 17
humor, humor-mind channel 105, 106
James J. Hurtak 15, 16, 33, 108, 180, 182, 184,
254, 258, 264, 268, 270, 271, 272, 273, 283, 312, 319
hypnosis 86, 102-105, 111
I Am 29
I Ching 147
immaculate conception 72
insanity 251
intent 22
intuition/psychicness 138-143
Iridology 159-160
Dr. Bernard Jensen 159, 162, 163
Jeremiel 254
Jesus viii, 18, 26, 27, 34, 37, 38, 42, 44, 48, 55, 56, 60,
64-74, 83, 88, 97, 111, 149, 182, 186, 192, 195-197,
234, 240, 256, 257-259, 264, 265, 271, 272, 280-287,
290, 297, 306, 309, 315, 317
Jesus debate 64
judgment 23, 226-228
Brugh Joy, M.D. 2, 50, 54, 83, 84, 108, 157, 316
Kali Yuga 186, 273

S. Kapp 136
karma 20, 37–42 positive & negative list 39–41
karma bank 41
Godfre Ray King 18–33, 184, 235, 255, 273, 277, 280–282, 319
Kirlian photography 51–52
Krishna 56
Kundalini energy 53–55
Leo 144
Lemuria 182–183
Libra 145
Light Brotherhood 186, 187
listening 219
lost soul(s) 32
love, God's love 74, 81–84
Lucifer 187
Shirley MacLaine 12, 30
Mahabharta 257
mantra 120
Maitreya 260
Management Consultant List 278
marriage (see sex and relationships)
Master teacher 253–254
matter 107
Jaime Maussan (Sixty Minutes, Mexico City) 279
meditation 27, 28, 58, 126–134, 297–303
Melchizedek 68, 180, 254, 257
Drunvalo Melchizedek 5, 25, 47, 56, 81, 140, 180, 181, 183, 185 (Sun-flare story), 187, 188, 192, 264
merkabah 273
metaphysics i, viii, 1, 2, 9–13, 21, 22, 37, 39, 40, 48, 49, 51, 52, 79, 136, 137, 179, 205, 219, 229, 242, 246, 275, 309
Metatron 15, 20, 180, 254–255, 276
Michael 254, 276
Dr. Norma Milanovich 149, 180–182, 261, 271, 320
mind 42, 85–107
mission 134
mistakes 244
Robert Moody, M.D. 101
money velocity 244
Mohammedanism (Islam; Muslim) 198
morphogenic fields 88–89
muscle testing 164
music 122
music of the spheres 201, 203
Namaste 285
nature spirits 203
Near-Death Experience (NDE) 7, 19, 29, 34, 101
New Age 11

new Souls 31–33, 53, 68, 69, 294
neuroses 248–251
Sheldon Nidle 71, 149, 180, 261–262, 320
non-attachment 219–222
Nostradomus 37, 258, 309
numerology 146
objective world 107
occult practices 49
old Souls 31, 47
Om (cosmic hum) 121
omega Orion 15
Omniscient 74
Omnipresent 74
Omnipotent 74
One-hundredth-monkey theory 89
Order Form 325
Organizational Transformations, ix, 277–280
Dean Ornish, M.D. 133, 157, 167
Orion 184
palmistry 146
paranormal experiences 7
past-life regression 67
peace 195
personality 23
Peter, Jesus disciple 67–68, 71, 73, 280–282, 307, 310
phone readings 146
photon belt 261–262, 272
physical body 79
physical human brain 85
physical eyes 80
physical heart 81
Pisces 145
placebo effect 103
Planet of the Cross 179–188
pleasure 224–225
Pleiades 184, 265, 267
polarity consciousness 187
Pope John Paul II 82
prayer 204–217
prayer chain 208
precognition 148
predicament anger 117
prematter 21
prosperity 243–244
prophesies 36, 37, 257–271
psychicness/intuition 138–143
psychics 142–149
psychokinesis 266
psychometry 146

purpose 134
Puttaparthi, India 59
quanta 20
quantum fluxuations 20
quantum physics 20, 21
Bhagwan Shree Rajneesh 16, 47, 96, 133, 167–
168, 232–234, 297, 298, 300, 301, 304, 316, 317
Rama 56
Raphael 254
realizations 80
real knowing 3
reincarnation 18, 36, 43–46, 47
relationships 237–243
relative truth vii
religious institutions 197
Religious Science 10, 17
resurrection 258
reverse–thought forms 21
John Robbins 172
Rosicrucians 10
Runes 147
Sagittarius 145
Sai Baba iii, viii, ix, 38, 57–64, 72–74, 77, 93, 108, 109,
129, 135, 143, 144, 156, 179, 193, 198, 257, 277, 316
Sai Baba's hospital (Sri Sathya Sai Institute
of Higher Medical Sciences) 156
saint 102, 123
Saint Germain 18, 179, 184, 235, 255, 273,
277, 280–282, 319
samadhi 134
Sariel 254
satguru 15–16, 168, 317
satori 125
Scorpio 145
seance 49
seeing experience 8, 60, 280
Self-realization, (enlightenment) 37, 90, 92, 93, 95,
106, 110, 115, 119, 122, 123–125, 132, 191, 297–302, 308
service to fellow humans 74, 223
Septimus 265
Seventh Golden Spiritual Age 79, 83, 190,
240, 256, 287, 291
sex 29, 235–301
shaman 104, 123
Rupert Sheldrake 89
sin 251
Sirius 180, 267
skin brushing 154
sleep 98–99
solution–finding mind 85, 93–94
Soul 12, 13, 19, 22–30, 32, 42, 46, 47, 56
too many to list)

Soul families 46
Soul mate 235–237
Soul time 108–109, 133
sound 12
Supreme Being Mind 85, 87–89
spirit 30
spirit band 20, 202
spirit guides 20, 202
spiritual ego 27
spiritual path 189–192
Spiritualism 10, 48–49
sub-conscious mind 86, 102–105, 111
subjective world 107
suicide 173
Taoism 198
Tarot 14, 146
Rebazar Tarzs (satguru) 15–16, 168, 317
telepathy 7, 147
"tenative shelf" viii
the path 189–192
the Universe 16
theta 85, 98, 137
third eye 138
thought forms 21, 22
thought molds 252–253
time 107–109
Time Lords 255
trance 36
trans-generational neurotic virus 249
truth 218, 299
twin flame 235–237
twin-ray souls 235–237
Paul Twitchell 15, 16, 33, 58, 101, 102, 135, 319
Photon belt 146, 261–262, 272
psychokinesis 266
Unity 10
U.S. Army Organizational Effectiveness
Center and School 277–280
Universal Church of the Master 10, 143, 285
Uriel 254
vegetarianism 157, 168–170
vibuti 62
Virgo 144
David Viscott, M.D. viii, 280
walk-in 181
war 193–194
Washta 180, 183, 185, 260, 267
weight loss 171
x-ray clairvoyant 148
yoga 147
Parmahansa Yogananda 38, 54, 122, 315
Zen 134

Order Form

You may order more copies of Cosmic Map – Metaphysics Demystified by Grandma Janis. Who of your friends and family would appreciate a copy? And how about holiday and birthday gifts?

Mail this order form with your check to:
Meadow Park Press
P.O. Box 14410
San Luis Obispo, CA 93406-4410

☎ Or get out your credit card and call **1-800-309-4645**

or Fax this order form to **1-805-782-9590** with credit card info

Name_____

Visa_____ Mastercard_____ Other_____

Card # _____ Exp. Date_____

The price is $17.95 ($22.95 Canada). Mailing costs plus applicable state tax totals $3.05 per copy. Total Fax, 800 or mail cost is $21.00 ($26 Canada).

Please send _____ copy/copies of Cosmic Map – Metaphysics Demystified by Grandma Janis at $21 ($26 Canada) total cost to each of the following

1. Name_____
   Address_____

   _____

   Message Phone_____
2. Name_____
   Address_____

   _____

   Message Phone_____

Order form continued on back

3. Name_____

   Address_____

   _____

   Message Phone_____

4. Name_____

   Address_____

   _____

   Message Phone_____

Circle one (for each book below).

Grandma Janis has two more books due out soon. Do you want to be notified when *Emaho, High-Tech Medicine Man* is published? One day an "ordinary" man named Donald reunited with his higher self. He brought in some of the Avatar powers, but was a little clumsy using them. Not for long. Rudolph Steiner in the last life, Emaho stepped forward as the most outstanding spiritual person Grandma Janis had ever met. It was a decade ago that she was his scribe for two and one-half years. He was her shaman teacher.

Yes, notify me.   **No**, don't.

Do you want to be notified when *Talk the Walk* is published? Real examples of how ordinary people are living the love in their lives, plus ideas for everyone on how to do this.

Yes, notify me.   **No**, don't.

✍ **Audiobooks Back Order Forms:** Send a SASE to Meadow Park Press indicating your interest. We will send you information just as soon as these tapes are available.